ABNORMAL PSYCHOLOGY
a perspectives approach

ABNORMAL PSYCHOLOGY
a perspectives approach

James D. Smrtic
Department of
Psychology and Human Services
Mohawk Valley Community College

AVERY PUBLISHING GROUP INC.
Wayne, New Jersey

CONTENTS

PREFACE

While studying abnormal psychology as an undergraduate, I questioned why the text was organized around the various mental disorders and not the major theoretical perspectives used to conceptualize and treat the disorders. For example, the text offered a symptomatic description of schizophrenia and then described the psychoanalytic, behavioristic, humanistic, medical and social perspectives' explanation of the disorder. By approaching the study of abnormal psychology in this fashion, I found it difficult to grasp the unique nature and orientation of each major perspective. It was difficult to understand why a specific type of treatment would be advocated by practitioners of a certain perspective without fully understanding the theory and background of the perspective first.

It seemed more logical and pedigogically sound to me to present the theoretical orientation of the perspective first, and then offer its explanations of the various disorders. Since theory is the vehicle by which we approach understanding and treatment of the disorders, it seemed to make more sense to present the theoretical basis of the perspective first.

I halfheartedly vowed that when I wrote my abnormal psychology book, it would employ a perspectives approach. My vow remained unfulfilled for a number of years -- I was preoccupied with the typical indulgences of the undergraduate and had not yet endured the rites of passage of graduate school. It was only after teaching abnormal psychology that my interest in this endeavor was rekindled. My students were experiencing the same frustrations that I had.

Thus, the book has been written. I have used it with my students. I find that after studying the major perspectives, students perceive that there are numerous ways to view the cause of a particular disorder, as well as many prescriptions for treating it. They wrestle with each perspective, trying to decide which is the most relevant and valid for understanding abnormal psychology. They become convinced of the superiority of one perspective only to find that their opinions change as they study the next. They realize that the experts don't agree; that there are many ways to view a problem. They are led into making their own evaluations.

I am convinced of the superiority of the perspectives approach for the study of abnormal psychology. This book is designed for those of similar conviction.

As we are well aware, our society is in a continual state of flux. So are the psychiatric and psychological professions. An intense controversy currently exists between the two professions regarding the system used to classify, diagnose and treat mental disorders.

Until January 1, 1980 both professions recognized *Diagnostic and Statistical Manual of Mental Disorders,* Second Edition (DSM-II) as the official document for the classification of mental disorders. Since the beginning of 1980, the American Psychiatric Association has recognized *Diagnostic and*

Statistical Manual of Mental Disorders, Third Edition (DSM-III) as its document. As of January of 1980 the American Psychological Association had yet to fully recognize DSM-III. It is likely that it will be some time before it does.

According to Robert Spitzer, chairman of the Task Force on Nomenclature and Statistics of the American Psychiatric Association, "The purpose of DSM-III is to provide clear descriptions of diagnostic categories to enable clinicians and research investigators to diagnose, treat, study, and communicate about the various mental disorders. It is hoped that comprehensive descriptions and the provision of diagnostic criteria will result in greater agreement among diagnosticians and will help to reduce the number of instances in which a single diagnostic label is used in vastly different ways by different mental health workers" (Foreward, DSM-III Draft, January 15, 1978). I hope that Spitzer is correct in the concerns expressed.

DSM-III eliminates the traditional classification of neurosis, a major classification in DSM-II. The traditional neurotic disorders have been renamed and classified elsewhere. It also includes new diagnoses, such as post-traumatic stress disorder, which may apply to Viet Nam veterans or released hostages.

Although DSM-III seems to correct some of the deficiencies of DSM-II, it has also been severely criticized. Some contend that DSM-III is overzealous in its consideration of some very common behaviors as mental disorders. For example, a person who had been smoking ten cigarettes a day and becomes irritable when attempting to quit experiences tobacco withdrawal; a person who becomes nervous after drinking two cups of coffee suffers caffeine intoxication. I have started drinking Sanka so I can honestly say I have no mental disorders when filling out insurance applications.

The ease with which normal people can be considered as having mental disorders should be a source of concern for civil libertarians. Americans are quick to criticize a Soviet mental health system in which dissidents are labeled insane to justify commitment to mental hospitals. Is it preposterous to speculate that diagnoses of tobacco or caffeine addiction could be used to commit American dissidents?

Psychologists and social workers contend that DSM-III views the causes of mental disorders as largely organic, therefore requiring medical treatments. Since psychologists and social workers cannot provide medical treatments, they would be driven from the mental health profession. By classifying just about anything that causes people distress as a mental disorder, psychiatrists stand to gain a "windfall" in insurance reimbursements. The insurance industry is giving careful scrutiny to DSM-III.

The current controversy poses a difficult problem in writing this book. Although I have firm commitment to providing students with the most recent information possible, it does not make sense to give an in-depth description of a classification system that is not yet fully accepted. Lags inevitably occur between the inception and application of policy. The government may decide that America should convert to the metric system, but few of us actually use it. Likewise, even if the American Psychological Association recognizes DSM-III, it will be a while before it is universally used. Indeed, I have observed that many *psychiatrists* are still using DSM-II to diagnose patients. Apparently, they are unfamiliar with DSM-III or still prefer DSM-II.

Unfortunately, neurosis cannot be eliminated by executive decree. Although eliminated from DSM-III, the emotional and behavioral phenomena of neurosis still exist. We may change the label, but we cannot change the nature of the disorder. If "a rose by any other name smells as sweet", neurosis by any name remains equally distressing.

Should DSM-III be universally recognized and employed, the impact on the mental health field would be of monumental significance. The issue is of lesser importance for the student taking a first course in abnormal psychology.

This is an abnormal psychology book. I will therefore use the terminology currently recognized by the psychological profession (DSM-II) in Chapter 3 - The Psychological Disorders. However, I will also provide DSM-III nomenclature, in parenthesis, for the equivalent disorder. This will aid both students and instructors in making the transition from DSM-II to DSM-III terminology.

I will continually "test the waters" of the mental health profession. Should conditions warrant, further revisions will be made in a subsequent edition of this book.

James D. Smrtic
February 8, 1980

Reference

Diagnostic and Statistical Manual of Mental Disorders, (Third Edition) (Draft), The Task Force on Nomenclature and Statistics of the American Psychiatric Association, January 15, 1978.

ACKNOWLEDGMENTS

The writing of this book has been a personal ambition of mine for quite some time. I now know why authors express such lavish thanks to so many people in their acknowledgments. They do so because the writing of a book would simply not be possible without the help of so many others.

Special thanks to Jude and Jennifer for tolerating a man often absent or grouchy during the writing of the book. I am truly indebted to the authors and publishers whose works are included in this book, and have graciously permitted me to use their works, often without charge. I express my gratitude to George Strong, Jaak Rakfeldt, and Jerry Brown for being receptive of the book since its beginning, and for helping me to clarify my thinking regarding the perspectives approach to abnormal psychology. To Mike Sewall, John Stratton, John Rybash, Elin Cormican, Joe Fallon and Rob McAndrews, I express my appreciation for their technical and moral support. The assistance of Charles Rogers and Keith Corneau was very beneficial in the writing of the chapter on abnormality.

Thank you, Ed Murphy, not only for proofreading the entire manuscript, but for serving as a personal inspiration to me throughout my teaching career. The library staff, particularly Audrey Sotendahl and Elaine Yerdon, has been extremely helpful in researching the book. Thank you, Julie Basile, for taking time from your busy schedule to type the manuscript and other correspondence. Thanks to Avery Publishing Group for thinking enough of my ideas to publish the book.

If I have forgotten anyone, please forgive me. You were there when I needed help. I have been remiss.

James D. Smrtic

PERMISSION CREDITS

Chapter 1
DIRECTION

Lenny Bruce, social and cultural commentator, was thrown in jail in the 1960's for saying some things in his comedy routines that one might today hear on prime time television. Lenny made some interesting comments about his friends' reactions to the now famous televised debate between John Kennedy and Richard Nixon during the Presidential campaign of 1960:

> I would be with a bunch of Kennedy fans watching the debate and their comment would be, "He's really slaughtering Nixon." Then we would all go to another apartment, and the Nixon fans would say, "how do you like the shellacking he gave Kennedy?" And then I realized that each group loved their candidate so that a guy would have to be blatant - he would have to look into the camera and say "I am a thief, a crook, do you hear me, I am the worst choice you could ever make for the Presidency!" And even then his following would say, "Now there's an honest man for you. It takes a big guy to admit that. There's the kind of guy we need for President (Bruce, 1966, p. 232-233)."

After reading Bruce's comments, it becomes obvious that each of the spectators witnessed the same debate. The picture on the television that each saw was the same. They each heard the exact same dialogue at the exact same time. Although each of the spectator's *sensations* of the debate were identical, it is of extreme importance to note that each spectator's *perceptions* of what he saw and heard were drastically different. This same phenomenon can be observed in many situations such as figure skating competition, gymnastics, or professional boxing matches, particularly those in which Muhammed Ali participated. Whenever human beings are exposed to any event it is quite likely that each individual's subjective perception of that event will be unique, or different from anyone elses.

Within American politics there are thousands of people who are all considered politicians. Although all are politicians, they are further distinguished by party affiliation. There are Democrats, Republicans, Liberals, Conservatives, and an endless stream of smaller political parties. But, as we have all probably observed, Democrats don't agree with Republicans, Republicans don't agree with Socialists, and the Socialists do not agree with the Conservatives. While all politicians are concerned with the same objective problems, such as inflation, unemployment, or foreign affairs, their subjective ways of interpreting these dilemmas, and their recommendations for dealing with these issues, are different. It is difficult to find political "experts" agreeing.

I had previously thought that if we were to find any field in which the experts consistently agree with each other, this field would be medicine. After all, one man's hernia is pretty much the same as the next man's. But, alas, this is not the case. While watching a television talk show involving a panel of medical "experts", I became appalled and horrified at what I witnessed. Since childhood I had been told that meat was a good source of necessary protein. One doctor immediately alerted me to the fact that I was clogging my blood vessels with cholesterol by eating meat. The point was made that large amounts of Vitamin E should be taken to promote good health, prompting another expert to rebut that Vitamin E is merely a placebo and large doses can be toxic. Although most doctors recommend drugs to control high blood pressure, a doctor on the panel said that these drugs have serious side effects and that proper treatment of high blood pressure can be accomplished through dietary changes. Finally, an oriental specialist advocated the sticking of pins into the human flesh to cure whatever ails the person. Emotionally drained and frustrated I slumped back in my chair wondering, "Who's right? Who really knows? Can we ever find any experts in a field that agree?"

This is a book about abnormal psychology. I would really like to be able to tell you in this book that within the field of abnormal psychology there is general agreement regarding the causes and therapeutic treatment of abnormal behavior. However, as you may already suspect, this is certainly not the case. A common saying in psychological circles is that "wherever there are two psychologists, there are three opinions."

Within the field of abnormal psychology we are faced with one common objective, behavioral phenomenon for observation. This is that there are some people whose behavior is in some way different from the way most other people behave. We may call this behavior abnormal, maladaptive, or self-defeating. The abnormal behavior may represent a serious problem for the individual or it may not. However, experts in the field of abnormal psychology will disagree as to how and why this person's abnormal behavior developed in the first place. They will also disagree as to how best change his behavior so that it may become more normal and allow him to become more satisfied with his behavior.

As previously mentioned, in American politics there are a number of political parties whose members agree on some basic political issues. In abnormal psychology there are also groups of psychologists whose members also are in general agreement about basic psychological issues. This is not to say that there are whole groups of psychologists that totally agree on important psychological issues, but that there are groups of psychologists that share a common theoretical orientation, a common psychological vocabulary, and a common way of viewing the nature and treatment of abnormal behavior. These groups of psychologists that share similar orientation, vocabulary and notions of causation and treatment regarding abnormal behavior represent *perspectives* in the study of abnormal psychology. The individual perspectives that comprise the study of abnormal psychology can be compared to the individual political parties that comprise the American political system. The debate and controversy among the experts who represent the individual perspectives for the study of abnormal psychology is every bit as real, intense, and emotionally charged as is the controversy that exists between the political parties in the politician arena.

The purpose of this book is to familiarize the beginning student with the perspectives approach to the study of abnormal psychology. Each of the five major perspectives will be presented individually so that you may begin to appreciate the unique nature of each of the perspectives. A description of each perspective will be followed by selected readings that will extend your understanding of the theory and practice of that perspective. Questions follow each article so that you can test your understanding of the material.

However, before we can delve into the perspectives that explain abnormality, some preliminary clarification is necessary. In Chapter 2, "Abnormality", we will investigate the nature of the distinction between normal and abnormal behavior so that we will better appreciate the nature of the phenomenon we are investigating - abnormal behavior. Chapter 3, "The Psychological Disorders", will describe the behavioral symptoms of the major psychological disorders (neurosis and psychosis), so that you will become familiar with the diagnostic and classification terminology used in clinical psychology and psychiatry.

Once you have developed an understanding of the characteristics of abnormal behavior and the classification system used in describing the different kinds of psychological disorders, the study of the individual perspectives can begin.

Chapter 4, "The Illness Perspective", represents the point of view that people who behave abnormally are "mentally ill" and therefore require medical interventions in dealing with their problems. The illness perspective is currently a very popular one, and has been since drug treatments for behavioral problems became wide-spread in the 1950's.

Chapter 5, "The Psychoanalytic Perspective", reflects the theory of Sigmund Freud, the most influential figure in the development of clinical psychology and psychiatry to date. Freud felt that incompletely resolved sexual conflicts in early childhood were of great importance in the development of abnormality in the adult.

Chapter 6 is entitled "The Learning Perspective" and represents the point of view of behavioristic psychology in relation to abnormality. The learning perspective views abnormal behavior as behavior that is simply learned, just like any other type of behavior. Abnormal behavior patterns develop because of faulty systems of reinforcement that the individual has been subjected to throughout life. Since abnormal behavior is learned behavior, it can also be "unlearned" and substituted with adaptive, normal behavior.

Chapter 7, "The Humanistic Perspective", describes a relatively new way of thinking about the person who behaves abnormally. The humanistic view of man is one that is optimistic, enthusiastic, and stresses the unique quality of every human being. Humanistic psychology is ever mindful of the importance of personal integrity and freedom for the effective functioning of the human being. Humanistic psychology is becoming more relevant in an American society where many ask "Who am I? What is my significance?" Humanistic psychology endeavors to answer these questions.

The final perspective, "The Social Perspective", is the subject of Chapter 8. Unlike the other perspectives, which had their roots in psychology or psychiatry, the social perspective is an application of sociological theory to aid in the understanding of people who behave abnormally. Proponents of the social perspective argue that we unjustly label people as being "mentally ill" simply because they do not behave the way most everybody else does. The social perspective is becoming more relevant today as the national movement to deinstitutionalize mental patients progresses. It is critical of what psychiatry and clinical psychology have been doing in the past.

Each of these perspectives offers a unique understanding of abnormality. Each uses its own vocabulary, sees abnormality as resulting from different factors, and offers different therapeutic alternatives for the individual. Once again we see that it is difficult to get the experts to agree. If after reading about the different perspectives you find yourself asking, "Who is right? What is the best way to conceptualize abnormal behavior? What is the best way to deal with abnormal behavior? Does anybody really know?"; if you find yourself more confused about the nature of abnormality after you have read most of the book than before -- don't dismay. You feel exactly like a serious student of abnormal psychology should feel -- confused.

Chapter 9, "Clarification", is designed to "put the perspectives into perspective". Various strengths and weaknesses of the perspectives will be pointed out so that we might finally come to some conclusions about the worth and validity of the perspectives that explain abnormal behavior. I will explain under which circumstances particular perspectives are the most valid and relevant.

But, if even after completing the book, you are still somewhat confused about the field of abnormal psychology, please don't feel dismayed. You see, you just can't get the experts to agree.

Reference

Lenny Bruce, *How to Talk Dirty and Influence People,* (Chicago: Playboy Press, and New York: Pocket Books, 1966).

Chapter 2
ABNORMALITY

In Chapter 1 the words "normal" and "abnormal" are used a number of times. All of us have some idea of what is generally meant when we say that behavior is either normal or abnormal. When we assess our own behavior or the behavior of others we frequently try to make some evaluation of the normality of the behavior. But specifically, what does it mean to be normal? Is it normal to smoke marijuana? Is it normal to get married or divorced? Is it normal to find religious fulfillment in shaving your head and living in a commune in Wyoming? Is being normal good? Is being abnormal bad? These are very difficult questions to answer. Unfortunately (or perhaps fortunately), there is no easy, objective, clear-cut way to distinguish normal behavior from abnormal behavior. There is no clear-cut dividing line which has normality on its left and abnormality on its right. The situation is not hopeless, however. There are some useful ways of looking at the concept of normality that can help to determine if behavior is normal or abnormal. On the societal level there must be some definite ways of determining if an individual's behavior is sufficiently abnormal to warrant his involuntary commitment to a mental hospital. We shall now begin to explore a variety of approaches to the understanding of normality, so that the terms normal and abnormal may take on some specific, rather than general, meaning for us.

THE STATISTICAL APPROACH TO ABNORMALITY

One way that we can approach the concept of abnormality is from a statistical point of view. Quite simply, normal behavior is statistically frequently occurring behavior. It is common behavior. It is the type of behavior that most people demonstrate most of the time. Conversely, abnormal behavior is statistically infrequently occurring behavior. It is relatively uncommon. It is the type of behavior that is not demonstrated frequently by many people. Normality implies usual behavior. Abnormality implies unusual behavior.

The statistical approach to abnormality can be understood quite easily by analyzing the possible outcomes of flipping ten coins simultaneously a great number of times. Since there are two sides to a coin, one a head and the other a tail, there is a one in two chance that any coin will show a head when flipped, and a one in two chance that the coin will show a tail (neglecting, of course, the remote possibility that the coin will stand on its edge). If a person had a lot of spare time and the perseverance to see it through, he would find that if he flipped these ten coins one million times and analyzed the outcome of each toss of the coins, that outcomes of the nature of five heads and five tails would be the most frequently occurring outcome. Somewhat less frequent would be an outcome of six heads, four tails or four heads, six tails. Somewhat less would be seven heads, three tails or seven tails, three heads. Lesser yet would the outcome be eight heads, two tails or eight tails, two heads. Less frequent yet would be an outcome of nine heads, one tail or nine tails, one head. The least frequent outcomes, occurring very rarely, would be for the coins to show all ten heads or all ten tails. Thus, from a statistical point of view, it would be relatively normal to toss the ten coins and have an outcome of five heads, five tails result, as this is a frequently occurring event. It would be abnormal to toss the coins and have an outcome of ten heads or ten tails result because these outcomes occur extremely rarely.

At the outset of this chapter the question, "Is being normal good?" was asked. That was a loaded question, as the answer to this question depends on the situation involved. We could substitute the word "conformist" for the word normal, and I imagine that some might say that conformity is undesirable because it connotes a person who lacks individuality and always follows the crowd. We could also substitute the term "team player" for normal and most people would agree that cooperative behavior has its advantages. Depending upon the situation involved, being normal or abnormal may be either good or bad. For example, in New York State hundreds of thousands of people buy lottery tickets. Only a small proportion of the tickets purchased are winning tickets. Therefore, to have bought a losing lottery ticket is normal. I think we can agree that in this instance being normal has no advantage. Conversely, to have purchased a winning lottery ticket is abnormal, but obviously, it is advantageous to be abnormal in this instance.

During the Viet Nam War the American government held annual draft lotteries. Those who "won" the lottery were invited to serve in the United States Army. The year in which I was involved it was relatively abnormal to be selected, as more were not selected than selected. I had always thought that winning a lottery was a good outcome to have happen to you; a sort of beneficial, abnormal outcome. What a curious feeling I had when I discovered I had "won" the only lottery of my life. I didn't know whether to marvel at the statistical significance of my selection, or be angry at the fact that I had been drafted. As you can see, it is not always easy to tell if being abnormal is good or bad. The decision is situation specific.

Let us now direct the discussion to the issue of behavioral abnormality. For any particular specific human trait or ability, it is probable that any individual will demonstrate that trait or ability to relatively the same degree as do most other people. The concept of human intelligence represents a good example of such a trait. Over the past fifty years literally millions of Americans have been given intelligence quotient tests that are designed to measure intelligence. On the standardized intelligence test a score of 100 is considered normal. Statistically speaking, the score of 100 on the intelligence test should be the score that would divide the total population in half, if the total population were to take the intelligence test. Half of the total population would get a score of 100 or above, the other half would get a score of 100 or below. Although technically a score of 100 is defined as normal intelligence, the actual range of scores on the intelligence test that are considered as normal is much broader. The normal range for intelligence test scores is considered to be between 85 and 115. It is expected that approximately 68% of the population's scores would fall in this range. I.Q. scores between 70 and 85 are considered as being low normal scores. Approximately 13.6% of the population scores in this range. Likewise, I.Q. scores between 115 and 130 are considered as being high normal scores. Approximately 13.6% of the population would also score in this range. If we include both high and low normals along with normals, we find that about 95 percent of the population has normal intelligence.

Those persons exhibiting the most extreme deviations from the score of 100, or normal intelligence, are designated as mentally retarded or mentally gifted. Those exhibiting scores of 70 or below are regarded as retarded; those with scores of 130 or above are termed mentally gifted. About 2.1% of the population falls in each of these categories (Kagan and Havemann, 1976, pp. 415, 435-436). Graphically, the distribution of intelligence scores would appear as the following:

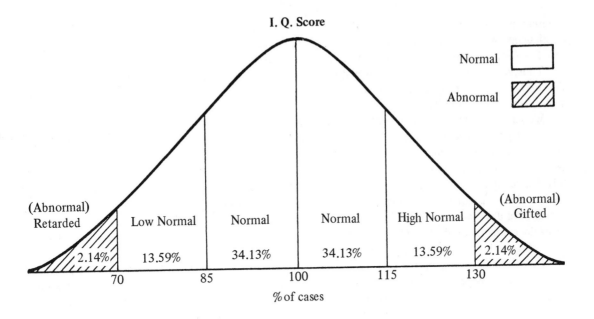

If the population of the United States is about 215 million people, this means that about 143 million people in the country have normal intelligence. If we include in this figure those who are of low normal or high normal intelligence, the number of people with normal I.Q.'s rises to about 205 million. Most people have normal I.Q.'s.

Since only about five million Americans are considered as retarded, it is quite uncommon for an individual to be considered retarded. It is also quite uncommon for a person to be considered mentally gifted since there are also only about five million Americans in this category. Both the mentally retarded person and the mentally gifted person are abnormal from a statistical viewpoint. However, we may consider retardation as a negative abnormality and giftedness as a positive abnormality. We might consider the mentally retarded person as demonstrating the trait of intelligence to a relatively small degree, and the mentally gifted person as demonstrating the trait to a relatively great degree.

The same kind of analysis that was just made with intelligence could be made with any human trait. Let us examine the trait of sociability. If we were to survey a large number of people with the intent of discovering how sociable they are, it could be expected that most people would have a small group of very close social friends, and a larger group of friends that they were not so close with, perhaps business associates. Most people belong to some social or civic organization. Many people would have some kind of religious affiliation that would necessitate them occasionally meeting socially with others of the same faith. Most people would associate with their immediate family on a day to day basis and with more distant relatives on special occasions, such as birthdays and holidays. It could be expected that this is the degree to which most people demonstrate the trait of sociability. The behavior described could be considered as normal social interaction.

There are also a relatively few people that are extremely introverted. They may have very few social contacts, do not belong to any religious, social, or civic organizations, do not associate with relatives, and live alone. The reclusive hermit may live alone in a cabin in the mountains with virtually no contact with the outside world. This is statistically abnormal, as there are very few people that demonstrate the trait of sociability to this very small degree.

On the other extreme are a relatively few people that are extremely sociable and feel compelled to belong to numerous organizations. They demand continual contact with family and friends. They continually give others what they feel is badly needed advice and serve as carriers of news between many

7

different people. They feel as though they must always be consulted by their associates and included in all plans. We may call these people busybodies, gossips, or nosey. It is abnormal to be like this as very few people demonstrate the trait of sociability to this degree.

Thus, it is possible to describe normal sociability, and most people demonstrate normal sociability. The hermit is abnormal because of an under demonstration of the trait; the gossip, because of over demonstration of the trait.

We can also use the characteristic of cleanliness as an example. It could reasonably be expected that most people wash their face and hands about three times a day. Most people bathe daily, or perhaps more frequently in hot, humid weather. Most people change their clothes daily. This could be considered as normal demonstration of cleanliness, as most people demonstrate the characteristic to approximately this degree. It is abnormal for a person to never bathe, wash or change his clothes as very few people are like this. It is equally abnormal for a person to wash his hands sixty times a day, change his clothes ten times a day, take ten baths daily, avoid waste baskets, and turn off light switches with his elbows to avoid contamination. The latter could be considered as demonstrating some of the symptoms of a psychological disorder called obsessive-compulsive neurosis.

Let us finally consider the trait of generosity. If we were to survey a large number of people to determine how generous they are, we might expect that most people would contribute some money to their favorite charities, give presents to close friends and relatives on special occasions, loan friends money if their need was great, and maybe toss a dollar or two in the collection plate in church. We might consider this typical demonstration of the trait of generosity.

Should a person demonstrate the trait of generosity to an unusually small degree the person would be referred to as a miser. The Guiness Book of World Records describes the world's greatest miser as Henrietta Howland Green who left an estate of 95 million dollars at the time of her death in 1916. Despite her wealth, she ate only cold oatmeal as she was too cheap to heat it. Her own son had to have his leg amputated as she was too cheap to take him to a doctor, instead delaying until she could find a free clinic for him. Very few people would be this miserly, and this is why Ms. Green's behavior is abnormal. It would also be very unusual for a person to give up all his material wealth to charity, dress in rags, and live in unnecessary poverty. Recently, a wealthy man appeared on a television talk show with bags full of money. He distributed the money to the crowd. As you might expect, the crowd was very enthusiastic. The reason why such an event was worthy of television coverage was that it is very uncommon to see a person distributing "free" money. Thus, over demonstration of the trait of generosity can also be abnormal.

The purpose of the preceding discussion was to point out that one fruitful approach to understanding abnormality is along statistical dimensions. Thus, the person whose behavior is abnormal regarding a multitude of behavioral and personality traits and characteristics is the person who is most likely to have his overall personality considered as abnormal. The mentally retarded individual, who lives alone in a one room apartment and shuns social interaction with other people, washes and bathes in ritualistic fashion many times daily, is excessively miserly and hoards pennies in a sack hidden under his bed, is the type of individual whose overall behavior is likely to be considered as abnormal. Statistically, abnormality is the result of an accumulation of abnormal personality and behavioral characteristics demonstrated by an individual.

THE CULTURAL APPROACH TO ABNORMALITY

Another way of viewing abnormality is from a cultural point of view. In order to explain the cultural view of abnormality it is helpful to borrow a term from sociology. This term is cultural relativism and it roughly means that what is considered to be normal behavior will vary from culture to culture. If we examine cultures throughout the world we will begin to realize that different groups of people have very different ways of doing essentially the same thing. That different groups of people have different techniques, customs, or systems of social organization is not really important. The important thing is that these groups of people are successful in achieving their objectives. No matter what customs groups of people use to obtain their goals, the success they have in attaining their goals is the most important criterion.

We live in middle-class oriented, contemporary American society. Within this society we have developed complex codes of conduct that constitute normal behavior in this specific cultural setting. We become so familiar with, and accustomed to, our way of life that often we have a tendency to view any behavior that does not fit in with the way in which people behave in our culture as being inferior, primitive, weird, threatening, or abnormal. We surround our eyes with cultural blinders that make us view behavior within very limited cultural guidelines. We view behavior that conforms with middle-class contemporary American values as moral, right, and normal. Conversely, behavior and customs that are different from what is accepted as normal in our culture are viewed as immoral, incorrect, and abnormal. I shall now point out how normality varies from culture to culture so that we may better understand the culturally relative nature of the concept of normality.

The most basic issue that all cultures have to deal with is the manner in which they rear children and enhance their socialization into the particular culture. In contemporary American culture it is traditional for one man to marry one woman and then to jointly share in the rearing and socialization of their biological children. We view this family structure as normal, since this is the way most families are organized in our society. However, one does not have to be the biological parent of a child in order to do an effective job of rearing and socializing that child. The effective social adaptation of adopted children proves that you do not have to be the biological parent of a child to do a good job in the rearing of that child. As we examine cultures throughout the world, it becomes apparent that there are equally effective ways of rearing and socializing children other than the style of family organization and rearing practices characteristic of contemporary America. Nevertheless, these different ways seem unusual to us because of our cultural bias.

The Nayar are a group of people which inhabit the Malabar coast of India. The marriage and family systems of the Nayar are very different from ours. The village astrologer is designated the responsibility of selecting which young males will be united with which pre-pubescent girls in a ritual marriage. After each young man has tied a gold ornament around the neck of his bride the couple enters seclusion for a three day period while the rest of the village celebrates on a grand scale. After the ceremony the couple will not reside together, and the girl is free to have sexual relations with anyone she choses, within certain caste restrictions. The bride has no further obligation to her husband, except to attend his funeral and bring her children with her, no matter who the biological father of the children was. The husband has no further obligation to his bride once the ceremony is completed. The two people may continue to have sexual relations in the future, but the husband has no priority over the other men of the neighborhood (Gough, 1959).

Although this is normal tradition in the Nayar culture, such an occurrence in our culture would be extraordinary. We would suspect the sanity of the father who consulted the astrology column in the morning paper to find out which boy in the neighborhood would be the best ritual husband for his ten year old daughter. We would be more amazed when after the selection the father let his daughter have a trial marriage with the boy for three days and then told her to be promiscuous and have as many illegitimate children as she desired. Furthermore, the husband would not be expected to pay any child support expenses, but the girl would be expected to weep at the funeral of the man who left her years ago when they were children.

As we look at the tradition of the Nayar from our cultural point of view we might be tempted to write off the customs as those of a primitive, immoral, ignorant group of people. However, closer analysis shows us that such is not the case. In some ways the "primitive" system of the Nayar has

9

distinct advantages over the American family system.

In American culture the illegitimate child often starts life "with two strikes against him". Because his/her father is not the legal husband of his/her mother, and probably does not live with her, the child will begin to perceive that he is different from his "legitimate" peers when he is asked in kindergarten "Who is your Daddy?" Father-son Cub Scout outings will be difficult for the child, even if "Uncle Art" (mother's current lover) accompanies him. Although a "Big Brother" may take the child fishing on Saturday, the community will not let the child forget that he is illegitimate, and as soon as the child's peer group's vocabulary improves he may be referred to as a bastard. The lot of the American illegitimate child can be an uncomfortable one.

In comparison, the Nayar culture does not really have the equivalent of what we would call an illegitimate child. A child's biological father may be one of any number of men, and as long as he is of suitable caste, the child is viewed as being "legitimate". Nayar women may have a number of lovers at any given time so exact paternity is often difficult to determine (Gough, 1959). The point is that the Nayar do not stigmatize the child whose biological father is not his mother's legal husband, as is often the case in the United States.

In the Nayar culture, the birth of children strengthens the mother's family lineage. The care of children thus becomes the responsibility of the mother's family. They are willing to accept the responsibility of rearing newborn children, even those we would call illegitimate, as it means that the family line will be perpetuated.

In our culture, the determination of custody of the illegitimate child is often a sticky issue. Of course, if the mother wishes to keep the child she is generally allowed to. However, if the mother does not want to keep her illegitimate child, the child may ultimately be placed in an orphanage, which is not a very good place for a child to be reared. The Nayar do not have these problems.

In American culture, if both biological parents of the child die, the responsibility for the care of the child is often uncertain. Brothers, sisters, or parents of the deceased may take over the rearing of the children, but this often poses an undue hardship on the new caretakers. Thus, the child with two deceased parents may be adopted, placed in a foster home, or an orphanage. In any event the child will have to cope with the emotional loss of his parents in a new, strange environmental situation.

The Hopi Indians of the northern Arizona desert have a family system that is organized around the mother. It is common for a mature woman, her daughters, and granddaughters to occupy the same residence. This arrangement may last throughout life, and all children would live in this same residence. In fact, the Hopi term "mother" not only applies to the child's biological mother, but also to aunts and other women of the same generation within certain family guidelines (Queen and Habenstein, 1974, pp. 50-51). Thus, if a child's biological mother were to die, the child would not be displaced into a new, strange home environment. He would remain where he had been living. There would also be an ample supply of women, which the child was already accustomed to calling mother, to take over the responsibility for rearing the child. This provides a built-in social welfare system within the Hopi culture. They take care of their own. Perhaps there is a lesson to be learned by American politicians from the Hopi.

The point of the preceding discussion was to point out that there is nothing sacred, or inherently superior, in the American family structure. It is a good family structure, and it works quite well. However, there are other family structures that work equally as well as ours, and in some cases are superior to it. We still have the tendency to judge as abnormal any family structure that is different from ours.

The designation of sex roles is another phenomenon that is culturally relative. There is no doubt that today sex roles are changing in this country. The traditional view of the female was that she was naturally nonaggressive, submissive, and passive. The man was viewed as aggressive, dominant and active. Today the aggressive, business oriented woman is not as conspicuous as she would have been thirty years ago. Sex role designation changes with time.

Sex role designation also differs from culture to culture. Anthropologist Margaret Mead analyzed three separate societies on the island of New Guinea to determine if there were universal differences in role and temperament between the sexes.

The Arapesh, regardless of sex, is expected to be gentle, responsive, and unaggressive. Both parents share in the rearing of the children, and when a woman gives birth, both are said to be "having a baby". In the Arapesh society, men are said to look haggard and worn out when rearing children. This is very different from our culture where it is common to hear things like "Why shouldn't he look good. *She* had the children!"

Among the Tchambuli, women are assigned the role of provider and the men take care of domestic concerns. Women work together in groups and men arrange social activities, devote themselves to hobbies, and gossip. Women are sexually aggressive and the men's emotional life centers around the women. This is essentially the opposite of traditional American role designation.

The Mundugumor men and women are both sexually aggressive and violent. Neither relishes child rearing. Sexual relations are characterized by much biting, scratching and fighting (Broom and Selznick, 1973, pp. 125-127). Although such sexual behavior is normal among the Mundugumor, it may be considered abnormal or "kinky" in our culture. Sex role designation, as we know it, is not universal. However, we still develop expectancies of people based on sex and what our concept of appropriate role behavior is. Men that violate our expectancies may be viewed as effeminate "sissies"; women as radicals.

All cultures throughout the world use cosmetics, jewelry, clothes or other adornments to decorate the body. Unusual techniques of decoration, in comparison to our standrads, are practiced by the Tchikrin, a little known group of people from the central Brazilian wilderness. Plugs of wood are inserted in the infant's ear lobes. These plugs wll be eventually replaced by larger ones to make the holes in the ear lobes larger. Dowels are inserted in the boy's lower lip. Mothers save the plugs as the children outgrow them and also save the baby's desicated umbilical cord. At puberty boys are given penis sheaths to wear and will be given their first lip plugs, which will eventually be replaced by a saucerlike plate that is four inches in diameter and will drastically change the shape of his face. Although both men and women have elaborately painted bodies, a girl who has reached reproductive age becomes identifiable to potential suitors by the broad black stripes that are painted on her thighs, breasts, and upper arms. She learns that it is intensely sexually stimulating to pluck an eyebrow from her boyfriend's face with her teeth while engaging in sexual foreplay (Turner, 1971).

The practices of the Tchikrin appear unusual, if not bizarre, to us. However equivalents to the techniques of the Tchikrin exist in our culture. Although the holes made are not as large, ear piercing is very common in American women and becoming more common in American men. Where Tchikrin mothers save their children's outgrown plugs and umbilical cords, what loving American mother does not keep Freddie's first pair of shoes, a lock of hair after the first trip to the barber, or the first of his baby teeth? The pride that the Tchikrin boy feels when he is given his first penis sheath at the time of puberty is probably not too different from the exhilarating feeling the American male gets when he puts on his athletic supporter for the first time in eighth grade gym class.

It may sound cruel to make children wear saucerlike plugs in their mouths that will make their lips beautifully protrude as adults, but, as I can attest from personal experience, it is no more cruel than making American children wear braces on their teeth because of an American aversion to teeth that are not perfectly aligned.

Sexually eligible Tchikrin women are designated by bodies which are painted in stripes. This is not too different from sexually eligible American females who attend dimly lit, smoke-filled singles bars with "help stamp out virginity" lettered on snug fitting T-shirts that cover braless torsos. Her face may be covered with a variety of cosmetics (many of which are made from by-products of urine), and she may have a butterfly tatooed on her thigh.

With the current American interest in sexual fetishism, it would be risky to wager that eyebrow plucking with teeth will not become a new turn-on.

Let us relate all of this to the concept of normality. The point is that what is considered as normal behavior is arbitrarily determined. What is normal in one culture may not be normal in another. However, when an evaluation of the normality of an individual's behavior is made, the criteria for evaluation are the standards and customs of the society in which the individual resides.

By combining the statistical and cultural approaches to abnormality, it follows that abnormal behavior is behavior that is infrequently demonstrated within a specific cultural setting. The person who demonstrates a multitude of behaviors that occur only infrequently in contemporary American culture has a high likelihood of being considered abnormal. The behavior of the person may be normal in other cultures, but the cultural standards of contemporary American society are the criteria of evaluation. While this kind of determination may not be moral or just, it is the reality of the situation.

SUCCESS AND NORMALITY

The success of an individual can often be an important factor in determining the acceptability of his behavior. Two people may demonstrate essentially similar behavior but society's reactions to each person might be quite different depending upon the success of each individual. There is an old saying that rich people who behave in an unusual manner are eccentric, whereas poor people who behave the same way, are just plain crazy. The successful businessman, who supplements his income by selling real estate in his spare time, is considered diversified. The policeman, who supplements his income by working as a security guard, is "moonlighting".

Success is a term that is difficult to define, but certain elements that would contribute to a person's success would be wealth, fame, popularity, and expertise in some area. Howard Hughes, American billionaire who died in 1976, is a prime example of an individual whose unusual behavior was largely excused as eccentricity. At the age of twenty Hughes had a two million dollar a year income and he later became famous for the transcontinental and round-the-world flying records he set in the 1930's. He was a successful motion picture producer, aircraft manufacturer, and real estate investor. He had love affairs with many of Hollywood's most beautiful actressses. Although throughout his life his behavior was abnormal in terms of contemporary cultural standards, words such as shy, reticent, and secretive were used in his description (Current Biography, 1941). The words reclusive, introverted, and anti-social might have been used to describe someone not as successful as Hughes.

On April 19, 1976, Time Magazine reported that for the last ten years of his life, Hughes lived as a recluse in a twentieth floor penthouse in Acapulco, Mexico. He was sheltered from the light of day by black curtains sealed with masking tape around the windows of the one room in which he spent most of his time. The room included a glass partition to protect him from germ contamination from his servants. He often ate only cakes that were measured with a ruler to make certain that they were perfectly square. One of the world's richest men was malnourished.

An Associated Press story of June 14, 1978, describing the legal proceedings for the determination of Hughes' estate, reported that "Hughes' conditions in these last years of his life resembled that of a chronic psychotic patient in the very worst of mental hospitals." A patient in any mental hospital in the country who showed behavior as "aberrant and as regressed as Hughes would be classified as psychotic."

What is interesting is that it is only after his death that words such as psychotic are used officially to describe Hughes. This may be because there is no longer a fear of reprisal from a powerful, vindictive Howard Hughes.

Ray Kroc started out with a few hamburger stands and ultimately created the multi-million dollar McDonald's fast food empire. Throughout his career, Kroc has been thought of as flamboyant and eccentric. He has also been extremely successful. A number of years ago Kroc purchased the San Diego Padres, a major league baseball team that has not been known for its athletic prowess on the baseball diamond. When frustrated and dismayed over his team's ineptness on the field, he would chastise his team verbally over the public address system at the stadium. Ray Kroc's baseball team was not a success on the field, and it was now that the Padre fans began to question the state of mind of Kroc.

Mark "The Bird" Fidrych is a baseball pitcher for the Detroit Tigers. While pitching, he often kneels on hands and knees and pats the dirt on the pitching mound. He frequently talks to the ball and gives it instructions regarding the path it should take. He audibly talks to himself. When he is healthy, he is one of the best pitchers in baseball. He is idolized by the fans and 50,000 people may join in a standing ovation for him. His unusual behavior is thus interpreted as being the eccentricities of a successful athlete. Were he not successful it would be likely that fan reaction would be one of ridicule and rejection, rather than respect and adulation. The distinction between genius and insanity may be a fine one. Often, this distinction is based upon the success that the individual enjoys.

QUALITIES OF NORMALITY

The statistical, cultural, and success approaches to normality all stress the importance of society's interpretation of behavior. Let us now look at some qualities of normality from the individual's point of view. All people desire to be happy. Thus, personal satisfaction with one's own behavior could be considered as an important determinant of normality. By personal satisfaction I do not mean that the person is always pleased with his behavior and the way that his life is going. Being normal does not mean being perfect. Normal people have financial, employment, marital, or health problems. However, despite problems, the normal person is still generally satisfied and content with life.

Normal people are generally able to experience pleasure. The inability to experience pleasure is called anhedonia and is often characteristic of mental patients. Contrary to the popular characterization of mental patients being in a blissful world of their own, such is not the case. Many such people do not experience pleasure and emotions such as joy and happiness. They are in a perpetual state of subjective distress. Thus, we could include personal satisfaction and the ability to experience pleasure as characteristic of the normal person.

Normal people are generally in control of their behavior. They have the ability to act or not, depending upon desire. Their behavior is purposeful and goal directed. There is an element of consistency to their behavior. There is predictability to their behavior based on what they know about themselves. Since they know themselves, they understand the motives they have for behaving in the manner they do (London, 1968, p. 4).

Ultimately, normality means the person is able to function effectively in a day to day manner that is acceptable to him. The normal person is generally satisfied, but not without problems.

We have now approached the concept of normality from a variety of points of view. But what does all this mean for the individual? Because a person demonstrates behavior that occurs statistically infrequently in contemporary American culture, is unsuccessful and is not satisfied with his behavior, does this mean that this person is sufficiently abnormal to be placed in a mental institution? Not necessarily. Once again we have run into a complex issue.

People come to receive psychiatric or psychological assistance in a variety of ways. Although many individuals receive attention voluntarily as out-patients, others are hospitalized in mental institutions, which are generally state operated. The conditions by which people enter mental hospitals are numerous. Before the process by which people enter institutions can be described, I should explain something about the staffing structure of the mental hospital.

Psychiatrists are generally designated leadership roles in the mental hospital. Psychiatrists are medical doctors with additional training in psychology. Psychiatrists can prescribe drugs and use other forms of medical treatment in addition to psychotherapy. Psychologists have graduate training in psychology and have earned either M.A. or Ph.D. degrees. Psychologists cannot prescribe drugs or perform medical treatments, but generally have more psychological training than psychiatrists. Psychiatric social workers generally have contact with the patient and his family and may perform psychotherapy. Psychiatric aids, or attendants, assist the patients in their daily routine and have the most direct contact with the patients. Psychiatrists, psychologists, social workers, nurses, and aides generally comprise the therapeutic team in the mental hospital.

The mechanics of entering a mental hospital vary from state to state. Some people may enter the hospital through informal admission. The individual experiencing distress merely applies at the hospital and indicates that he is in need of help. He may leave whenever he wishes. This type of admission may be more characteristic of private rather than state hospitals.

Voluntary admission occurs when the patient appears at the hospital stating that he is sick and needs help. He will sign papers asking for treatment. He may leave at will, providing he has given the hospital a few days notice of his intention.

Medical certification is a form of commitment. In an admission, the patient is free, within guidelines, to leave the hospital when he wishes. In a commitment, the patient must stay in the hospital, at least for a specified time limit. In a medical certification, a relative of a person requests that the individual be examined by a doctor (interestingly, the doctor need not be a psychiatrist). If the doctor feels that hospitalization is needed, he can sign the necessary papers that would commit the person. Usually the person would have to stay in the hospital for about two weeks. Some states require two doctor's signatures.

In legal commitment, the individual is taken before a judge for a sanity hearing. The police, doctors, or relatives may initiate the proceedings. A doctor, not necessarily a psychiatrist, is present to advise the judge. The judge then determines if the person is to be committed. The duration of the commitment may be indefinite (Milt, 1969, pp. 76-78). It is estimated that at any given time there are 350,000 patients being held on involuntary status in American mental hospitals (Torrey, 1974, p. 86). The term commitment has a negative connotation. People who work in private mental hospitals are often quick to point out that patients are admitted, not committed, to their hospitals.

It is difficult to specify the precipitating conditions that will lead to the hospitalization of an individual. Generally, a person will not enter an institution as long as he is generally satisfied with his condition and is not harmful to others. Of course, many people voluntarily enter hospitals because they are not satisfied with the way they feel or behave. Whether or not a person is harmful to others is a very difficult question to answer. There are some clear-cut instances where people have demonstrated that they represent real danger to the safety of others. It is relatively easy to determine in these instances that the individual should either be placed in a mental hospital or prison. Although Charles Manson or David Berkowitz may have been content to murder people, it was very obvious that they represented potential danger to society. Decisions like these are not that difficult to make.

Other instances are not so clear-cut. The question sometimes arises as to whether the state has the right to protect an individual from potential harm to himself. *Newsweek*, September 29, 1975, reported the case of Robert Friedman. Friedman was arrested for begging on a Chicago street. Questioning of Friedman revealed that he was carrying $24,087 in small bills in his attache case. With the support of Friedman's family, a judge signed a commitment order that placed Friedman in Chicago-Read Mental Center for an indefinite period. Although Friedman may have been content with his behavior, it was apparently felt that it was not in Friedman's best interest to allow him to roam the streets of Chicago carrying many thousands of dollars in small bills. Chicago authorities were severely criticized for committing an individual who represented no real danger to others. On the other hand, it would have been probable that the authorities would have again been criticized if they had allowed Friedman to go free and he had been robbed of his money and murdered. "Didn't anyone care about this sick individual?"

might have been the outcry. Decisions of this nature are difficult to make, because whatever the authorities do, their decisions can be criticized.

The point has also been made that decisions of commitment, such as in Friedman's case, are not made for the protection of the individual, but because the individual is a troublemaker or merely offends the general public. A significant proportion of individuals have been committed to state hospitals over the years, not because they were violent or suicidal but because they were a nuisance to society (Ulmer, 1975). This notion will be elaborated upon in the chapter on the social perspective.

The responsibility for initiating commitment proceedings generally rests with the family of the potential patient. This is particularly true in cases of alcoholism, drug addiction, or physical abuse, where family members are often reluctant to bring the problem to the attention of the authorities. Once the family initiates the proceedings, there is a good chance that the individual will be committed.

In summary, two general criteria in determining admission to mental hospitals are the personal satisfaction of the person, and the possible danger or threat that the individual represents to himself or others. People may voluntarily admit themselves if they are not content or satisfied with their condition. Commitments may be ordered when individuals represent threat or danger to themselves or others. The last criterion is a very ambiguous one and difficult to deal with in reality.

In this chapter we have viewed the concept of normality from a variety of perspectives. The notion of normality should have some more specific significance for us now. We have also investigated the process involved in becoming a mental patient and the criteria used in making decisions regarding entrance to a mental hospital. We are now ready to describe the variety of psychological disorders and their behavioral symptoms.

References

Maxine Block, editor, *Current Biography: Who's Who and Why* (New York: The H.W. Wilson Company, 1941)

Broom and Selznick, *Essentials of Sociology* (New York: Harper & Row, 1973)

Kagan and Havemann, *Psychology: An Introduction* (New York: Harcourt Brace Jovanovich, Inc., 1976)

Perry London, *Foundations of Abnormal Psychology* (New York: Holt, Rinehart and Winston, Inc., 1968)

Kathleen Gough, The Nayars and the Definition of Marriage. *The Journal of the Royal Anthropological Institute of Great Britain and Ireland*, 89 (1959): 23-24.

Harry Milt, *Basic Book on Mental Illness* (Maplewood, New Jersey: Scientific Aids Publications, 1969)

Queen and Habenstein, *The Family in Various Cultures* (Philadelphia: B. Lippincott Company, 1974)

E. Fuller Torrey, *The Death of Psychiatry* (Radnor, Pennsylvania: Chilton Book Company, 1974)

Terrence S. Turner Tchikrin: A Central Brazilian Tribe and Its Symbolic Language of Bodily Adornment. *Natural History*, 78 (October 1969): 50-59, 70.

A. H. Ulmer, Implications of California's New Mental Health Law, *American Journal of Psychiatry*, 132 (1975): 251-254.

SELF TEST: MEASURING COMPREHENSION
Chapter 2

1. By combining the statistical and cultural approaches to normality, what does it mean to be normal?

2. Is it normal to smoke marijuana? Why?

3. What are the two general criteria for determining if a person should be admitted to a mental hospital?

4. What are the different proceedings by which people become patients in mental hospitals?

5. Do you feel that the criteria for determining commitments are fair and just? Why or why not?

Chapter 3
THE PSYCHOLOGICAL DISORDERS

Human behavior is a variable phenomenon. It is not the sort of thing that easily lends itself to clear-cut diagnostic classification. It would be presumptuous to think that individuals could be neatly and easily plugged into diagnostic categories based upon their behavior. Scientific psychology is thus challenged by the variable nature of human behavior. Such may not be the case with other sciences, chemistry in particular. A chemist may analyze a particular compound and definitely classify it based upon its characteristics. He may examine a tasteless, odorless, colorless liquid and discover that this compound is also capable of existing in solid and gaseous states. He may also determine that this compound is composed of two parts of hydrogen to one part of oxygen. He will determine this compound to be water. He will also know that any other compound that demonstrates the same characteristics and has the same chemical composition must also be water. This method of analysis doesn't work as well with people. Although the classification of psychological disorders is a difficult task, it is a task that has been taken on within clinical psychology and psychiatry. A workable classification system of psychological disorder is in use, although the model used has not received universal approval.

The two major classifications of psychological disorders are the neurotic disorders and the psychotic disorders. Just as there was no clear-cut dividing line between normal and abnormal behavior, there is no clear-cut dividing line that exists between normal behavior and neurotic behavior. Nor is there a clear-cut dividing line between neurotic behavior and psychotic behavior. It is difficult to determine just where normality ends and neurosis begins. It is also difficult to tell where neurosis ends and psychosis begins.

There are a number of different kinds of psychological disorders that are considered neurotic, just as there are a number of different kinds of psychotic disorders. Before the specific types of neurosis and psychosis can be described, it is necessary to provide some general guidelines that are used in distinguishing the behavior of the neurotic from that of the psychotic.

One way that the behavior of the neurotic can generally be distinguished from that of the psychotic is along the dimension of severity. The overall condition of the neurotic is not as severe and debilitated as that of the psychotic. The neurotic, to be sure, has his share of difficulties, but he is still capable of maintaining relationships with others and struggling through his daily life. The psychotic, on the other hand, may cease functioning as a social person, and find himself incapable or disinterested in conducting his daily routine. The neurotic may continue to work. The psychotic probably won't. The neurotic's overall functioning ability is impaired. The psychotic's ability to function normally is virtually destroyed.

Whether or not the individual is in contact with reality is another key distinction that can be made between the neurotic and psychotic. Neurotics are generally in touch with reality. Although judgement may be impaired, neurotics have accurate perceptions of time, place, and identity. They know the correct time of day, day of the week, and month of the year. They know where they are. They realize that their ability to function is impaired. They are aware of their condition. Psychotics are characterized by a break with reality. They may not have accurate perceptions of time, place, or identity. Their perception of the world around them is very much different from the way that others perceive the world. They may not be aware of the fact that their ability to function is impaired. Although psychotics are not always out of touch with reality, episodes of breaking with reality are often a prime determinant of a diagnosis of psychosis.

The condition of the neurotic is typically more stable than that of the psychotic. The neurotic may exist in his impaired condition for years. He may be able to function relatively normally for long periods of time, with periodic aggravation of his condition during times of stress and tension. Assuming the neurotic were not undergoing psychotherapy or medical treatment, it could be reasonably expected that his condition today would be pretty much like it was a month ago, or pretty much like it will be a month from now. There is an element of consistency in the condition of the neurotic. Psychotics frequently undergo drastic changes in their condition. They may be out of touch with reality for a period of time, then return to reality. At times they may be capable of carrying on meaningful conversation, at other times incapable. The emotional condition of the psychotic is also likely to be unstable. At times he may be extremely depressed and crying out loudly. Within a few moments he may be in a euphoric emotional state. The neurotic may have the long range goal of getting back in control of his life so that he can be more satisfied with himself. The psychotic may express specific wishes and goals in one breath, and then contradict himself in the next. Statements such as, "I have big plans for the future! I will live forever!", may be immediately followed by, "My life is miserable. I wish I were dead." There are elements of stability and consistency to the behavior of the neurotic. Instability and inconsistency are more characteristic of the psychotic.

In terms of treatment, the neurotic would be more likely to be treated with psychotherapy alone than would be the psychotic. The psychotic would be more likely treated with both psychotherapy and medical treatments. Many neurotics are under the out-patient care of psychologists, who cannot legally administer medical treatments. Other neurotics are under the care of psychiatrists and will receive medical treatment. However, most psychotics receive psychiatric treatment, thus increasing the likelihood they will be treated medically, as well as psychologically. Institutionalized neurotics usually do receive medication. Still in all, the psychotic is more likely to be treated with both medical and psychological interventions than the neurotic.

The psychotic is also more likely to be institutionalized than the neurotic. This is not to say that neurotics are never institutionalized. They often are. However, the duration of time spent in the hospital is usually shorter for the neurotic than the psychotic. Many psychotics will live for years in mental hospitals. Some spend almost their entire lives in the hospital. This is rare for the neurotic. Because neurotics are in contact with reality, they are moderately capable of taking care of themselves, attending to their personal hygiene, and avoiding dangerous situations. Psychotics often cannot take care of themselves, do not attend to their personal hygiene and may not appreciate danger in situations, such as throwing lit matches on the floor, thus necessitating their hospitalization.

Disturbances of the affective domain refer to disturbance of an emotional nature. Disturbances of the cognitive domain refer to disturbances of logic, thought, and reasoning ability. The neurotic is likely to experience intense, irrational feelings of guilt, sorrow, anxiety or fear. These are impairments of the affective domain. The psychotic will likely experience these same feelings. However, the psychotic is also likely to demonstrate disturbances of the cognitive domain, such as illogical thought process, inability to reason effectively, and hallucinations. Thus, the neurotic's major impairment is in the affective domain, where the psychotic is likely to be impaired in both the affective and cognitive domains.

In the previous discussion I have purposely avoided making absolute statements about the distinctions between neurosis and psychosis. I have avoided the use of the word "always" in making this distinction and instead used words such as "generally" or "typically". As previously mentioned, it is difficult to concretely distinguish the behavior of the neurotic from that of the psychotic. The major distinction lies along the dimension of severity. The condition of the psychotic is more severely and drastically impaired than the condition of the neurotic.

We can now begin to examine the different kinds of neurotic and psychotic disorders. I will first describe the behavioral symptoms that would likely lead to a diagnosis of a particular type of neurosis. Five major types of neurosis will be described. A case history will then be offered as an example of neurotic behavior. I will then describe the major classifications of psychosis, and offer a case study of psychotic behavior.

THE NEUROTIC DISORDERS

A. Anxiety Neurosis   *Anxiety Disorder (DSM-III)

The neurotic individual demonstrating the symptoms of anxiety neurosis could be characterized as being in a chronic state of vague, free floating, unfocused, fear and apprehension. Chronic disorders are disorders of relatively long duration. If a person has chronic bronchitis, he has had the condition for quite some time. Likewise, the neurotic individual described as suffering from anxiety neurosis will have been plagued by extreme feelings of anxiety for prolonged periods of time. All of us have days on which we feel particularly anxious. We may awaken some morning with a tense feeling in our stomach. We may be nervous about the exam we must take, the hopeless love relationship we feel we must terminate, or the bill that is due that we don't have the money to pay. These feelings of tension and anxiety do not mean that we have become neurotic. They simply mean that we have problems that need solving. After we take the exam, terminate the relationship, or pay the bill, the feelings of anxiety diminish. Such is not the case with the anxiety neurotic. The feelings of anxiety do not appreciably diminish, even after solving problems. The anxiety is chronic.

The terms vague, free floating and unfocused used in describing the fear and apprehension of the anxiety neurotic refer to the fact that there is often no identifiable factor that is making the individual so anxious. The individual may be in a state of panic, but when asked why he feels such extreme fear, he may reply, "I don't know quite why I feel like this. Something bad is going to happen. I don't know when, how, or why. I just know it will." Feelings of impending doom are characteristic of him. These feelings may persist for years.

The anxiety may often be accompanied by feelings of restlessness, irritability, excessive appetite, and dizziness. A person may encounter difficulty in sexual performance. The person's concern with his physical health may be exaggerated. He may have a pain in his chest and imagine that he is having a heart attack. He may run from doctor to doctor because of his preoccupation with his health (Milt, 1969, pp. 21-22). Nothing seems to work for him, though.

Our era has been called "the age of anxiety". Whether or not Americans today are confronted with more potentially anxiety-provoking situations than in the past is debatable. In the past, people became anxious over such events as natural disasters, starvation and disease. Today, we additionally have the threat of nuclear war and the loss of the significance of the individual in a technological society to be concerned with. Nevertheless, anxiety is a primary symptom of most of the different classifications of psychological disorders. It is the primary characteristic of the anxiety reaction (Lief, 1967, p. 857).

We all have problems. We all suffer periodic anxiety. We all worry. These things are not neurotic. They are normal. However when a person is in a state of chronic anxiety, for reasons that are unclear to him, is excessively concerned with his health and because of these factors experiences great distress, and an inability to conduct his life style in the way that he wishes, the person may be described as an anxiety neurotic.

*For further information regarding DSM-III terminology see the Preface.

B. Phobic Neurosis

Phobic Disorder (DSM-III)

The phobic neurotic is characterized by acute fear, which is experienced when particular objects or situations are encountered. Acute fear refers to fear that is extremely intense and of sudden onset. This contrasts with the chronic feelings of anxiety experienced by the anxiety neurotic. The phobic may be able to effectively function for long periods of time, as long as the stimulus or situation that produces the fear is not encountered. Where the anxiety of the anxiety neurotic is vague, free floating and unfocused, the fear of the phobic is situation specific and generally predictably occurs when the individual is in a specific situation or in the presence of a certain stimulus.

Phobias can be developed to just about any situation or object. Some of the more common phobias are claustrophobia (fear of enclosed places), acrophobia (fear of heights), and agoraphobia (fear of the outdoors). In one case, I encountered a woman who had a phobia of telephones. She was relatively able to function unless she was in a room in which there was a telephone. She would become intensely anxious and become quite distressed when confronted with a phone. As you can imagine, the list of possible phobias is virtually endless. In his first inaugural address in 1933, Franklin Delano Roosevelt is quoted as saying "The only thing we have to fear is fear itself." He probably didn't realize that he was inferring that Americans are phobophobiacs, or people who fear fear.

Both anxiety neurotics and phobics realize that their functioning ability is impaired. In fact, phobics will often admit that their phobias are irrational. Although irrational, the phobias are apparently uncontrollable, and despite his wishes, the phobic experiences intense, acute, situation specific fear. Many phobics demonstrate essentially the same symptoms as do anxiety neurotics prior to their first phobic episode. Following the first occasion the anxiety becomes focused on a particular event or object. (Frazier and Carr, 1967, p. 901).

All of us have fears of specific situations or stimuli. Many of us do not like being in high places, seeing smakes, or being in closed places. This does not mean that we are phobic neurotics. We only cross the fuzzy boundary between normality and neurosis when our ability to function becomes drastically impaired. If you are so afraid of heights that you cannot climb stairs, so afraid of snakes that you won't go outside for fear of seeing one, or so fearful of being in closed spaces that you cannot walk through the hallway that leads to your office at work, your functioning ability is becoming impaired and you are not doing the things that are important to your. Determining what constitutes drastic impairment involves a subjective decision that only the individual can make. But generally, the more drastically impaired the condition of the individual becomes because of his fear, the greater is the likelihood that his behavior should be considered as symptomatic of phobic neurosis.

C. Depressive Neurosis

Depressive Episode/Chronic Depressive Disorder (DSM-III)

The depressed individual is characterized by chronic feelings of sorrow, guilt, melancholy, grief, and apathy. Chronicity is an important criterion in the diagnosis of depression. We all have days when we feel "blue" or "down in the dumps". The depressed person has these feelings on a prolonged basis. These feelings may persist for months or even years.

Depression usually follows a loss that the individual has experienced. The types of losses that can be serious enough to trigger depression are many and varied. The loss of a loved one, job, or physical health are some of the more common events that preceed depression. Women, who give birth to normal babies, sometimes go into depression. The baby that had been inside her for nine months is now living in the external environment. This is a type of loss. Some people who undergo surgical operations and have an organ removed become depressed. When people do things that they know are wrong and in violation of their personal moral codes they often experience intense feelings of guilt and become depressed. In this case, self-esteem has been lost (Mowrer, publication pending).

Depression is usually accompanied by a slowing down of the person's physiological processes. The person may lose weight because of loss of appetite. He may complain of chronic fatigue, although he has difficulty falling asleep. As his diet becomes worse and he becomes less physically active, he may become constipated (Milt, 1969, p. 22). Headaches, tightness of the muscles, and various body pains are among the physical complaints.

The depressed person may have feelings of self-doubt and have an extremely poor self-concept. His speech may be slow and monotone. Where he used to look forward to going to work, just getting up in the morning becomes a difficult task. His chores around the house are left undone. Although he used to watch his children play little league baseball, he stops going to the games. The garden just never gets planted.

Depression is a very serious problem. It is estimated that between ten and twelve million Americans are depressed (Fieve, 1975, p. 181). Although this estimate may be too high, it is still indicative of a serious national mental health problem. Depressed people are very likely to attempt or commit suicide. Ronald Fieve, pioneer in lithium treatment for depression and manic-depression, estimates that 80% of those individuals who attempt suicide are depressed. (The Thin Edge-Depression, 1975).

Another classification of depression is called the psychotic depressive reaction. It is distinguished from depressive neurosis in that in addition to the usual symptoms of depression, the person also is out of touch with reality. (Diagnostic and Statistical Manual, 1968). Technically, depressive neurosis that is being described is considered a neurotic disorder. It was previously mentioned that neurotic disorders are generally less severe than the psychotic disorders. Regarding depression, it could be argued that a person's condition could hardly be more severe than in the case where a person tries to kill himself. However, most depressed people who contemplate or attempt suicide are in touch with reality. Their existences are painful and they decide that they are better off dead than alive. Depression is a difficult disorder to classify. Depression, by itself, is not a fatal disorder. Its effects can be.

D. Hysterical Neurosis

Hysterical neurosis is sub-divided into two types.

1. Conversion Hysteria   Somatization Disorder/Conversion Disorder (DSM-III)

The conversion hysteric is characterized by the demonstration of physical ailments without medical cause. Conversion reactions may take the form of blindness, deafness, paralysis, or muteness. The person may seem unconcerned about his symptoms. Upon thorough medical examination no organic defect or malfunction can be discovered to explain the ailment. The person may demonstrate uncontrollable episodes of vomiting, hiccupping, or defecation. Rarely, a woman may develop a false pregnancy, complete with morning sickness and swelled belly. The conversion hysteric must be distinguished from the malingerer, or faker. Malingerers will often fake physical symptoms to collect insurance money, get released from the military, or even to get committed to a mental hospital. Their performances are worthy of Academy Awards. The conversion hysteric actually believes that he is physically afflicted (London, 1968, p. 348).

The ancient Greeks' felt that conversion hysteria occurred only in women and resulted from abnormal movements of the woman's uterus. Hystera is the Greek word for uterus (Nemiah, 1967, p. 871). We know today that it occurs in both men and women. In the late 1800's, Sigmund Freud proposed that conversion hysteria resulted when a person was subjected to severe trauma and failed to react to the traumatic situation. Because the person did not react to the trauma, psychological energy which should have been used to produce action was left in the person's system, and then *converted* into a physical symptom (Freud, 1962).

Trauma, or potential trauma, often preceeds the onset of hysterical symptoms. R. Peter Mogielnicki has observed parents who came to an emergency room at a hospital with a variety of physical complaints like blindness, paralysis of arms, nausea, and shortness of breath. In a couple of cases it was found that the parents had strong urges to physically abuse their children, and that these thoughts were prominent on their minds when their ailments began. In another case a man developed a paralysis in the arm that he used to beat his child. Mogielnicki suggests that patients who appear at emergency rooms with hysterical symptoms should be questioned about the issue of child abuse as a way of detecting possible cases of it (Mogielnicki et al, 1977).

2.   Dissociative Hysteria   Dissociative Disorder (DSM-III)

To dissociate means to separate. In dissociative hysteria the individual is separated from his awareness of personal identity. His normal state of consciousness is altered.

Amnesia is a type of dissociative hysteria. In amnesia, the ability to remember is impaired. The amnesiac block may be for a specific traumatic portion of a person's life, or it may be a total block of his past. Amnesia may be temporary or long lasting. In extreme cases the person may be unable to recognize his family and does not know who or where his is (London, 1968, p. 348).

Somnambulism, or sleepwalking, can be serious enough to be considered as dissociative hysteria. In somnambulism the person gets up in the middle of the night and begins walking in a semi-conscious state. He appears to be in contact with his surroundings, but as if the surroundings are a part of what he is dreaming. If questioned, his response will likely be related to what he is dreaming (Milt, 1969, pp. 25-26). The person may or may not be aware of the episode the next morning. Recently I read of a woman, who during a somnambulistic state, walked outside her house and laid back down in a snowbank. By the time she was found in the morning, she had frozen to death.

Multiple personality is a type of dissociative hysteria in which the person demonstrates totally different personalities at different times. It is as if a number of people were living in the same body. It is the type of situation illustrated in the story of Dr. Jekyll and Mr. Hyde. The book "Three Faces of Eve" is a documented example of a woman who had alternately gone through three distinct changes in her personality during her life. Cases have occurred in which murderers claim that it was not them who had killed, but someone else who had taken over their body. The Associated Press reported on July 17, 1978 that Gail Tate had brutally murdered her four children. She said she felt that she was "under a voodoo curse". Throughout her court appearance she made no response and just stared at the carpet. Also in July of 1978, Lemuel Smith confessed to his psychiatrist that he had committed three Albany, New York area murders because he was driven by the spirit of a non-existent brother whom Smith felt had died before his own birth. During that summer, Immanuel David, described as a religious fanatic, committed suicide. Before his death, "He believed that he was the Holy Ghost, Jesus Christ, and God - all three at the same time," according to Salt Lake City police Sgt. Brent David. Four days after David's death, his wife and six of their children also were killed by falling from their 11th floor balcony. Witnesses said some of the children were thrown by their mother. Others jumped willingly.

Multiple personality is a particularly difficult disorder to diagnose. It is difficult to distinguish between a person who truly does have multiple personalities and a person who may feign the disorder to avoid criminal responsibility for his actions. Innocence because of insanity, such as multiple personality, is becoming a more common plea.

Because of the split personality aspect of multiple personality many people often incorrectly confuse multiple personality with schizophrenia. While the schizophrenic may demonstrate a split personality, schizophrenia differs from multiple personality in many ways. These distinctions will be clarified in the discussion of schizophrenia, a type of psychosis.

E.   Obsessive-Compulsive Neurosis   Obsessive-Compulsive Disorder (DSM-III)

An obsession is a preoccupation with unwanted ideas or emotions. It is a feeling or idea that is constantly pervading an individual's consciousness. A compulsion is an irresistible impulse to act, regardless of the rationality of the motivation. Thus, in obsessive-compulsive neurosis, the person is beset with unwanted feelings and emotions that compel him to do things of a repetitive, ritualistic nature in a vain attempt to satisfy the obsession. The obsession is the mental or cognitive element of the disorder; the compulsion is the behavioral component. The obsession may function as a defense to keep other painful, traumatic, remembrances from entering the person's consciousness. The person often demonstrates intense anxiety if prevented from completing the ritual (Diagnostic and Statistical Manual, 1968, p. 40).

The obsessive-compulsive neurotic develops rituals which are attempts to avoid or escape intense anxiety (London, 1968, p. 347). The rituals can take almost limitless forms. One of the more common obsessions centers around concern with health and cleanliness. The obsessed individual may literally wash his hands sixty times a day. Gloves will be worn continually to avoid contamination. Door handles are avoided. "In one case, a patient went so far as to go about on roller skates while cleaning the house in order not to become soiled" (Milt, 1969, p. 24). A few winters ago, when a flu epidemic was predicted, a doctor described to me the compulsive behavior of a nurse who was working for him. He described her as so obsessed with the possibility of getting the flu that after every patient left the doctor's office the nurse would go through a fifteen minute ritual of sanitizing the office. Any object that the patient had touched was wiped clean. She sprayed disinfectant around the room and on the chair in which the patient had been sitting. The doctor was concerned that he would have to fire the nurse because she was not doing her job because of her compulsive behavior. All of us are concerned with our health and cleanliness. However, when the point is reached that we are no longer able to perform our job or conduct our lives in the way we are accustomed to because of the compulsive aspects of our behavior, we may then consider the behavior as being neurotic. Whether or not behavior is considered as neurotic is a matter of degree.

Other obsessions may center around money, power, dieting, gambling, or the desire to commit crimes such as arson (pyromania), or theft (kleptomania).

We have now described the symptoms of the five major classifications of neurosis. This list is not meant to be all-inclusive, as there are a few other disorders that are considered neurotic. Those I have described are the most common forms and are sufficient for our purposes.

A PORTRAIT OF NEUROSIS
from *Memoirs of an Amnesiac*
Oscar Levant

Dramatist S. N. Berman once observed that if Oscar Levant "did not exist", he "could not be imagined". He was an extremely gifted pianist, actor, composer, and radio and television personality who was known for his cutting, caustic wit. I can vaguely recall from my childhood seeing Levant on the Steve Allen and Jack Parr television shows. I remember a disheveled looking, humorous, piano player who continually smoked cigarettes. Besides being talented, he was also neurotic. Throughout his life he behaved in a bizarre manner and spent the last ten years of his life as a recluse. As he once said, "There is a thin line between genius and insanity. I have erased that line." Levant demonstrated the symptoms of a variety of the types of neurosis we have described. As you read this first person account of what it is like to be neurotic, look for the behavioral symptoms of specific types of neurosis.

* * *

Instant unconsciousness had been my greatest passion for ten years. During the most acute phases of my mental depression, which lasted many years, my most unabated obsession was instant unconsciousness. For a short interval I was administered eighteen electrical shock treatments, which had dire results. However, they had one incalculable pleasure—each shock treatment was preceded by an intravenous injection of sodium pentothal. Afterward I was hooked on intravenous injections of pentobarbital (Nembutal), which had an even more luxurious and longer lasting unconsciousness. This addiction was discontinued—it was short lived. I not only ran out of doctors, but out of veins. During these comatose seizures, the only exercise I got was stumbling, tripping and falling into comas. My deterioration was bottomless. At one time I was in a state of apathy and then later lapsed into a deep depression. During the deep depression period, where I became zombie-like, I would get nostalgic for the good old apathy days. Incidentally, "apathy" and "deep depression" are precise terms in psychiatric terminology.

I would endlessly complain at the prospect of consciousness. Once I told June, "You ought to hit me on the head." But after I'd said it I was frightened because I'd made such a remark, and the barbiturate dose she gave me didn't work, due to my fear. Yet it's true: I had an insatiable craving for unconsciousness. It was my only surcease. I rated the drug Demerol over sex as the ultimate pleasure at one time. Now I don't have access to either. Speaking of Demerol and just for the record, it has been many years since I've been administered this deleterious narcotic.

The other day I was walking upstairs and I was breathing heavily. "You know, walking upstairs is just as bad as sex," I complained. "I get the same reaction from both. Terrible chest pains."

The horrors of my subconscious had left me with a fanatical disbelief in myself, which displays sound judgment. I was an inert, happy-go-lucky derelict who could have been created by Gogol.

* * *

Rituals have taken the place of religion for me. These superstitions started the second time I appeared on *Information Please* in the late 30's. (The first time I appeared I didn't even know what the show was all about.) I had a cup of coffee in a drugstore in Radio City before the program and left a dime tip. This began the whole pattern. From then on, every time I was to appear on that show, no matter how late I was, I dropped into that drugstore, sat on the same stool, ordered a cup of coffee and left a dime. Often I didn't even drink the coffee. I never changed my clothes till I had a bad show. From this simple beginning, my program of rituals has become as complex as the Canadian Air Force exercises.

Today my rituals are more elaborate and they increase with my anxieties as the years go by. At times I have to perform some of these rites in front of my wife, and she sneers. This deflates me and I beg for her tolerance; I can't give up either my rituals or my wife. When guests are there I try to perform them covertly, or if the compulsion is strong, I perform them flagrantly, but I am deeply embarrassed. The rites give me something—not necessarily peace of mind, but a kind of puerile comfort and security.

In 1952 I had a heart attack. After I refused to go to the hospital, the doctor told me that I should undress and get to bed. I did, but I insisted on performing all my undressing rituals, even with the heart attack.

I usually perform them when I dress or undress, when I go to bed, and when I open a pack of cigarettes. Everything that is pleasurable, I give a pagan benediction.

A few years ago someone suggested that I read Spinoza. The first chapter in this particular volume was about superstitions and rituals. Here was my faith! Spinoza said rituals are all based on fear. My faith destroyed, I put down the book. My rituals are automatic, mechanical and absolutely necessary, and I perform them without thinking. But when I occasionally forget one, I feel a temporary euphoria, but it is evanescent. A sixth sense (I lack the other five) tells me that I am in serious difficulties.

When I button my shirt, for example, I always button the lowest button first. When I take off my shirt, I do it from the top down. When I turn on water faucets the first time, I tap each faucet with both hands eight times before I draw the water. After I've finished, I tap each of them again eight times. I also recite a silent prayer. It goes: Good luck, bad luck, good luck, Romain Gary, Christopher Isherwood and Krishna Menon. I also tap my clothes.

There's no symbolism involved in the count of eight. I started out with smaller numbers but—due to inflation and increased anxiety—it's now eight. I skipped seven. I don't like the number seven.

I stir my coffee four times one way with a teaspoon . . . then pause a moment . . . then two times more. I recently added two more stirs but discarded them because they took too long. The coffee got cold.

My napkin has to be on the left side before I put it down. If the cream pitcher has a crack, I have it removed. I don't allow any cracks at the table; I demand an absolutely pristine, unadulterated topography.

When I play the piano—a form of tactile therapy—I always play a few bars of the Fourth Etude of Chopin, Opus 12, and as I finish playing I always add a few bars of the same, a few bars of the Eighth Etude, and then the coda of the prelude from the Prelude and Fugue in C minor of Bach's "Well-Tempered Clavichord." Then I go back to Etude 4, Etude 8, and then a little bit of Etude 4 again. I finish every practice period that way. I guess that's because I'm the fourth child. This has been with me for many years.

George Gershwin used to practice the First Etude of Cramer in C major. When I resumed concert playing after Gershwin died, I adopted that and also always wore the specially inscribed wristwatch he once gave me. Then I suddenly gave up the Cramer Etude. Fortunately I have given up anything associated with George. It was too obsessive.

A girl I liked before I was married once gave me a pair of gloves. Before a concert, I'd touch the gloves; I don't remember how many times in those days—the economy was different then. Later my wife gave me some gloves and I discarded the first pair.

I used to drive to Edgemont Hospital in Hollywood for shock treatments in 1956. Every time I passed a funeral parlor I would be sure that there was no cigarette in my hand. I would also stop breathing until the traffic lights changed and the car moved on. If anyone in the car spoke, I would become very disturbed physiologically. One of the funeral parlors has now been replaced, but I still observe my obeisance. I never look.

I have many bottles of the pills I take. Some are tranquilizers. I gave up vitamin pills, although my doctor and wife insist that I take them. I never was convinced of the efficacy of vitamins. They were introduced publicly, incidentally, by the St. Louis Cardinals when they were called the Gashouse Gang. They presented vitamins to the public—public relations they call it—but in my lexicon it was *chutzpah!*

Yet there is a certain method in my method, to uncoin a phrase. The sequence remains fixed. I take certain pills first, second, third and so forth. Then I arrange them in a precise order on the table. That's fixed, too. It's like finger painting by a monkey.

All my medicine bottles must be placed with their backs toward me, including the Sweeta; I never look at the fronts of the bottles. I also have a collection of old medicine bottles which nobody is allowed to touch although I'd like to get rid of them. If they're touched my day is ruined. They symbolize unfortunate experiences.

When I go into the bathroom, I put the index fingers of both hands on the slit of the door and silently count to eight. I repeat this once more. On my exit, I also do this twice. I always keep the toilet seat covered at all times. If anything is one quarter of an inch out of place in my bathroom, I lapse into a deep funk. I raise hell. Pandemonium breaks out.

I cannot stand an open door. Every closet door has to be closed.

When I'm taking off my trousers or pajama pants, the count is eight. But when I lie down on my bed, I lean my head to one side on my pillow and silently count to five twice. I have rigid rules about my pillows—which side they're on.

It takes a long time for me to open a package of cigarettes. It calls for the count of one to five twice over, and I take the tinfoil off during the latter half of the second count. If June talks during this ritual, I'm not allowed to rebuke her anymore because she'd beat the hell out of me, but I throw the pack away and wait until she leaves the room before I start opening another. Mine is always the most mangled pack of cigarettes around. The tinfoil must go into the silent butler and the paper into the wastebasket. But I allow very few things in my wastebasket. If it is anything of evil, sinister or possible catastrophic design, I put it in my wife's wastebasket.

* * *

When I'm in the hospital or if I'm not doing well in my career, I'm more relaxed about this ritualistic straitjacket. If I have nothing impending I relax, but as my engagements increase I get worse. I'm like a ballplayer on a streak.

In the middle and late 50's I was in hospitals constantly. I was committed every time I drew a breath or took an extra twelve pills—which never affected me much because I'm not suicidal.

Recently we were watching the *Eleventh Hour* on television. As the advice and behavior of the psychiatrist team became more and more appalling my wife shouted, "You're quacks, both of you!"

Last year in the book review section of *The New York Times* there was an irate article by a psychoanalyst who did not approve of commitments, which he felt were often the worst possible of terrors and punishment. I read it and thought it was completely justified and was inflamed; my wife had committed me so many times. I took the article to her.

"Just read this!" I demanded.

She read it and shrugged. "You don't know what I've been through," she replied.

Ethel Merman once said to me, "Oscar, your wife sure loves you."

"She's pretty noncommittal about showing it," I grumbled.

June yawned. "I guess I'll have to throw myself in front of a streetcar to prove it, Ethel."

"There are no streetcars anymore," I pointed out in my usual literal fashion.

Ethel replied, "They go uphill in San Francisco." I've been pondering that one.

Florence, the best maid we ever had, used to come on Wednesdays. I always dreaded that day because my wife would have Florence dust the table in my bedroom where I keep my newspapers and magazines. They each have to be in just the right position. The most sanctified object on that table was my latest copy of the London *Observer*. One day Florence touched it while she was dusting. I exploded. She sat on a chair and cried. Then I apologized; I'm always dreadfully contrite at a time like this. I got down on my knees and begged her to forgive me. But she left and never came back.

I complained to one psychoanalyst about my wife—not about anything irrational, but that she touched magazines or other objects that were quite holy to me. I told him I'd get into a cold sweat and a kind of paralysis and absolute congealed hysterics when this happened.

The doctor said, "You can't blame your wife for behaving normally."

I tried to use this as an antidote, but it doesn't work.

I find most forms of exercise repugnant and aimless; walking without an objective, dull and pointless. Also fatiguing. Psychologically it is important to know this although few may consider my views on the matter significant. It was better and more meaningful when I used to go shopping with my wife, when we had an objective, going from one store to another or going to a friend's house. Then the walking took on briskness and purpose.

It's the difference between practicing at the piano in your room and playing a concert. There is no tension in your room. The audience that you have to overcome (overwhelm is the better word) isn't there. Even playing in a room full of people, which I haven't done for a long time, creates tension and therefore makes the playing more important. No matter how much you practice, I discovered years ago when I was concertizing, you are never in shape until after five or six concerts in front of the public.

I bought a bicycle in the spring of 1958. I rode up to Pamela and James Mason's, and he was so excited about it that he was envious. He took his daughter Portland's tricycle and got on it and we both rode through the streets of Beverly Hills.

I finally gave up riding it. It was too strenuous, what with the traffic in Beverly Hills and the Tanner buses with the tourists. Every time I left my house the bus would stop and the driver would point his finger and give a lecture about me. I'd run in terror.

Recently I've had a yen for gefullte fish. There are two makes: one is taboo in my home—it's called Mother's (an unfortunate commercial title); the other is Manischewitz. My wife bought some, but it was put on top of a couple of cans of sardines. When I was in my prime, I was an egomaniac and didn't allow my wife to buy the best sardines—the King Oscars—which bear my name. I felt there should be only one king in the house. But I finally compromised and let her buy Oscar Mayer products. Yet this jar of gefullte fish was on top of the sardines I wanted and I suddenly saw that it was Mother's. So I didn't have sardines for three months.

I finally got up the courage to order my wife to throw out the jar of gefullte fish. A couple of days after it disappeared she told me that it had been Manischewitz all the time. I have neurotic eyes. (Sometimes I have neurotic ears, too.) But I still didn't have sardines for three months because I was afraid that if I touched them, I'd get contaminated by my neurosis. It's quite volatile.

Food confuses me. An unscrupulous doctor who used to prey on my weakness, using extortionist rates, was once giving me shots and placebos and a few pills. My taste buds were dulled, as they are now, too. Suddenly I could only eat chili con carne. I'd eat it about 12:30 as night. I had always loathed chili con carne before.

I like tart things. One midnight recently I told one of my daughters to bring me some salad with sardines and herring on it. She was aghast, but that's my Ovaltine before I go to bed.

My food obsessions change. The other night my daughter Lorna reminisced about the time I regressed to complete infantilism. We were having dinner and tapioca pudding was served. A wild glint came into my eyes and in the presence of my wife and children I shrieked at the top of my voice, *"I love this more than anything in the world!"* I had to be withdrawn from tapioca pudding slowly. It was one of the few times I wasn't committed to achieve withdrawal. I just had a teaspoonful less every night. The last time it was served to me it looked like soap shavings. At the table I sometimes discourse on the cynicism of the blintz, particularly our homemade variety, or the bottled anger and rapelike aggressiveness of Coca-Cola.

About a year before my tapioca kick, I had a passion for chocolate—especially chocolate mousse and chocolate parfait. Whenever I was in New York, I'd sit in a completely reclining position at Le Pavillon and watch the waiters serve chocolate mousse. It became a hobby. I had so many chocolate stains on my suit that when the waiter would come with mine I'd say, "Just serve it on my lapel."

* * *

One time in the 40's I was taking my usual train trip to California from New York. During the stopover in Chicago I was restive and suddenly took a plane. My untrammeled fears about flying and the fact that it was Yom Kippur provided an opportunity to broaden the spectrum of my superstition rituals. I created a new ritual which I retained until recently. I "read" punctuation marks, including parentheses, exclamation points, commas—even accents on French words and dollar signs. I mutely say all of them in my mind. On this trip I repeated phrases ten times, in case I missed a word or forgot a comma. (When the late President Kennedy was revealed as a speed reader, it took me three hours to read the article about it.) This includes Walter Winchell, with the three-dot form of journalism. Actually there are four, but I consider the first one a period, then I do the three dots. This form of journalese is characteristic of many of the trenchant modern American writers. (The style is trenchant but the content is as phony as whipped cream in a chain drugstore.) It's quite tedious and limits my reading time. And I know it's all a conspiracy to deny me pleasure. I love reading.

* * *

In New York in the old days, my shirts had to be put in backwards in the drawers. At that time I always smoked the cigarette of my sponsor. In those days it was Lucky Strike and they had a bad habit of putting the packs carelessly into cartons. Some cartons had them upside down. I would never touch those. Lux Soap disturbed me a lot . . . L.U.X. They had "Lucky Lager" which always makes my squirm. Olympia Beer must be pretty distressed—they use a horseshoe. I shudder at the hard-pressed situation where they have to appeal to the public with "Lucky" or a horseshoe. That's pretty inane and unimaginative. I have great contempt for that. Both words are taboo with me. When the Lucky Lager commercial is on, I don't smoke until the commercial is over—or with Olympia Beer, either. I never smoke a cigarette when there is a commercial with an umbrella in a closed room. As a matter of fact, an open umbrella any place is taboo. I desist from smoking.

Speaking of superstitions, Truman Capote and I finally met recently. I'd read an interview with Capote in the *Paris Review* several years before and knew that he was as superstitious as I.

He said he never allowed three cigarette butts in an ashtray. Since then, in my bedroom—the high altar of my rituals and the place where I'm most tyrannical—I've cut mine down to one butt per ashtray.

* * *

Until 1958, if one of my friends was sick, I'd cut him off and not see him again. I viewed it as a personal affront to me. Also when someone once asked, "Do you remember me?" I replied giddily and with some joy, "Fortunately I'm suffering from amnesia."

When I'm in the mood, I vary the reply to this question. A woman once tricked me by asking, "Do you remember when you and I were in the earthquake?"

I dismissed her beautifully. "Every moment is an earthquake to me," I replied.

And to another woman who squirmed up to me at a party with the classic query, I answered, "No," and when she told me her name, added, "I make it a point never to remember you." Then I added guiltily, "Because I see you so seldom."

I have acrophobia. It's not only the fear that I'll jump off high places, it's that if I do . . . well, I hate mingling with strangers.

I won't get dressed unless my wife urges me to. And I'm indifferent to my appearance. Years ago Stanley Marcus, of the Neiman-Marcus Department Store in Dallas, Texas, introduced himself to me. "We're supposed to look alike," he said. We both stared at each other in mutual horror.

When I was young, I looked like Al Capone but I lacked his compassion. Once my composer friend David Raksin told me that he was taking his three-year-old son to the San Diego Zoo to see the gorilla. I told him to bring the child to my house and save the trip.

Apparently I enjoy self-chastisement. When I used to speak of the lunatic fringe, I didn't know I was going to head it.

People often ask me why I moved to the West Coast from New York. I like to explain that it was because the eastern waves aren't big enough for surfing. "Besides," I used to cry, "how can I go back to New York when my daughter is the chief pompon girl at Beverly High?"

I understand that President Kennedy once considered me to head the physical fitness program. It was politics. I could have delivered the mental illness vote in a solid bloc. Instead, he chose Stan Musial, who has the Polish bloc.

I get glimmers of my real character from time to time. Once a Beverly Hills cop stopped me when I was trying to enter my own house, and was going to arrest me because I looked so furtive.

"Do I look like a criminal?" I asked indignantly.

"You sure do," he replied.

I took him into the house and had my wife identify me.

At one time I was a pretty good driver, except I refused to back up my car and I never knew how to get into a parking place.

Once I was going over the speed limit and a cop stopped me and gave me a ticket and told me what mileage I was doing. I said, "But I was humming the last movement of the Beethoven Seventh Symphony," and I sang it to him, in its furious tempo. Then I said, "You can't possibly hum the last movement of Beethoven's Seventh Symphony and go slow." He agreed. I didn't get a ticket.

A psychiatrist once diagnosed my troubles as "an abdication of will." I wake up, and the feeling of terror is so knife-edged . . . just the idea of waking up and facing a day of inertia and fear makes me long for a return to the unconscious. That's one reason why I address sleep with such great reverence; I can escape fear and melancholia.

Once you're in a mental hospital, you might as well make up your mind to look after yourself and recognize my axiom: The patient is never right.

A few years ago when I was suffering from a nutritional deficiency and had anorexia they were feeding me pureed food, catering to my womblike regression. I hit upon a brilliant idea to supplement my nutrition.

"Why not give me Metrecal?" I asked the doctor. He was impressed by my ingenuity. That's how much they get accustomed to routine. But the Metrecal disagreed with me.

As for the axiom, I recall being given a sleeping medicine called Somnos, a form of chloral hydrate with alcohol in it. One night in the hospital my Somnos dose tasted weak, flaccid, and apparently watered and it proved inefficacious that night. I told the head nurse that the dose was inadequate. She protested that it was the regular dose. I raised hell. The next morning my doctor bawled me out for questioning the word of the nurse. He practically accused me of being irreligious, his faith in the staff was so prodigious. Later one of the nurses admitted that I had been right. What had happened was that the bottle was nearly empty, it was a Saturday night, and they had forgotten to renew the order.

On the psychiatric floor at Mount Sinai Hospital, which I've been in and out of from 1956 to 1962, the regime is strict and confining, particularly for the deeply depressed and catatonic patients. I don't believe that confining a deeply depressed patient in a solitary cell helps anyone—except the hospital administration. The attendants are nearly always Irish Catholic, for some reason. I once commented that you needed a permit from Pope John to get two Bufferin there. The meals come on the typical hospital schedule. I told Dorothy Parker that dinner was at quarter to five P.M. "That makes for a nice long evening," she replied.

I used to have an excellent memory, but when I was giving piano recitals "With Com-

ment" (that was how it was billed), one of my remarks was that I was writing a book to be called *Memoirs of a Man Suffering from Amnesia.* I did indeed suffer from amnesia after my shock treatments. One time when I was home either recuperating or just treading water—I can't remember which—I was watching a television picture of an old English film starring Sir Ralph Richardson.

June entered the room and asked, "What are you watching?"

I explained that it was an absorbing story in which Richardson played the role of a man who had an attack of amnesia—and I was anxious to see how it came out.

June sighed, "You saw that movie last week," she said.

I'm so guilt-ridden that when I watch *The Defenders* on television and the jury shuffles in and the judge says, "Have you reached a verdict?" I start to panic. When the foreman stands up and says, "Yes, Your Honor," and the judge add, "Will the defendant please rise?" I always stand up. And get hysterically happy when the jury finds me guilty.

Years ago there was a play called *The Amazing Dr. Clitterhouse* which was later made into a movie with Edward G. Robinson. At the end of the second act the judge orders the protagonist to stand, and announces, "You are guilty," and the man falls down.

When I got up for a smoke after that second-act curtain, I fell right down. It was complete neurotic association. Actually, about four attorneys general in different administrations could sue me for monopoly of guilt.

During the summer of 52, I again went east to play at the Lewisohn Stadium in New York.

Before the concert all the strength left my body. It was unbearable neurotic hysteria which included a psychogenic paralysis. During the performance I lost my coordination. I managed to finish the concert but after that ordeal I declared a hiatus.

In 1953 I spend most of my time in bed in a dazed, drugged loneliness, days and nights fading into one another without meaning.

Ahead—although I didn't know it then—was nearly a decade of addictions and withdrawals, of commitments and subtle revolts of my subconscious which would manifest themselves in anguish.

It all blends into a phantasmagoria, a gray blur in which people and events emerge now and again and then recede. I remember hospital beds, a parade of doctors, homosexual male nurses, friends and fellow patients coming and going. Above all, I remember the never-ending desire for those drugs which would give me instant oblivion, the wild and neurotic quest for unconsciousness. Woven through the warp and woof of this fabric of terror and pain were threads of manic elation, deep depression and fantasy.

In trying to recollect those years, incidents fade into one another and perspective vanishes. The details and chronology are not easily recalled.

SELF TEST: MEASURING COMPREHENSION
Chapter 3

1. What are the major distinctions between neurotic and psychotic behavior?

2. Generally speaking, at what point does behavior cease to be normal and become neurotic?

3. What are the major distinctions between the anxiety and phobic reactions?

4. Referring to the selection by Oscar Levant, indicate specific behaviors of him that are symptomatic of the following types of neurosis.

   a) anxiety neurosis

   b) phobic neurosis

   c) depression

   d) conversion hysteria

   e) dissociative hysteria

   f) obsessive-compulsive neurosis

THE PSYCHOTIC DISORDERS

A. Schizophrenia
Schizophrenic Disorder (DSM-III)

Schizophrenia is currently the greatest challenge faced by the fields of psychology and psychiatry. It is estimated that there are 320,000 hospitalized schizophrenics in the United States. The chances are one in a hundred that any individual will be hospitalized as a schizophrenic at some time in his life. Schizophrenics occupy two thirds of all beds in mental hospitals (Lehmann, 1967, p. 593).

Schizophrenia, previously called dementia praecox, has puzzled mankind for thousands of years. The term schizophrenic has been used to describe the most severely impaired chronic cases in locked wards in mental hospitals to "anyone who wanders in the hospital door looking befuddled..." (Haley, 1965). It is a confusing disorder. Although theories of schizophrenia are many, we do not really know what causes it. Treatments are virtually limitless, but we don't know how to cure it. We don't conclusively know if it can be best understood through medical, genetic, or psychological approaches. The behavioral symptoms that may be considered as part of the schizophrenic syndrome are almost endless; yet no two schizophrenics will demonstrate the same constellation of symptoms. When put in its simplest term, schizophrenia means pretty much the same as the layman term "crazy".

Often, when people hear the word schizophrenia applied to an individual, they infer that the person has a "split personality". This is a misconception. It is true that the prefix "schiz" does mean split, but it does not necessarily mean that the schizophrenic individual has a split personality. Split personality is more an accurate description of multiple personality, a type of dissociative hysteria, already discussed. The "schiz" in schizophrenia really refers to the split the person has made with reality. The schizophrenic is at least at times out of contact with reality. To the observer it seems that the schizophrenic lives in a world of his own. The prefix "schiz" also refers to a split in emotion that is often common in schizophrenics. They are often emotionally withdrawn and do not have close interpersonal relations with others. They may laugh wildly in a sad situation or sob in a happy one. The affect, or emotional behavior, of the schizophrenic is impaired.

Many schizophrenics experience hallucinations. They may see things that do not exist. The size, shape, and brightness of things they really do see may continually change. They may hear sounds that do not exist. They will answer aloud to imagined voices. They may experience tactile hallucinations, such as the feeling that there are fingers wrapped around their throat strangling them. They may also suffer delusions. Delusions are false beliefs that the person holds. Schizophrenics may believe that they are being followed, persecuted, or under governmental scrutiny, when in reality such is not the case. They may believe that they are immortal and that nothing can harm them. They may feel that television shows are made for them, and provide them with important, personal messages.

Disturbances of logic, thought and language, or disturbances of the cognitive domain, are common in the schizophrenic. A schizophrenic may reason "The Virgin Mary was a virgin: I'm a virgin; therefore, I'm the Virgin Mary", or "John is Peter's father; therefore, Peter is John's father" (Lehmann, 1967 (a), p. 624).

The language of the schizophrenic may be incoherent and seem to ramble on endlessly without coming to any point or conclusion. He may confabulate, or confuse fact with fantasy in his conversation. If he reaches a point in the conversation where he cannot remember what really happened in a particular instance, he may make something up to substitute for the information he has forgotten. A schizophrenic's speech is often echolalic. Echolalic speech involves almost exact repetition of what has just been said to the patient. The question, "How are you today?" asked of the schizophrenic, may be followed by a response of "How are you today?" This can be taken as an indication that although the patient is capable of speaking, he really does not understand what he is saying. He appears remote, detached and disinterested in his surroundings.

The schizophrenic may create neologisms, or new words. These words seldom mean anything to anyone but the individual himself. During the course of conversation the schizophrenic may use words that sound as though they should have some meaning. He may use proper sentence structure, grammar, and voice inflection in his speech. However, the key word in a sentence is often a neologism that is not part of our language and has significance only for the schizophrenic. The insertion of neologisms in the language of the schizophrenic is reminiscent of a professional comedian performing double talk.

The neologism may express a concept that he cannot otherwise express. The neologism may be a form of linguistic shorthand for the schizophrenic by which he attempts to relate the content of a whole paragraph in a single word. Lehmann (1967, pp. 627-628) describes the meaning that a neologism had for one schizophrenic patient.

> "A schizophrenic woman who had been hospitalized for several years kept repeating, in an otherwise quite rational conversation, the word "polamolalittersjitterstittersleelitla." The psychiatrist asked her to spell it out, and she then proceeded to explain to him the meaning of the various components, which she insisted were to be used as one word. "Polamolalitters" was intended to recall the disease poliomyelitis, since the patient wanted to indicate that she felt she was suffering from a serious disease affecting her nervous system; the component "litters" stood for untidiness or messiness, the way she felt inside; "jitterstitters" reflected her inner nervousness and lack of ease; "leelitla" was a reference to the French le lit la (that bed there), meaning that she was both dependent on and feeling handicapped by her illness."

The appearance of the schizophrenic may be quite deteriorated. He may not wash, shave, change his clothes, or take care of his personal hygiene. His manners may be extremely crude. He just doesn't care how he appears to others.

The preceeding are some of the common symptoms associated with schizophrenia. There are also numerous, more specific sub-classifications of schizophrenia. One such sub-classification is catatonic schizophrenia. In addition to the usual psychotic symptoms of the patient, the catatonic patient may be characterized by states of complete stupor. He may become almost perfectly still. His arms and legs may be contorted in bizarre fashion and he may remain in this position for hours on end. If his arms or legs are repositioned by an aide, he may then assume this new position. This puppet-like characteristic of the catatonic schizophrenic is called waxy flexibility. After a long period of being mute and motionless, the catatonic may suddenly and without reason demonstrate brief, violent outbursts of destructive behavior (Lehmann, 1967, p. 631).

In addition to his psychotic symptoms, the paranoid schizophrenic is characterized primarily by the presence of severe delusions. The delusions may be of grandeur. The patient may feel that he is immortal and that nothing can harm him. He may believe that he is Christ or some other religious or political figure. Because of his feelings of invincibility and power he may be quite likely to attempt or commit suicide, as he feels he cannot possibly die. Delusions of persecution are often common. The person may be suspicious, reserved and careful. He may feel that everyone is "out to get him". He may also be prone to outbursts of physical violence. In one case in which I was involved, a young man developed paranoid thoughts after he had swindled the government of welfare and unemployment money. He became extremely concerned that he would get caught. He imagined passersby on the street as F.B.I. agents. He perceived secret messages in radio and television programs. He fled the area to question an old college friend about her role in the imagined governmental investigation of him.

It is likely that many transient hobos, who run scared from town to town, never staying in one place very long, and attempt to avoid pursuers that do not really exist, are really undiagnosed paranoid schizophrenics. It is also plausible that many prostitutes are undiagnosed paranoid schizophrenics. Many girls who eventually become prostitutes were physically and sexually abused by members of their family during their earlier lives. It is understandable that they would develop feelings of persecution. These justified feelings of persecution may eventually become exaggerated and delusional, motivating a girl to flee to a large urban area where she feels she will be safer. Once in a new, strange, scary city, she may find some sense of security in a pimp, who assures her that he will protect and take care of her. Because she is easily deluded, she may come to believe that she is her pimp's only lover, even though she sees him daily with his other prostitutes.

As previously mentioned, the symptoms of schizophrenia may differ somewhat from case to case. However, if a person is out of contact with reality, suffers hallucinations and delusions, is prone to extreme emotional outbursts, or prolonged periods of emotional withdrawal, is generally confused and disoriented, and demonstrates impairment of thought and language, a diagnosis of schizophrenia would be most probable.

B. Manic-Depression   Schizoaffective Disorder (DSM-III)

Manic-depression is a form of psychosis in which the individual becomes severely handicapped by extreme emotional states. The manic-depressive may also demonstrate the common symptoms of psychosis, such as the break with reality, hallucinations, delusions, and disordered thought, but it is commonly thought that the development of these psychotic symptoms occur as the result of the extreme and crippling emotional experiences of the manic-depressive (Cohen, 1967, p. 676).

A manic person has limitless energy. He is enthusiastic, bubbly, and inspired. He can work for days on end with very little sleep. He has fantastic goals for the future. No task is too large, complex, or difficult for the manic individual. Thousands of ideas continually race through his mind. He cannot sit still. He is always on the go. He has unbelievable self-confidence.

A depressed person is listless, lethargic, sad, apathetic, and melancholic. His expectancies for the future are bleak. He is plagued by self-doubt. Depression is the converse of mania.

Manic-depressive psychosis can take a variety of forms. The classic case of manic-depression is called circular manic-depression. It involves alternating periods of mania and depression. The person may be manic for a period of time and suddenly and unpredictably slide into a period of severe depression. After a period of depression, he may then again enter the manic phase. Commonly, the person may enjoy relatively long periods of remission, or normalcy, between the manic and depressive phases. The person may suffer one episode of mania and then enter long term depression, or one episode of depression and then enter long term mania. In a case in which I was involved, a woman had gone into depression for a two month period following the birth of her child about twenty years ago. Since that time she has had numerous periods of mania, in which she becomes incoherent, flighty, uncontrollably active, and out of touch with reality. The depressive phase has not recurred. Circular manic-depression is the diagnosis when the individual has had at least one manic and one depressive episode at sometime (Diagnostic and Statistical Manual, 1968, p. 37).

Manic-depressive illness, manic type, consists of only manic episodes. Manic-depressive illness, depressed type, consists of only depressive episodes. It is to be distinguished from neurotic depression in that in manic-depression, depressed type, the person may become stuporous, break with reality, hallucinate, and develop delusions. The degree of overall impairment is greater than in neurotic depression.

Manic-depressives can be terrifically productive people when in their manic phases, providing their cognitive disorganization is not so extreme that they are rendered helpless. Controlled mania is common in high achievers. A psychiatrist once told me that if it were not for manic people, nothing would ever get accomplished. I don't fully agree with his belief, but often a mild, controlled state of mania can be conducive to achievement. Bert Yancey was one of America's best professional golfers a few years ago. He won almost $700,000 on the professional tour throughout his career. He has also been a manic-depressive for about two decades. David Kindred, of the Washington Post writes:

> "In the winter of 1974, Yancey was floating on a high. He knew it, he says today, and as all manic-depressives would, he loved it. The high is intoxicating. It is a feeling the manic-depressive craves just as the alcoholic thirsts for the bottle's deliverance from life's pain.
>
> He didn't know what to make of it in 1960, but now Yancey recognizes the symptoms of his illness. "I couldn't sleep. I went for three nights and four days without sleeping. When you're high your mind just works and works constantly. That's when you're creative. You get really charged up."
>
> "What happens," Yancey said, trying to explain the catalyst of his manic highs, "is that when you succeed, believe it or not, you become depressed. For me, anyway, you become depressed because your body feels now it has to succeed again and again . . . so my body was saying 'Man, I'm tired. I'm tired of this. I'm depressed because we can't keep up this pace.' So a manic episode follows (Kindred, 1978)."

Ronald Fieve, previously described as an expert on manic-depression and pioneer of lithium carbonate treatment for it, feels that some of history's most productive and creative people have been manic-depressives. Ernest Hemmingway, the famous writer, was a manic-depressive whose extremes of mood made national headlines. He spent great amounts of time writing and if he wasn't writing he was hunting, fishing or fighting, anything to keep active. He referred to his depressive episodes as his "black-ass days". He eventually killed himself during one of those episodes. Abraham Lincoln suffered numerous serious episodes of depression. During one such episode his friends had to keep razors and knives away from him for fear that he would kill himself. Fieve also feels that Theodore Roosevelt and Winston Churchill were manic-depressives (Fieve, 1975, pp. 116-145). Famous singers Rosemary Clooney and Tony Orlando have had serious manic-depressive episodes.

Fieve estimates that there are between ten and twelve million manic-depressives in American (Fieve, 1975, p. 181). Many are diagnosed and treated for the disorder. Others are never diagnosed or treated and struggle through their lives plagued by their recurring extreme mood swings. The compulsive gambler who is observed talking to himself aloud as he violently throws crumbled tickets to the ground at a race track, the successful manic stock investor who is occasionally absent from the stock exchange because of periodic bouts with depression, or the housewife, who cannot find the energy to get out of bed or care for her house one week and the next week buys new curtains, rugs and appliances and cannot seemingly spend enough time caring for her house, are possible examples of undiagnosed, struggling, ambulatory manic-depression.

C. Other Psychoses

Functional disorders are those in which no definite causative, or etiological factor, can be identified for the disorder. Organic disorders are those in which some physical, biological, biochemical, or genetic factor has been identified as the cause of the disorder. It is a matter of great debate as to whether the neurotic disorders and psychotic disorders, such as schizophrenia and manic-depression, should be considered as functional or organic disorders. Although currently we are unable to definitely determine what the organic factor may be in all types of behavioral disorders, the point has been made that because we currently cannot find organic etiological factors in all cases of behavioral disorder, does not mean they don't exist (Ausubel, 1961). With more comprehensive research, we may be more successful in finding these organic etiologies in the future.

Although it is a matter of debate as to whether there are organic etiologies in the neuroses and psychoses, there are certain types of psychoses in which organic factors are the causes of these disorders. I will now describe some of the types of psychosis in which there are identifiable, organic etiologies.

1. Korsakov's Psychosis   Alcohol Amnestic Syndrome (DSM-III)

Korsakov's psychosis results from the chronic abuse of alcohol. Deterioration of the nervous system can be identified. Along with other symptoms of psychosis, the person is likely to be confused, disoriented in time and place, suffer from amnesic blocks and confabulate. Delirium tremens, in which the person shakes, becomes terrified, and is likely to experience severe hallucinations, such as being attacked by animals or having bugs crawling all over him, may precede the psychosis. The organic etiology is the damage done by chronic over-use of alcohol (Solomon, 1967, p. 463).

2. General Paresis   Dementia (DSM-III)

General Paresis is a type of psychosis that results from untreated syphilis. Because of spirochetal invasion, the brain and nervous system suffer severe, permanent damage. The disorder develops in about 5% of syphilitics and usually about five to fifteen years after the initial infection. Along with the common psychotic symptoms, the person may demonstrate bizarre delusions, slurred speech, paralysis, poor reflexes, and extremely poor personal hygiene. At one time paresis accounted for 10% of all admissions to mental hospitals (Mulder and Dale, 1967, p. 781). Penicillin has been used extensively and effectively in the treatment of syphilis. During the 1950's the number of cases of syphilis dropped dramatically. However, it was estimated that in 1970 the number of syphilitic Americans had risen to one million (Strange, 1971). Apparently many people incorrectly feel that syphilis is no longer a threat. It is likely that in the 1980's there will be a tragic, unnecessary resurgence of general paresis in this country.

3. Huntington's Chorea   Dementia (DSM-III)

Huntington's chorea is a progressive nervous disorder that ultimately leads to death. There is no known cure, or effective treatment for it. It is a disorder that is inherited. All people who develop Huntington's chorea have a parent who also had the disorder. It is passed on through the influence of a dominant gene, which means that about half of the children born of a parent with Huntington's chorea will develop the disorder (Rainer, 1967, p. 38).

The person may demonstrate the common symptoms of psychosis accompanied by gradually increasing difficulty in movement, loss of coordination, depression, tremors, and impaired speech. Woody Guthrie, American folksinger, died of Huntington's chorea. He was often mistakenly taken to be drunk because of his impaired coordination and speech. The disease usually begins to afflict the person between the ages of 30 and 50 and death usually results in about 15 years (Solomon, 1967, p. 461). Huntington's chorea is a particularly tragic disease. The person who has a parent with Huntington's chorea may suffer extreme anxiety wondering if he will become afflicted with the disease. Because the disease does not begin to affect the person until about age thirty, the possible victim of Huntington's chorea will be faced with the tremendous ethical decision of whether or not he should have children, and possibly pass along the trait to them.

Other types of organic psychosis can be brought on by brain damage, poisoning, tumors, or other types of infection.

We have now described the major classifications of psychosis.

References

Diagnostic And Statistical Manual of Mental Disorders (Second Edition) (Washington, D.C., American Psychiatric Association, 1968).

Diagnostic and Statistical Manual of Mental Disorders (Third Edition) (Draft), The Task Force on Nomenclature and Statistics of The American Psychiatric Association, January 15, 1978.

David P. Ausubel, Personality Disorder *Is* Disease, *The American Psychologist*, 16, (1961), 69-74.

Robert A. Cohen, Manic-Depressive Reactions. In Freedman and Kaplan, editors. *Comprehensive Textbook of Psychiatry* (Baltimore: The Williams and Wilkens Company, 1967).

Ronald Fieve, *Moodswing: The Third Revolution in Psychiatry* (New York: William Morrow and Company, 1967).

Frazier and Carr, Phobic Reaction. In Freedman and Kaplan, editors. *Comprehensive Textbook of Psychiatry* (Baltimore: The Williams and Wilkens Company, 1967).

Sigmund Freud, On the Psychical Mechanism of Hysterical Phenonema: A Lecture (1893). *The Standard Edition of the Complete Works of Sigmund Freud*, Volume III (London, The Hogarth Press, 1962).

Jay Haley, The Art of Being Schizophrenic, Voices, 1, 1965.

Dave Kindred, Golfer Bert Yancey's Long Struggle. *The Daily Press*, Utica, New York, March 27, 1978.

Heinz E. Lehmann, Schizophrenia I: Introduction and History. In Freedman and Kaplan, editors. *Comprehensive Textbook of Psychiatry,* (Baltimore: The Williams and Wilkens Company, 1967).

Harold I. Lief, Anxiety Reaction. In Freedman and Kaplan, editors. *Comprehensive Textbook of Psychiatry* (Baltimore: The Williams and Wilkens Company, 1967).

Perry London, *Foundations of Abnormal Psychology* (New York: Holt, Rinehart, and Winston, Inc., 1968).

Harry Milt, *Basic Book on Mental Illness*, (Maplewood, New Jersey, Scientific Aids Publications, 1969).

Mogielnicki, Mogielnicki, Chandler, and Weissberg, Impending Child Abuse. *The Journal of the American Medical Association*, Vol 237, No. 11, March 14, 1977.

O. Hobart Mowrer, There May Indeed be "Another Way", Reply to James D. Smrtic, Publication Pending.

Mulder and Dale, Brain Syndrome Associated With Infection. In Freedman and Kaplan, editors. *Comprehensive Textbook of Psychiatry* (Baltimore: The Williams and Wilkens Company, 1967).

John C. Nemiah, Obsessive-Compulsive Reaction. In Freedman and Kaplan, editors. *Comprehensive Textbook of Psychiatry* (Baltimore: The Williams and Wilkens Company, 1967).

John D. Rainer, Genetics and Psychiatry. In Freedman and Kaplan, editors. *Comprehensive Textbook of Psychiatry*. (Baltimore: The Williams and Wilkens Company, 1967).

Seymour Solomon, Clinical Neurology and Neuropathology. In Freedman and Kaplan, editors. *Comprehensive Textbook of Psychiatry*. (Baltimore: The Williams and Wilkens Company, 1967).

M. Strange, VD: The Clock is Ticking. *Today's Health*. 1971, 49, 16-18, 69-71.

The Thin Edge, "Depression", Produced by WNET, New York State Education Department, 1975.

A PORTRAIT OF PSYCHOSIS
from *Personality Development and Psychopathology*
Norman Cameron

Norman Cameron, who has been associated with the Institute of Human Relations at Yale University, has had great experience in the practice of psychoanalysis, or Freudian psychotherapy. Of all of the cases that Cameron has described, I feel that the case of Joan R., a schizophrenic, is the most interesting. Although Cameron's psychoanalytic bias is evident in his presentation of Joan's case, the constellation of symptoms characteristic of the schizophrenic is vividly described. As you read about the psychotic behavior of Joan, try to make distinctions between her condition and that of Oscar Levant, whose neurotic behavior was previously described.

A Schizophrenic Reaction In An Adolescent Girl

Joan R., A Kansas City high school girl, was admitted to a psychiatric clinic after she had attempted suicide by drinking iodine. We shall begin with her childhood. She had suffered the loss through death of two important mother figures, one when she was two years old, the other when she was fourteen. These are critical ages in personality development, ages when a mother figure plays her most significant roles. Joan's mother had been ill for some time before her death, so that the little girl lacked the ego support which should have been available to her for the structuring of her early personality. At fourteen, when an adolescent normally lives through in altered form the edipal conflicts of early childhood, Joan's foster mother died, and Joan was again left with no one to help her build her adolescent personality. To further complicate matters for Joan, her foster mother was her father's sister, a domineering widow with a daughter of her own. It will be simplest if we present briefly the patient's life history.

As we have said, Joan was two years old when her mother died. Her father's sister moved at once into the home, taking Joan's mother's place, and bringing with her Peggy, an eight-year-old daughter. We shall see how Joan tried to repeat what her foster mother had done as soon as death left her place vacant. Peggy's mother was an anxious, probably superstitious woman who encouraged Joan to be over-dependent. The two girls apparently hated each other. When Peggy's mother died, Joan was fourteen and Peggy was a grown woman of twenty. The household now consisted of Joan, Peggy and Joan's father, a scholar with little psychological understanding.

To her father's surprise Joan showed no sorrow over the death of her foster mother. Instead, she tried at once to take her place in the home, just as her foster mother had immediately taken her own mother's place. She became self-assertive, arrogant and demanding. The home, she said, was now hers, and Peggy could henceforth obey her orders. Joan's father spent the next two years trying unsuccessfully to keep the peace between these two girls, rivals for control of the home.

Without a mother figure and without a stable personality of her own, Joan soon got out of control. She continued for the time being to be affectionate to her father, but she also behaved toward him as a nagging wife rather than as a young adolescent daughter. She openly criticized his appearance and his ways, even in front of guests. She demanded that he give her more attention and more money. She reminded her father that her foster mother, her father's sister, had been afraid of the house, often saying that there was a curse upon it. She protested violently against his going out in the evening and leaving the latchkey under the mat, where strangers might find it. As we shall see Joan was already beginning to develop delusional fears in relation to this evening situation. Toward Peggy, her grownup cousin, she remained relentlessly hostile. Once during a quarrel over the radio she bit Peggy severely, giving her a wound that took two weeks to heal. From other evidence it is clear that Joan's emotional problems, with which no one helped her, were precipitating a general personality disorganization.

When Joan was sixteen her cousin married. This removed her rival from the home; but it also left Joan, in a state of emotional turmoil, alone in the house with her father. Her attitude toward him abruptly changed. She no longer gave or accepted tokens of affection. The hate that she had visited upon her cousin she now directed toward her father. She behaved insolently toward him, accusing him even before visitors of mistreating her. These accusations, which completely mystified her father, were actually the product of delusional experiences that she was having, experiences in which weird primary process fears and wishes had escaped repression and were mingling with preconscious and conscious organization. What these were we shall soon see. Whenever Joan had frightening dreams she would make her father join her in bed, as her aunt had always done, but later she would rail against him for having done this and accuse him of mistreatment. He was greatly disconcerted by all this contradiction and confusion; but he did not know what to do about it. He thought she would outgrow it. One night he came home late to find his daughter thrashing about the room with a cane—killing snakes, she said. She used to keep her light on all night long because she was having "frightening dreams," which were probably delusional and hallucinatory experiences rather than dreams.

As might be expected, after the aunt's death, when Joan was fourteen, her school work grew poorer and poorer. She seemed bored, inattentive and irritable. By the time she was fifteen and a half she needed a tutor to keep her from being dropped from school. Eventually even this help was not enough. When she was sixteen, Joan was dropped from school, and her father was told to consult a psychiatrist. The psychiatrist recommended immediate treatment, but his recommendation was not followed. Joan simply stayed at home.[1]

Joan showed a corresponding decline in her social relationships. Undoubtedly because of her personality defects, and because she was overdependent upon her foster mother, Joan had never reached an adequate level of social skill. She frightened and repelled the neighborhood children with her temper tantrums and uncompromising demands. As an adolescent she was far too much involved in the rivalry with her cousin for domination of the home, in her own revived edipal conflicts and her preoccupations with frightening experiences to be able to interact normally with her peers, the boys and girls around her.

The climax came when Joan was sixteen, a year before she came to the hospital. She bought a new dress for a high school dance, but when her escort arrived she refused at first to see him. After considerable persuasion she finally consented to go with him; half an hour later she returned home without her escort. Perhaps she knew that her father had arranged to have her escorted when he found that nobody had invited her to the dance. At any rate this was her last social engagement. Following Joan's withdrawal from school, her father arranged little parties for her, "to help her get well," but she would shut herself in her room until the guests left the house. The best he could do about the situation was to engage a housekeeper.

During the months between leaving school and entering the hospital Joan was living in a nightmare. She was afraid to sleep at night because of all that seemed to be going on. During the day she lay around the house, preoccupied, worn out and doing next to nothing. Her behavior became obviously strange, reflecting the hopeless confusion of her thinking. For example, her father gave her forty dollars to buy some clothes, and she spent it all on history books which she never read. On another occasion she went out and spent twelve dollars on cosmetics, but a few days later she destroyed the lot. She got up early one morning, collected all the playing cards in the house and burned them, saying that they were sinful. She began talking about religion, the church, sin, charity and the hereafter. She gave the housekeeper five dollars because she had to be charitable "to get to heaven."

Joan said that all her troubles came from masturbation. At fifteen she concluded without telling anyone that this was driving her crazy. Her conclusion increased her already intolerable guilt, anxiety and confusion, and contributed to her belief that she would burn in hell for her sins, and that her hands were diseased. "I have leprosy!" she said at the hospital, "look at my hands. But that's not punishment enough for all my evil. Faust, yes, he gave himself to the devil. That's what I've done. Don't touch me! You'll be sorry, you'll get leprosy too!"[2]

The girl's unconscious material, which ultimately emerged and overwhelmed her, seems to have appeared first as anxiety dreams and frightening nighttime fantasies — of snakes, assault, strangers in the house and murder. "I used to read stories and things," she said, "and then I'd go to bed and lie awake and think about them. I'd be scared silly to be in the room by myself. That house is so spooky." The last statement repeats what her foster mother had always said. When Joan closed her eyes and tried to sleep, she would have horrible visions, and see faces that seemed to grow enormous.[3] She thought men were walking on the roofs, which were flat and connected with one another, and that they were climbing in the window. Eventually a man across the street seemed to control the house; and she began hearing voices. Finally a man's voice dominated, telling her to do whatever she was told.

Joan now used weird delusions to reconstruct the reality that she had lost in her steady regression and disorganizations, delusions which would help explain her previously unconscious fantasies, now fully conscious. Her home, she told herself, was now the headquarters of a dope ring. Her father had been murdered and an imposter put in his place. "My father wouldn't treat me the way this man has treated me," she said. "My father and I were friends. This man will get into bed with me. I've been love-starved and forsaken; and I thought someone was bringing in opium." The similarity of this tale to the common dope ring mystery story is obvious, and its appeal is probably to the same unconscious needs.

In her fantasies, which Joan considered real, people seemed to beat her and tie her up. They seemed able to read her mind, to control her by reading her thoughts. She tried to keep back her thoughts; but the effort hurt the back of her head.[4]

Joan began having horrible dreams and fantasies of killing her father and other people, of cutting them up and chewing their flesh, of being God, and of being murdered as a sacrifice.[5] She felt at times that she was someone else, that her body was changing, that she might be going to have a baby, that she had a brain tumor and was going crazy.

In the hospital, where people listened to her when she spoke, some of her sadomasochistic fantasies became obvious. Joan said that her suicidal attempt was an act of self-punishment. She was going to hell for her sins, she thought, and the quicker she got there the better. "I thought it would make me suffer. If I hadn't become so hardened it would have hurt terribly." At times she was sure she would be executed for her crimes, which seemed real to her, or that she would get life imprisonment. She wished that she would "get black smallpox or something." She said, "I hot hipped on the subject of Christianity. I thought I should torture myself. . . . I try to figure out ways of torturing people. It seems I have been in so much pain; and I want other people to have the same thing."

Joan had many outbursts of rage. One night a nurse found her trembling and wringing her hands. "I think I'm pushing people's eyes in. I'm dreadfully wicked. . . . It's those awful thoughts that go through my head." Once in the daytime she cried to a group of patients, "If I had the strength of Christ I would kill every one of you! Yes, I would kill you all because a more horrid doom awaits you than death." There is a sign of confusion between herself and the others in this histrionic statement. Another day Joan became angry and struck an inoffensive depressed patient. "That's nothing in comparison with what I'm going to do," she cried, "I'm going to chop off your heads, every one of you. You'd better go home and chop of your families' heads. . . . You're not going to keep me here and make me bear children!" In the more permissive atmosphere of the hospital, Joan was giving vent to the violent aggression that she had felt for years at home.[6] After expressing it, she excused herself on the grounds that she would be saving the patients from something worse by killing them.

There were grandiose delusions also. Joan said that she felt she had a powerful influence over people and was responsible for everything that happened. She thought that she might get superhuman ideas, "such as how Christ turned water into wine — I had to find out how it done." As God, she thought, she must suffer to help others; and because of her sins she ought to kill herself. But the attempt failed. "So," she said, "I came to the conclusion that I would have to forget. As time goes on, I'll forget all my troubles, my experiences and so forth." This was just what Joan seemed

to be achieving. She expressed, in well-organized secondary process speech, the disintegration which she was experiencing, and to which she was resigned.

Years before, when her foster mother died, Joan had begun a struggle at home with a tangled personal situation involving real persons, her father, her cousin and herself. For such a struggle, with one one around to understand her, Joan's personality organization was unprepared. As time went on, this shared social community was gradually replaced by the even greater complexities of Joan's delusional pseudocommunity, with its mixture of real and imagined persons, of fact and reconstructed delusion. Now she seemed to be making a final retreat. She was withdrawing into an autistic community which consisted mainly of fantasied persons and action with the background of her own private fantasies.[7]

There were two definite catatonic episodes. One day, while telling her therapist that she liked dreamy states, Joan slipped into a stupor. Her eyes closed, her eyeballs rolled upward, and her limbs went limp. Her eyelids resisted opening, however, and her jaws and limbs grew stiffer as they were manipulated. When she was left alone she soon recovered. Another day Joan was lying on her side on her bed, just before lunch, when there was a sudden loud clap of thunder close by. Joan instantly became so rigid that the nurses could pick her up and place her in a sitting position with no more change in her posture than if she had been a statue. Then the lunch trays arrived, and an experienced nurse began coaxing her gently and spoon-feeding her. After about ten minutes of this, the girl suddenly got up, rubbed her eyes as though she had just awakened, and ate her lunch with the others as if nothing had happened.

Therapy was unsuccessful with Joan. She slept well at night without medication, in spite of occasional disturbing dreams. In the daytime she spend most of her time daydreaming. She became less and less communicative, her talk developed more and more disorganization. She was frequently observed talking excitedly to herself. Sometimes she smiled and laughed as though she were hallucinating. Often she stood straight against the wall with her hands high above her head; but she would give no explanation of this posturing. Her father decided to place Joan in a state hospital near her home. Her prognosis for social recovery was poor.

---

[1]Bower, E. M., Shellhamer, T. A., and Daily, J. M., "School characteristics of male adolescents who later became schizophrenic," Amer. J. Orthopsychiat., 1961, 30, 712-739.

[2]Compare this with the neurotic compulsive reaction to soiled hands, as in the case of Sally J., who washed and scrubbed her hands when she had evil thoughts.

[3]Such changes in size have been reported by normal adults who have studied their visions when falling asleep. Cf. Silberer, H., "Report on a method of eliciting and observing certain symbolic hallucination-phenomena," in Rapaport, D. (Ed.), Organization and Pathology of Thought. New York: Columbia Univ. Press, 1951; Isakower, O., "A contribution to the pathopsychology of phenomena associated with falling asleep," Internat. J. Psychoanal., 1938, 19, 331-345.

[4]When adults anticipate a small child's actions, it must seem to the child that they know his thoughts. Such childhood experiences are probably the origins of this common form of schizophrenic delusion.

[5]Cannibalistic dreams are not rare among neurotic persons. Such dreams and the fantasies of this patient probably revive early childhood feeding fantasies which, in the adult, take on a more definite form.

[6]There is a recent discussion of sadomasochism in relation to aggression in Gero, G., "Sadism, masochism and aggression," Psychoanal. Quart., 1962, 31, 31-42.

[7]For a comparison of pseudocommunity and autistic community, see Cameron, N., and Magaret, A., Behavior Pathology. Boston: Houghton Mifflin, 1951, Chapters 13 and 14.

SELF TEST: MEASURING COMPREHENSION
Chapter 3

1. What behavioral symptoms would likely lead to a diagnosis of schizophrenia?

2. What behavioral symptoms would likely lead to a diagnosis of manic-depression?

3. What is a disorder of the affective domain?

4. What is a disorder of the cognitive domain?

5. What is a functional disorder?

6. What is an organic disorder?

7. Joan was described as a schizophrenic in the preceeding case study. Which sub-classification of schizophrenia describes her? Why?

8. What are the major differences between the overall conditions of Levant, described in the previous article, and Joan?

Chapter 4
THE ILLNESS PERSPECTIVE

The first of the five major perspectives we will cover is the illness perspective, or the medical model. It is the oldest of the perspectives. It is also probably the most popular, and the one with which the layman is most familiar. The illness perspective employs a medical approach to the treatment of psychiatric disorders. The treatments employed within the illness perspective are usually medical in nature (as in drug therapy), surgical (as in psychosurgery), or electrical (as in electroconvulsive therapy).

Although the illness perspective has made its most rapid advances during the twentieth century, the use of medical types of treatments for psychiatric disorders has been employed for thousands of years. Electroconvulsive therapy has been employed as a treatment for depression by contemporary psychiatry since the 1930's. It involves the passing of an electrical current, sufficient to produce a convulsion, through the patient's brain. However, thousands of years ago the technique of applying an electric eel to the skull of the patient was practiced by the ancient Greeks and Egyptians.

American psychiatry began using the major tranquilizers during the 1950's. Reserpine is one such tranquilizer. However, the rauwolfia root, from which reserpine is made, has been used as a tranquilizer for centuries in India and by "primitive" West African witchdoctors (Torrey, 1972).

The technique of psychosurgery, or the performance of surgical operations on the brain, is currently a very controversial topic. However, psychosurgery is not really new, either. The technique of trepanning was used in ancient Peru to treat what today would probably be called epilepsy. Trepanning involved the drilling of holes in the patient's skull to allow evil spirits to escape from his brain. Throughout history, shamans, or medicine men, have been given the responsibility of treating the equivalent of modern day psychiatric disorders in numerous cultures. Shamen would often use drugs, heavy smoking, alcohol and rhythmic drum music in the treatment of their patients (Mora, 1967). Although the medical model has made terrific advances recently, it is apparent that the use of medical treatments for psychiatric disorders is thousands of years old.

The basic theoretical orientation of the illness perspective involves a re-application of terms and concepts of physical medicine to the behavioral realm. In physical medicine, when a person is in a state of health his body functions normally and he feels well. However, this state of physical health can be disrupted. For example, a person may suffer a heart attack and have damage done to his heart. The person is physically ill, and symptoms such as pain, decreased activity level, and poor blood circulation may result. Medical treatments, such as drugs or surgery, may be employed to help improve the patient's physical health.

The same basic conceptualization is employed by the illness perspective in the treatment of psychiatric disorders. When the structure and function of the brain and body are normal, the person is in a state of mental health. His behavior is normal, and he feels psychologically well. However, this state of mental health can also become disrupted. Should the structure or function of the brain or body become abnormal, the person may become mentally ill, and behavioral symptoms result. The illness perspective then employs medical interventions to correct the physical disorder, so that the behavioral symptoms of mental illness can be eliminated. The concepts of health, illness, symptoms, and treatment are used in similar ways in both physical medicine and the illness perspective.

Because laymen understand the concept of physical illness and its need for medical treatment, they can accept the notion that when we behave abnormally we are mentally ill, and require medical treatment. Thus, the basic theoretical orientation of the illness perspective has received general public acceptance.

For the chapter on the illness perspective, I have selected articles which accentuate the theory and techniques of this perspective. The first article, "Should Some People Be Labeled Mentally Ill?", by Albert Ellis, investigates the validity of the concept of mental illness, as it is currently used. The second article, "It's Not All in Your Head", by Seymour S. Kety, describes advances made in drug treatment for psychiatric disorders. The final article of the chapter, "The Promise and Peril of Psychosurgery", by Richard Restak, describes the techniques of psychosurgery and discusses ethical concerns regarding its use.

References

George Mora, M.D., History of Psychiatry. In Freedman and Kaplan, editors. *Comprehensive Textbook of Psychiatry*. (Baltimore: The Williams and Wilkens Company, 1967).

E. Fuller Torrey, M.D., What Western Psychotherapists Can Learn From Witchdoctors. *American Journal of Orthopsychiatry*. 42 (1), January, 1972.

SHOULD SOME PEOPLE BE LABELED MENTALLY ILL?

from *Journal of Consulting Psychology, 1967*
Albert Ellis

People whose behavior has been sufficiently abnormal to warrant mental hospitalization are commonly referred to as "mentally ill". Proponents of the illness perspective are apt to use the term mental illness. Since the general public understands the concept of physical illness, proponents of the illness perspective feel that it is appropriate to reapply the concept of illness to the behavioral realm to describe people who behavior is "ill".

However, critics of the use of the term mental illness are quick to point out that evidence of "sick brains" must be found to warrant the term's usage. They also point out that evidence of "sick brains" in people who are labeled as mentally ill is rare. To have been at one time labeled as mentally ill can have strong prejudicial effects on an individual.

Professional opinion regarding the use of the term mental illness is strongly divided. Most professionals are either strongly in favor of, or strongly against, the use of the term. The following article, by Dr. Albert Ellis, is a unique, objective investigation into the advantages and disadvantages of using the term mental illness to describe abnormal behavior.

The question considered is whether it is proper to label some people mentally ill in view of the social discriminations, self-denigration, interference with treatment, impeding of social progress, and unscientific close-mindedness which may ensue when this kind of labeling is employed. It is shown that it is not the labeling process itself which is necessarily harmful, but that if such terms as "mental illness" are operationally defined and if the individuals so described are not negatively evaluated as persons, it may be possible to employ these terms scientifically and usefully.

For the last two decades there has been increasing objection by a number of psychologists and sociologists (as well as an even greater number of nonprofessional writers) to labeling certain people as "mentally ill" or "emotionally sick." Thus, Szasz (1961, 1966) has vigorously alleged that the concept of mental illness "now functions merely as a convenient myth." Mowrer (1960) has contended that behavior disorders are manifestations of personal irresponsibility and sin rather than of disease. Whitaker and Malone (1953), as well as many other experiential and existential psychotherapists, have held that emotional disturbance is a rather meaningless term because practically all therapists are just about as sick as their patients. Keniston (1966) and a number of sociological writers have insisted that individual psychodynamics are not nearly as important as has commonly been assumed in the creation of human alienation and insecurity, but that our technological society itself lays the groundwork for the growing estrangement of young people and, to one degree or another, makes us all emotionally aberrant.

The question of whether some individuals are especially "mentally ill" and should be clearly labeled so is of profound importance, since it affects decision making in the areas of hospitalization, imprisonment, psychotherapy in the community, vocational training and placement, educational advancement, and many other aspects of modern life. Siegel (1966) has recently reported that high school students who are hospitalized for emotional disturbance or who undertake psychotherapy without hospitalization, are frequently held to be poor risks for higher education and are consequently refused admittance to college. Obviously, labeling a person "mentally ill" has more than theoretical import.

To my knowledge, no dispassionate discussion of both sides of this question has yet been published. I shall, therefore, try to list the main disadvantages and advantages of labeling certain people "mentally ill," so that psychologists in general and psychotherapists in particular may be better able to see and cope with this problem. The main issues that have recently been raised in connection with diagnosing individuals as "emotionally sick" involve (*a*) social discrimination against the "mentally ill," (*b*) self-denigration by disturbed people, (*c*) moral responsibility and "mental illness," (*d*) prophylaxis and treatment of aberrant individuals, (*e*) social progress and emotional disturbance, and (*f*) scientific attitude and advancement in regard to labeling people "mentally ill."

Social Discrimination against the "Mentally Ill"

There are several discriminatory practices which seem to be inevitably connected with labeling an individual as neurotic, psychotic, or emotionally disturbed. When so diagnosed, either officially or semiofficially, he is often discriminated against in some practical ways—is refused jobs, kept out of schools, rejected as a love or marriage partner, etc. This discrimination is entirely unjust in many cases, since the sick individual is not given a chance to prove that he can succeed vocationally, educationally, or otherwise. In some instances, a person who behaves unconventionally or idiosyncratically may be adjudged psychotic and may be forcibly hospitalized. Consequently, his—and everyone else's—freedom of speech may be restricted by his incarceration of threat thereof. Siebert (1967) has noted in this connection:

The thing that has pained me for so long is that, while Americans will go to extreme lengths to protect a person's right to speak, there is really very little freedom in this country to express all of one's thoughts. I talked to many, many people in mental hospitals who were placed there because they revealed some personal thoughts to a relative or to a psychiatrist. Few citizens realize how easy it is to lock up a person who has "undesirable" thoughts [p. 11].

Practically all psychological labels today are inexact. What is more, they keep changing from diagnostician to diagnostician and from decade to decade. Thus, most of the patients whom Freud called neurotic would today be designated as borderline psychotic or schizophrenic reaction. Yet, once a person is psychiatrically labeled, he is treated as if that label were indubitably correct and as if it accurately describes his behavior. His remaining inside or outside of a mental institution, being employed or unemployed, or remaining married or unmarried may depend on the particular kind of labeling done by a given psychologist or psychiatrist who is in a certain mood at a special time and place.

Labeling some people as emotionally disturbed tends to set up a caste system, with consequent social discriminations. In most communities of our society, so-called healthy individuals are socially favored over the "mentally sick." But in some groups—Bohemian, hippie, criminal, or drug-taking groups—the reverse may be true, and the sick individual may be considered "in" and may be favored over the "square."

As an escapee from a New York mental hospital points out (Anonymous, 1966), individuals who commit clearly illegal acts, such as trespassing on others' property and refusing to support their wives, may be discriminated against once they are judged to be "mentally ill" by not being held morally responsible for their acts and not being given a stipulated prison term for committing these acts, but, instead, being indefinitely committed to a mental institution. These individuals are thus deprived of their moral (or immoral) choices and of being held accountable for such choices.

Our psychiatric terminology itself, as Davidson (1958) and Menninger (1965) indicate, is highly pejorative. Referring to people with behavior problems by such designations as "anal character," "sadistic," "castrating," "infantile," "psychopathic," and "schizophrenic" hardly helps their states of mind and adds grave doubts to the attitudes of life insurance companies, social clubs, officer groups, and other organizations about their eligibility. Nor, as Menninger (1965) points out,

is the patient, or ex-patient, the only sufferer from this situation. An entire family can be hurt by the diagnostic label attached to one of its members, because of the various implications such labels have in the minds of the various groups of people with whom that family comes in contact [p. 45].

With the very best intentions, then, psychologists and psychiatrists who are instrumental in labeling individuals as "mentally ill" may unwittingly subject these individuals to a variety of social and legal discriminations and may seriously interfere with their civil and their human rights. And not all psychiatric intentions are the very best! Redlich and Freedman (1966), while favoring involuntary commitment of psychotics in many instances, admit that "Certainly, commitments in many cases are entirely rational acts; however, in some cases there is evidence that psychiatrists and other involved

persons are motivated, in part, by counter-aggression toward very provocative patients [p. 780]." So, quite apart from the contention of groups helping ex-mental patients (during the last two decades) that many Americans have been and still are being railroaded by their relatives into institutions when they are not truly disturbed, there seems to be considerable evidence that commitment procedures leave much to be desired and that various discriminatory mistakes are made in this connection.

There is, however, another side to the story. Some individuals in our society, whatever we choose to call them, are clearly unfit to live unattended in the community—as even Szasz (1966) admits. Many of them should, perhaps, best be placed in regular prisons, even though today that solution is hardly ideal! Others, such as those who have committed no crimes but are obviously on the brink of harming themselves and/or other people, can hardly be incarcerated in jail, nor can they even properly be given determinate sentences in a mental hospital. If their behavior is sufficiently aberrant, they may well have to be placed in some kind of protective custody for an indeterminate period, and what better place do we have for this kind of treatment than a mental institution?

The main point here is that labeling an individual as "mentally ill," and thereby being enabled to send him for therapy either in a suitable institution or as an involuntary patient in his own community, frequently subjects him to unfair legal and social discrimination. Nonetheless, many other people, and sometimes this individual himself, may be unfairly discriminated against if this kind of procedure is not in some way followed. Take, for example, the case of a suicidal individual. Morgenstern (1966) states:

Since suicide is not only irrational—it punishes oneself for rage directed at others—but is also irrevocable, the psychiatrist and society have the human obligation to force reconsideration. All of us are at times tempted to do the irrational and the irrevocable, and I would doubt that, having been stopped, we were ungrateful [p. 4].

The seriously disturbed person, in other words, may well be unfairly discriminating against himself, even to the point of irrevocably harming himself in some major ways. Is it not, therefore, fair under these conditions to judge him ill and forcibly restrain him from his self-sabotaging, even at the expense of possibly discriminating against him in other ways?

Granted that this question may have no utterly agreed-upon, clear-cut answer, here is another that warrants asking: Assuming that legal and social discriminations may accrue to the individual who is labeled "mentally ill," is it not sometimes necessary to discriminate against him in this manner in order to prevent him from needlessly harming others? Mrs. Hyman Brett (1966), in a letter to the *New York Times* following its publication of Szasz' article, "Mental Illness is a Myth" (1966), puts this question in more detail:

What about the freedom and the liberties of the relatives of the mentally ill person who consistently refuses care? At the same time that we refuse to tamper with the mentally ill person's freedom are we not tampering with theirs? By returning the mentally ill member to his family we are chaining his relations to a life of dread, despondency, and frustration. When we allow the neurotic or psychotic the freedom to reject care we are allowing him at the same time another very special freedom: the freedom to drive his family over the border line into the realm of mental illness, too. For though his condition may not be a danger to society, it is a very grave and definite threat to the emotional stability of the members of his family [p. 4].

Mrs. Brett may exaggerate here, since family members of a "mentally ill" individual may, at least to some extent, choose whether or not to be unduly influenced by his illness. Her general point, however, seems to have some validity. For in giving a highly disturbed person his full civil rights, we may easily impinge upon those of others whom he may incessantly annoy, frustrate, maim, and even kill, his behavior ranging from playing his radio very loudly all night to mowing down some of his neighbors with a machine gun.

Just as the protection of the civil rights of Jews or Negroes does not extend to their rights to libel, injure, or slay non-Jews and non-Negroes, so may the civil rights of highly idiosyncratic individuals have to be curtailed when they infringe upon the similar rights of non-so-idiosyncratic others.

Self-Denigration by Disturbed People

Perhaps the most pernicious aspect of a person's being labeled "mentally ill" is that he not only tends to be denigrated by other members of his social group, including even the professionals who diagnose him, but also that he almost always accepts their estimations of himself and makes them his own. This is exceptionally unfair and pernicious; even if he can unmistakably be shown to be disturbed, he is obviously not entirely responsible for being so, but has been born and/or reared to be sick and is not to be condemned for his state of being.

It is true that an individual, unless he is in a state of complete breakdown, is somewhat responsible for his acts, since he performed or caused them and usually has some degree of choice in doing or not doing them. Not every psychotic murders, and under the old McNaughten rule there was some justification for our courts holding certain disturbed people responsible for their crimes, as long as it could be shown that they were aware of what they were doing when they committed these crimes and that they had some choice in their commission. There is no reason, however, why even thieves and murderers have to be condemned in toto or held to be worthless persons for their misdeeds. They are, like all of us, intrinsically fallible humans and to demand that they (or we) be infallible is unrealistic. They, moreover, are much different from and greater than their performances, and although we can legitimately measure and evaluate an individual's *products*, there is no way—as Hartman (1959, 1962) has shown—of accurately assessing his *self*. Finally, when we do assess a person as a whole for his performances, we inevitably make it impossible for him to have self-respect; for as soon as he does something wrong, which, being fallible, he soon must, we label *him* as bad and, thereby, strongly imply that as a bad *person* he has no other choice than to keep doing wrong acts again and again (Ellis, 1962).

This is what frequently happens when we pejoratively label an individual "mentally ill." Instead of indicating to him that some of his *behavior* is inefficient or mistaken, we insist that *he* is psychotic or sick, whereupon he logically concludes that he is probably unable to do anything efficiently or right, gives in to his illness, and keeps perpetuating ineffectual behavior that he actually has the ability to change or stop. To the degree that he feels denigrated by the label of "mental illness," he is likely to feel hopeless about acting in anything but a sick manner and likely to continue to act in a negative manner that is congruent with this label. Self-deprecation, as practically all psychologists and professionals agree, is one of the main causes of disturbed behavior. Labeling an individual as emotionally ill or schizophrenic often tends to exacerbate this cause.

It must be admitted, on the other hand, that people in our society are predisposed to condemn themselves in toto when they perceive that their performances are wrong or ineffective and that one of the best ways to help them to ameliorate or stop their self-denigration is to show them that they are basically immature or sick. They then are likely to conclude either that they are not truly responsible for their misdeeds or that even though they are responsible, they are not to be blamed or condemned. It is perhaps a sad commentary on our society that the only individuals who are not consigned to everlasting Hell for their sins are little children and sick adults, but the fact is that we do largely exonerate "mentally ill" people for their misdeeds and forgive them their sins. Until society's attitudes in this respect significantly change, labeling a person "ill" has distinct advantages (as well as disadvantages) in minimizing his self-denigration.

Moral Responsibility and "Mental Illness"

Mowrer (1960) and Szasz (1961, 1966) have persuasively argued that if we cavalierly and indiscriminately label an individual "mentally ill," we are thereby glossing over the fact that he is still responsible for a good deal of his behavior, that it is quite possible for him to change his performances for the better, and that (in Mowrer's terms) he is not likely to improve his condition until he fully acknowledges his sins and actively sets about making reparations and correcting them. By focusing on the illness of certain individuals, these writers would contend, we give them rationalizations for being the way they are and fail to teach them how to modify their self-destructive and immoral deeds.

Ellis (1962), Glasser (1965), Morgenstern (1966), and various other psychotherapists have recently emphasized the point that people are personally responsible for the social consequences of their behavior and that unless they admit that they can largely control their own destinies, in spite of the strong parental and societal conditioning factors that existed during their childhood, they are not likely to change their ineffectual behavior. As Morgenstern (1966) points out, labeling a person as "mentally ill" and involuntarily committing him to a mental institution frequently "reinforces the immature wish to avoid this responsibility, by blaming the illness for failure to achieve desired goals [p. 4]."

As usual, however, there is another side to the story. Ausubel (1961) heartily concurs with Mowrer that "personality disorders . . . can be most fruitfully conceptualized as products of moral conflict, confusion, and aberration [p. 70]," but he seriously questions the notion that these disorders are basically a reflection of sin; he demonstrates that most immoral behavior is committed by individuals who would never be designated as ill or disturbed and that many people who display disordered behavior are not particularly sinful or guilty. Moreover, Ausubel points out that not all "mentally sick" persons are truly responsible for their behavior:

It is just as unreasonable to hold an individual responsible for symptoms of behavior disorder as to deem him accountable for symptoms of physical illness. He is no more culpable for his inability to cope with socio-psychological stress than he would be for his inability to resist the spread of infectious organisms. In those instances where warranted guilt feelings *do* contribute to personality disorder, the patient is accountable for the misdeeds underlying his guilt, but is hardly responsible for the symptoms brought on by the guilt feelings or for unlawful acts committed during his illness. . . . Lastly, even if it were true that all personality disorder is a reflection of sin and that people are accountable for their behavioral symptoms, it would still be unnecessary to deny that these symptoms are manifestations of disease. Illness is no less real because the victim happens to be culpable for his illness. A glutton with hypertensive heart disease undoubtedly aggravates his condition by overeating and is culpable in part for the often fatal symptoms of his disease, but what reasonable person would claim that for this reason he is not really ill [pp. 71-72]?

Prophylaxis and Treatment of Aberrant Individuals

In several important ways labeling an individual as "mentally ill" may interfere with the treatment of any behavior problem he may display and may hinder the prevention of emotional disorder. For example:

1. Calling a person "mentally sick" frequently enhances his feelings of shame about his "illness," so that he defensively refuses to admit that he has serious behavior problems and therefore does not seek help with these problems.

2. A person who is set apart as being emotionally aberrant may become so resentful of this kind of segregation that he may refuse to acknowledge his "persecutors'" efforts to help him and may get into hostile encounters with them and others that only serve to increase his living handicaps.

3. In many instances, the "mentally ill" individual is forcibly incarcerated in an institution where he is kept from doing many things he enjoys and where his condition may become aggravated rather than improved.

4. Labeling a person as psychotic may easily imply, to himself and those who may be able to help him, that he is hopeless and that little can be done to get him to change his behavior. As Menninger (1965) indicates, psychological treatment today is carried out by many people in addition to psychologists and psychiatrists, and the cooperation of family members is often urgently needed. "Schizophrenia" and "mental illness" are such impressive labels that they induce many people to feel that only highly trained professionals, if indeed anyone, can work with sick people and to ignore the fact that less trained individuals can often be specifically shown how to help troubled humans.

5. By being encouraged to label other people as sick, many of us fail to consider adequately our own problem areas. If we are not seen as being totally ill, we easily assume that we have few or no shortcomings; when we can easily label others as neurotic or psychotic we tend to assume that we are not in the least in such a class. By an all-or-none labeling technique, we tend to gloss over our own correctable deficiencies.

6. Labeling individuals as "mentally ill" often bars them from various social, vocational, and educational situations where they would best learn how to help themselves. It sometimes interferes with adequate research into treatment, while focusing on more precise research into diagnosing or labeling. It consumes psychological and psychiatric manpower which might better go into treatment.

7. If people have close relatives who are labeled psychotic, they sometimes become so afraid of going insane themselves that they actually bring on symptoms of disturbance and begin to define themselves as "mentally ill."

On the other side of the ledger, if we have a clear-cut concept of "mental disease" and if we unequivocally refer to certain kinds of behavior as neurotic or psychotic, many benefits in preventing and treating "emotional disturbance" are likely to accrue. For instance:

1. If needlessly self-defeating and overly hostile behavior does exist and is to be fought

and minimized, the individual who exhibits it has to acknowledge (*a*) that it exists and (*b*) that he is to some degree responsible for its existence and, hence, can change it. This is what we really mean when we say that an individual is "mentally ill"—that he has symptoms of mental malfunctioning or illness. More operationally stated, he thinks, emotes, and acts irrationally and can usually uncondemningly acknowledge and change his acts. If this, without any moralistic overtones, is the definition of "mental illness," then it can distinctly help the afflicted individual to accept himself while he is ill and to work at changing for the better.

2. When an individual fully accepts the fact that he is emotionally disturbed, he often starts to improve (Redlich & Freedman, 1966). Why? Because (*a*) to some extent he knows why he is behaving ineffectively; (*b*) he can begin to define in more detail exactly what his sickness consists of and what he is doing to cause and maintain it; (*c*) he may accept his symptoms with more equanimity and tend to be less guilty about creating them; (*d*) he may be much more inclined to seek professional help, just as he would if he were physically ill.

3. By accepting the concept of "mental illness," a person can often accept and help others who are neurotic or psychotic. I have seen many parents with highly disturbed children who, after learning that their child's peculiar behavior is the result of a deep-seated disturbance which is biologically as well as environmentally rooted, became enormously less guilty and were able to sympathetically accept their child and do their best to help him ameliorate his symptoms.

4. There is an essential honesty about the full acceptance of states of "emotional illness" that is itself often curative. In the last analysis, almost all neurosis and psychosis consists of some fundamental self-dishonesty (Glasser, 1965; London, 1964; Mowrer, 1960, 1964) or some self-deceptive defense that one raises against one's perfectionistic and grandiose leanings (A. Freud, 1948; S. Freud, 1963). When, therefore, one fully faces the fact that

one is "mentally ill," that this is not a pleasant way to be, and that one is partially responsible for being so, one becomes at that very point more honest with oneself and begins to get a little better.

5. Accepting the fact that he is emotionally sick may give an individual an incentive to improve his lot. Most confirmed homosexuals in our society utterly refuse to admit that their homosexuality is a symptom of disturbance (Benson, 1965; Wicker, 1966[1]). They mightily inveigh against clinicians such as Adler (1917), Bieber et al. (1962), and Ellis (1965a), who insist that they are sick. As a result, relatively few mixed homosexuals come for psychotherapy, and of those who do come only a handful work to change their basic personality structure and to become heterosexually interested and capable. At the same time, many phobiacs admit their disturbance, come for therapy, and are significantly helped (Redlich & Freedman, 1966; Wolpe, 1958). This is not to say that all those who accept the idea of their being "mentally ill" work hard at becoming better. Far from it! But their chances are often improved, compared to those who insist that they are no more disturbed than is anyone else.

6. Psychotherapists are often more effective when they face the fact that their patients are "mentally ill." When they look upon these patients as merely having behavior problems, they work moderately hard with them and often become disillusioned at the poor results obtained. When they acknowledge that their patients often have basic, deep-seated emotional disorders, they know they are in for a long hard pull, work with greater vigor, expect many setbacks and limited successes, and take a realistic rather than an over-optimistic or over-pessimistic therapeutic view.

7. Whether we like it or not, it sometimes seems to be necessary for some individuals to be adjudged "mentally ill" and even to be forcibly incarcerated, if they are to be treated effectively. A dramatic case in point is the recent one of the Texas resident, Charles Whitman, who killed 16 innocent bystanders

shortly after he had gone for one interview with a psychiatrist and filed to return for further treatment, although he was found to be potentially homicidal. Redlich and Freedman (1966) remark:

As therapeutic interventions increase in intensity and scope, we more frequently encounter the question of a person impulsively leaving treatment when there appears to be a good chance that he could further improve his status and diminish his self-destructive behavior. Without some element of restraint, such a person might not have received therapeutic help at all. Nonetheless, it is probably best, both for society and for therapy of the patient, that coercion be restricted to the minimum necessary for the protection of life [p. 782].

Redlich and Freedman note how difficult it often is, as in the case of James Forrestal, Secretary of the Navy, who committed suicide while under psychiatric observation in a naval hospital, to adequately supervise persons of high position and eminence who are seriously disturbed. While their book was going through the press, Hotchner's (1966) *Papa Hemingway* appeared. According to Hotchner, Hemingway, because of his literary genius, was treated with unusual leniency by psychiatrists at the Mayo Clinic, and the day after he returned home from the Clinic he shot and killed himself. There is little doubt in Hotchner's mind that Hemingway might have lived for many more years if he had been honestly adjudged "mentally ill" and had been involuntarily treated.

8. If the facts of "mental illness" are forthrightly faced and it is recognized that numerous individuals in our population are predisposed, for biosocial reasons, to be severely disturbed, educational prophylaxis will tend to be stressed. For if none of us is truly sick, just because all humans have some problems of adjustment, it seems futile to teach people the principles of mental hygiene, methods of sound thinking about themselves, and ways of coping with reality. But if it is accepted that all of us are a bit "touched" and that some of us are more so, greater efforts toward prevention of "mental illness" may become the rule.

9. If the concept of emotional disturbance is admitted, proper surveillance of predis-posed individuals can be instituted for preventive, protective, and curative reasons. Thus, if a child or adolescent is known to have tendencies toward severe illness, he can be specifically watched to see when these are breaking out. He can be kep out of situations where he may inflict damage on others, can at times be placed in protective custody to safeguard himself and others, and can be regularly treated to minimize his sick tendencies. In this respect, I recall a patient who was referred to me by a psychologist almost 20 years ago because, although he was only moderately disturbed, his twin brother had just been institutionalized with a diagnosis of paranoid schizophrenia. I saw this patient steadily for a couple of years and since that time have been seeing him a few times a year. I believe that it is largely as a result of my treating him and seeing him through a number of incipient crises during these years that he has been helped to remain only moderately ineffective and never to be in danger of a serious break, although in my opinion he is clearly a borderline schizophrenic. Similarly, other incipient psychotics can, if recognized early enough, be helped to remain perennially incipient and prevented from overtly breaking down.

Social Progress and Emotional Disturbance

If we label people who display various adjustment problems or idiosyncratic ways of living as "mentally ill," we may impede social progress in various ways. Many of the world's great statesman, innovators, and creative artists have been "crackpots" who might well have been diagnosed as neurotic or psychotic and whose contributions to the world could have been (and in some cases actually were) sadly curtailed because of such labels. Thus, Dorothea Dix, who helped reform our mental hospital procedures, was opposed because she was deemed a "screwball," and Richard Wagner had difficulty getting some of his works performed because he was considered a "madman." In our own way, highly qualified people may not be elected to public office because of their unconventional and "crack-potty" views. Diplomats may not take with sufficient seriousness the statements of the Hitlers of the world because these leaders are seen as maniacs. Notable inventions may go unused because their inventors are considered "crazy."

Actually, an individual's aberrant or peculiar characteristics may have distinct advantages as well as disadvantages. Rank (1945, 1958) held that what is normally called neurosis is a creative process that may lead to beneficial and exciting aesthetic productions, and several other writers have noted the creative aspects of some psychotic states, but once an idiosyncratic individual in our society is labeled "mentally ill," it is assumed that his illness is wholly pernicious and that it must quickly be interrupted and abolished.

The very concept of illness or disease, as applied to emotional malfunctioning, may be socially retrogressive, since it limits thinking in this area. As Albee (1966), Rieff (1966), and several other students of mental health have recently shown, the medical or disease model of human disorder is restrictive and misleading, in that it implies that the afflicted individual has a specific handicap caused by a concrete organism or event and that his troubles can fairly easily be diagnosed and cured, as is the case in many physical disorders. Actually, what has been called "mental illness" appears to have multifarious causative factors and appears to be interrelated with the individual's entire existence and his global philosophy of life. It is therefore best understood and attacked on a philosophical, sociological, and psychological level rather than a narrow medical level, and those who practice psychotherapy (in itself a bad word because of its medical origins and implications) would aid their patients (another medical term!) in particular and the art of mental healing (!!) in general if they forgot about the illness or disease aspects of ineffectual behavior and focused in a more global way on the causes and amelioration of such behavior.

Viewing disorganized thought, emotion, and action as "mental illness" may again limit social and psychotherapeutic progress by supporting the concomitant view that only psychiatrists and other physicians are truly equipped to treat the emotionally disturbed, when, actually, some of the best theoreticians and practitioners in the field have been psychologists, social workers, marriage counselors, clergymen, and various other kinds of non-medical workers. Social progress is at present probably being seriously hampered in the field of mental health by professional opposition to nonprofessionals, such as intelligent housewives and college students, who have been found to be quite helful with sick individuals but who have often been kept from doing very much in this respect because their patients are designated as being "mentally ill" (Ellis, 1966).

As usual, much can be said in opposition to the view that diagnosing people as "emotionally sick" tends to hinder social and therapeutic progress. First, there is no good evidence to support Rank's (1945, 1958), view that neurosis is a creative process and that it should be cherished if artists and their public are to continue to make great progress. Nor is there any reason to believe that many of the outstanding innovators of the past and present would not be ignored and opposed by their contemporaries even if the latter could not call them "mentally ill" or "crazy."

As for the concept of "mental disease" aiding social reaction and blocking therapeutic progress, Menninger (1965) points out that modern medicine is not atomistic but holistic and that good physicians see disease in a broad, almost nonmedical (in the old sense of the term) way. He quotes Virchow, "Disease is nothing but life under altered conditions," and Engel, "Disease corresponds to failures or disturbances in the growth, development, functions, and adjustments of the organism as a whole or of any of its systems," (Menninger, 1965, p. 460) to show that the medical model of "mental illness" that Albee (1966) so severely criticizes is no longer typical of modern psychiatrists.

Ausubel (1961, p. 70) contends that to label personality disorder as disease not only would not hinder social and therapeutic progress but that the Szasz-Mowrer view of the "myth of mental illness" would "turn back the psychiatric clock twenty-five hundred years." The most significant and perhaps the only real advance registered by mankind in evolving a rational and humane method of handling behavioral aberrations has been in substituting a concept of disease for the demonological and retributional doctrines regarding their nature and etiology that flourished until comparatively recent times. Conceptualized as illness, the symptoms of personality disorders can be interpreted in the light of underlying stresses and resistances, both genic and environmental, and can be evaluated in relation to specifiable quantitative and qualitative norms of appropriately adaptive behavior, both cross-culturally and within a particular cultural context. It would behoove us, therefore, before we abandon the concept of mental illness and return to the medieval doctrine of unexpiated sin or adopt Szasz' ambiguous criterion of difficulty in ethical choice and responsibility, to subject the foregoing proposition to careful and detailed study.

Ausubel (1961, p. 69) also points out that labeling individuals with aberrant behavior "mentally ill" does not preclude nonmedical personnel from helping these individuals, since "an impressively large number of recognized diseases are legally treated today by both medical *and* non-medical specialists (e.g., diseases of the mouth, face, jaws, teeth, eyes, and feet)." Consequently, even if we maintain the concept of "mental illness," we can justifiably allow and encourage all kinds of professionals and nonprofessionals to treat the ill.

Scientific Advancement and the Label of "Mental Illness"

There would seem to be several impediments to the use of the scientific method and to the advancement of science when we label individuals "mentally ill." For one thing, this kind of labeling leads to over-categorization

and higher-order abstracting, which obscures scientific thought and leads to countless human misunderstandings. (Korzybski, 1933, 1951). To say that an individual is bad because his *behavior* is poor is to fabricate a sadly overgeneralized and invariably false description of him, as it is most unlikely that *all* his behavior—past, present, and future—was, is, or will be poor. Similarly, to label a person as a genius is to describe loosely and inaccurately, because it is likely that (at most!) he displays certain aspects of genius in only some of his productions—even if his name is Leonardo da Vinci; it is most probable that in many or most of the other aspects of his life, for example, his playing pingpong, making love, and cooking a souffle, he is far from displaying many aspects of genius (Ellis, 1965b).

This kind of overgeneralizing distorts reality and causes the unrealistic (and often unfair) condemnation or deification of a human as a whole for relatively isolated parts or aspects of his functioning. Just as an individual's good deeds do not prove that he, on the whole, is a genius, so his bizarre or dysfunctional acts fail to show that he is totally "mentally ill" or incompetent. Designating him in this manner may, therefore, lead to misapprehension and misunderstanding of his sick and healthy behavior.

Labels of all kinds promote close-mindedness rather than open-minded, experimental, scientific attitudes. Calling an individual "mentally ill" tends to put him in a niche, from whence his removal may never be considered. It encourages us to diagnose an individual's condition and then to forget about it because it has been neatly categorized, to rigidify our thinking in the field of mental health itself, and to help us forget that the patient's "illness" is more of a hypothesis than a well-established fact.

Szasz (1961) has contended that the concept of "mental illness" is antithetical to science because it is demonological in nature, in that it follows the lines of religious myths in general and the belief in witchcraft in particular and because it uses a reified abstraction, "a deformity of personality," to account causally for disordered behavior and human disharmony. Many other writers, such as Ellis (1950) and LaPiere (1960), have held that the Freudian Terms, in which most forms of emotional disturbance are put today (e.g., "weak ego" and "punishing superego"), are reifications that have no actual substance behind them and are hence mythical and misleading entities. The entire field of "mental health" appears to be replete with these kinds of myths.

While some of these objections to the diagnosis of "mental disease" are important (and others seem to be trivial), there is much to be said in favor of the notion that categorizations of this sort are, when carefully made, reasonably accurate and quite helpful to the cause of scientific advancement. Arguments in this connection include the following:

1. Although it is inaccurate to state that the individual in our culture who is usually labeled "mentally ill" is a much different kind of person from the healthy individual, or that he exhibits entirely aberrant behavior, or that he is a bad or lower kind of person because he sometimes behaves oddly, the fact remains that there is almost always some significant difference between the actions of this ill individual and those of another who is well. What is more, the existing difference is one that can usually (if not always) be detected by a trained observer, is fairly consistently evident, and leads to definite behavior of a self-defeating or antisocial nature. If the individual with aberrant behavior is not in any way to be labeled "mentally ill," neurotic, psychotic, or something similar, the peculiarity, undesirability, and improvability of his behavior is likely to be overlooked, some segment of reality will thereby be denied, and the essence of science—observation and classification—will be rejected.

2. There is considerable and ever-increasing scientific evidence to show that although the term "mental illness" itself is vague, the major characteristics which are subsumed under its rubric, such as compulsion, over-suspiciousness, phobia, depression, and in-tense rage, do exist and have observable ideational and physiological correlates. Thus, feelings of depression are usually accompanied by the individual's belief that "When I do the wrong thing, I am no good and will probably always remain worthless," and "If significant people in my life do not approve of me, I can't approve of myself." These feelings are, in addition, frequently accompanied by fatigue, poor appetite, insensitivity to stimulation, ineffective performance, etc. Objectively, therefore, some individuals can be described as being consistently depressed and in that sense, at least, may be thought of as being "mentally ill."

3. Some kind of general factor of emotional distress appears to exist in certain individuals, since they are observed to display various major symptoms (e.g., hostility, anxiety, and depression), while other individuals are practically symptom free. Thousands of years of observation would seem to attest to the existence of this general factor, as many of the descriptions of peculiar people in past centuries are amazingly similar to modern clinical descriptions. Recently, moreover, a great deal of evidence has accumulated which tends to show that people who display severe behavior problems are to some degree biologically different from others (Chess, Thomas, & Birch, 1965; Greenfield & Lewis, 1965; Redlich & Freedman, 1966) and that they can be reliably selected from the general population (Joint Commission on Mental Illness and Health, 1961). To ignore this evidence of "mental illness" would seem to be highly unrealistic; to acknowledge it would be to accept people as they truly are.

4. Although all self-defeating human behavior may well have the elements of social learning and may be best understood, as Szasz contends, by being studied in a sociological context and in the light of social deviance, the fact remains that the individual himself contributes significantly to what he accepts or rejects from his culture and, at times, may therefore be justifiably deemed sick or disordered. Anyone of us, as Messer (1966) observes, may be neurotically influ-

enced by dramatic television commercials which convince us that we have acid indigestion when we experience abdominal discomfort. Few of us would conclude, however, that the discomfort represents a demon tearing away the lining of our stomachs and that unless the pain stops we must cut outselves open to get at this demon. Those few, who gratuitously add their own distorted perceptions and thoughts to their socially imbibed neurotic ideas, may justifiably be diagnosed as psychotic, even though some of their notions (e.g., that demons could exist) are partially derived from their cultures.

5. Although we may concede Szasz' (1961) points that what we usually call "mental illness" is largely an expression of man's struggle with the problems of how he should live and that human relations are inherently fraught with difficulties, Ausubel (1961) demonstrates that,

there is no valid reason why a particular symptom cannot both reflect a problem in living *and* constitute a manifestation of disease. . . . Some individuals, either because of the magnitude of the stress involved, or because of genically or environmentally induced susceptibility to ordinary degrees of stress, respond to the problems of living with behavior that is either seriously distorted or sufficiently unadaptive to prevent normal interpersonal relations and vocational functioning. The latter outcome—gross deviation from a designated range of desirable behavior variability—conforms to the generally understood meaning of mental illness [p. 71].

Discussion

It would appear that there are important disadvantages as well as advantages in labeling people "mentally ill." Many of the disadvantages result from our tendency to include in the terms "mental illness," "neurosis," and "psychosis" not only a description of the fact that the afflicted individual behaves self-defeatingly and inappropriate to his social group, but also the evaluative element that he is bad, inferior, or worthless for so behaving. If this evaluative element were not gratuitously added, the term "mental illness," even though an abstraction that is not too precise,

might have descriptive, diagnostic, and therapeutic usefulness. It is a kind of shorthand term which can be used to describe the usual and fairly consistent state of a person who keeps driving himself to act ineffectually and bizarrely.

Thus, instead of saying, "He is mentally ill," we could say, "He is a human being who at the present time is behaving in a self-defeating and/or needlessly antisocial manner and who will most probably continue to do so in the future, and, although he is partially creating or causing (and in this sense is responsible for) his aberrant behavior, he is still not to be condemned for creating it but is to be helped to overcome it." This second statement is more precise, accurate, and helpful than the first one, but it is often impractical to spell it out in this detail. It is, therefore, legitimate to use the first statement, "He is mentally ill," as long as we clearly understand that it means the longer version.

A good solution, then, to the problem of labeling an individual "mentally ill" is to change the evaluative attitude which gives the term "mental illness" a prejorative tone and to educate all of us, including professionals, to accept "emotionally sick" human beings without condemnation, punishment, or needless restriction. This, to some degree, has already occurred, since the attitude that most of us take toward disturbed people today is much less negative than that taken by most people a century or more ago; much, however, remains to be accomplished in this respect.

Meanwhile, what is to be done? For psychologists, psychiatrists, psychiatric social workers, and other professionals, the following conclusions are in order:

1. The term "mental illness," or some similar label, is likely to be around for some time, even though continuing efforts can be made to change current psychological usage.

2. An individual who is "mentally ill" may be more operationally defined as a person who, with some consistency, behaves in dysfunctional ways in *certain aspects* of his life, but who is rarely *totally* "disturbed" or uncontrolled.

3. It is highly dangerous to evaluate a "mentally ill" person as you would evaluate his acts or performances. If he is sufficiently psychotic, he may not even be responsible for his acts. If he is less disturbed, he may be responsible but not justifiably condemnable for his deeds, since they are only a part or an aspect of him, and to excoriate him in toto for these deeds is to make an unwarranted and usually harmful overgeneralization about him.

4. Although most "mentally ill" individuals perform bizarre and unconventional acts, not all people who perform such acts are sick or ill. Neurosis or psychosis exists not because of an individual's deeds, but because of the overly anxious, compulsive, rigid, or unrealistic manner in which he keeps performing them.

5. Most "mentally ill" individuals are variable from day to day and changeable from one period of their lives to another. The fact that they act inappropriately today does not mean that their behavior was equally dysfunctional yesterday nor that it will be so tomorrow. Such people usually have considerable capacities for growth and can change radically for the better (as well as for the worse).

6. People, no matter how "mentally ill" they may be, are always human. We owe them the same kind of general respect that we owe to all human beings, namely, giving them the rights to survive, to be as happy as possible in their handicapped conditions, to be helped to function as well as possible and to develop their potentials, and to be protected from needlessly harming themselves and others.

If these approaches to individuals with severe emotional problems are kept solidly in the forefront of our consciousness and are actualized in our relationships with them, the question of whether to label them as "mentally ill" may well become academic.

---

[1]R. Wicker. Statement made on the Larry Glick Show, radio station WMEX, Boston, January 8, 1966.

SELF TEST: MEASURING COMPREHENSION
"Should Some People Be Labeled Mentally Ill?" By Albert Ellis

1. Specifically, what kinds of discrimination may be encountered by the individual who has been labeled as mentally ill?

2. What societal benefit may be gained through the labeling of a person as mentally ill and the consequent restrictions on the labeled person's civil rights?

3. Should people labeled as mentally ill be held responsible and accountable for their behavior?

4. Does being labeled mentally ill help or harm the chance that psychotherapy will be beneficial to the individual? Why?

5. Should behaviorally abnormal people be termed mentally ill? Why?

IT'S NOT ALL IN YOUR HEAD
from *Saturday Review*
Seymour S. Kety

As previously noted, many new drugs for the treatment of severe psychiatric disorders were developed in the 1950's. In some cases the drugs had desirable results in controlling psychotic symptoms. Some drugs, while controlling psychotic symptoms, had undesirable side effects. Some criticized the side effects as being just as bad as the psychotic symptoms.

Within the illness perspective continual attempts are being made to discover medical etiologies for psychiatric disorders. Recent research has taught us much about the functioning of the brain and has indicated ways of correcting imbalances in it. Although the word "cure" may be too strong to use in describing the effect of drugs in controlling psychotic symptoms, proponents of the illness perspective are optimistic that further research will allow us to better understand and treat psychiatric disorders with medical techniques.

In the following article, Seymour S. Kety reports some of the progress that has recently been made in our understanding of the brain and its relationship to mental illness. Kety also investigates the possibility that psychotic disorders may be genetically influenced. The article is a strong validation of the medical model and implies that when we finally unlock the mystery of mental illness, the key will be a medical one.

Mental illness, although not a major cause of death, like cancer or heart disease, nevertheless ranks as one of our most serious national health problems. More than 10 million Americans will experience one or more episodes of serious mental illness, which may last for only a few weeks or even for many years, before they reach old age. The care of the mentally ill, inadequate as it often is, costs this nation considerably more than $5 billion annually—and less easily calculated is the larger human cost to the victims and their families.

For two mental illnesses that at one time rivaled schizophrenia in severity and extent—general paresis and pellagrous psychosis—biomedical research discovered the causes: an invasion of the brain by the spirochete of syphilis for one, and a dietary deficiency of nicotinic acid for the other. This made possible their effective treatment and prevention through purely physiological reasons. As a result, these disorders have become practically extinct in America; where they do occur, the cause is a failure to utilize available knowledge.

But schizophrenia and the so-called affective disorders (depression and manic-depressive psychosis) have remained with us, and their seriousness is matched by our ignorance regarding them. We do not yet know their causes or understand the processes through which they develop. Their treatment, which has improved dramatically through the use of recently discovered drugs, still leaves much to be desired. However, over the past two decades substantial indications have revealed that these serious mental illnesses have biochemical underpinnings, and powerful new techniques and concepts have been developed which make the search for these remedies more promising than it has ever been before.

The idea of a biochemical cause of insanity is not new. The Hippocratic physicians of ancient Greece argued against the prevailing attribution of insanity to supernatural causes:

. . . and by the same organ [the brain] we become mad and delirious and fears and terrors assail us, some by night and some by day, and dreams and untimely wanderings and cares that are not suitable and ignorance of present circumstances, desuetude and unskillfulness. All these things we endure from the brain, when it is not healthy but is more hot, more cold, more moist, or more dry than natural, or when it suffers any other preternatural and unusual affliction.

The modern biochemical approach to mental illness can be traced to J. W. L. Thudichum, a physician and biochemist, who, nearly 100 years ago, hypothesized that many forms of insanity were the result of toxic substances fermented within the body, just as the psychosis of alcohol was the result of a toxic substance fermented outside. Armed with the hypothesis, he received a 10-year research grant from the Privy Council in England. He did not go to the mental hospitals and examine the urine and blood of patients; instead he went to the abattoir to obtain cattle brain and spent the 10 years studying the brain's normal composition. It is fortunate for us that he did that, because he laid the foundations of modern neurochemistry from which will come whatever we learn about the abnormal chemistry of the brain. If Thudichum had been less wise and courageous, or if Parliament had insisted on "relevant" research, what contribution could he have made with the little knowledge that existed at that time? What chances would he

have had to identify abnormalities in substances unknown in his day? He would have frittered away funds and wasted 10 years in a premature and futile search.

Thudichum, and the science of neurochemistry he founded, were concerned at first with composition and chemical structure. In the normal brain a large number of substances were identified that were later found to be abnormal in a substantial variety of neurological disorders. Fifty years ago biochemistry began to trace the complex metabolism by which foodstuffs and oxygen are utilized and energy is made available. This understanding was eventually applied to the brain, where its dependence on glucose was discovered, and the oxygen utilized in various mental functions could be measured. Application of this knowledge to the states of sleep, coma, anesthesia, and senile dementia soon followed. But the major psychiatric problems (schizophrenia and manic depressive psychosis and depression) remained unaffected. No known changes in chemical composition or structure account for these disorders; the brain uses just as much oxygen thinking irrationally as rationally.

Over the past 25 years there has been dramatic growth in the neurosciences and unprecedented knowledge of the brain and behavior. One major new concept is that of the synapse, the highly specialized junction between one nerve cell and another through which information is carried. Electron microscopy, biophysics, biochemistry, and pharmacology have taught us a great deal about the synapse's structure and function. Most novel and far-reaching is the knowledge that chemical mediators called "neurotransmitters" carry the message over a small gap (the synaptic cleft) that lies between the termination of one nerve cell and the beginning of another. Because sensory processing, perception, the storage and retrieval of information, thought, feeling, and behavior all depend upon the operation of these chemical switches, this discovery elucidated the focal points at which chemical processes and substances, metabolic products, hormones, and drugs could modify these crucial aspects of mental state and behavior. If there are biochemical disturbances in mental illness, they would be expected to operate there, and drugs that ameliorate these illnesses should exert their influences at synapses.

There are hundreds of billions of synapses in the human brain, and they are organized in a marvelously systematic way along pathways that neuroanatomists are mapping. A growing list of neurotransmitters is being identified, and these are found to be associated with particular pathways, functions, and behavioral states. The class of substances known as *catecholamines* includes *adrenalin, noradrenaline,* and *dopamine,* first identified in the adrenal gland or in the peripheral sympathetic nervous system. Catecholamines are now known to be important neurotransmitters in the brain, where they appear to be involved in emotional states such as arousal, rage, fear, pleasure, motivation, and exhilaration. *Serotonin,* first discovered in the intestine, has also been identified as a neurotransmitter in the brain, where it seems to play a crucial role in sleep and wakefulness, in certain types of sexual activity, and perhaps in modulating, damping, and balancing a wide range of synaptic activity that we are only beginning to understand. *Acetylcholine,* which is known to be the transmitter between nerve and muscle and is therefore crucial to every voluntary movement, has also been found to be involved in a very large fraction of brain synapses. There are other neurotransmitters, such as *gamma amino butyric acid,* certain amino acids and polypeptides discovered more recently, and undoubtedly many that are as yet undiscovered. The importance of the concept of chemical neurotransmission and its implications for medicine and psychiatry was recognized by the Nobel Committee, which made the award in 1970 to Julius Axelrod, Bernard Katz, and Ulf von Euler for their contributions to the understanding of acetylcholine and catecholamines as neurotransmitters.

Fundamental knowledge of the synapse and chemical neurotransmission has had important implications for the understanding and treatment of nervous and mental disease and represents an area of unusual promise for the future. At the same time that noradrenaline and serotonin were being identified in the brain, several drugs were discovered quite independently to exert important effects on mood. The first of these was *reserpine,* which has been found to be useful in the treatment of hypertension. In a small percentage of patients, however, reserpine produced a state of depression very much like that known to psychiatrists. At the same time scientists at the National Institute of Health made the important discovery that reserpine causes the disappearance of serotonin and noradrenaline from the brain.

A few years later a new drug, *iproniazid,* was introduced and found to be highly effective in the treatment of tuberculosis. It caused excitement in some patients, however, and was supplanted by other drugs equally effective and without such side effects. What was a deleterious property of iproniazid in the treatment of tuberculosis, however, became the basis for an effective treatment of depression. Iproniazid was found to block the enzyme, *monoamine oxidase* (MAO), that is responsible for inactivting biogenic amines, including serotonin and the catecholamines, in the brain. Thus, iproniazid exerted an effect on these transmitters opposite to that of reserpine, permitting them to rise in concentration and activity and exerting an antidepressant effect. A number of other *MAO inhibitors* were developed that were also effective in treating depression. Even more effective were a group of drugs, the *tricyclic antidepressants* such as *imipramine* and *amitryptaline*, that enhanced the synaptic actions of noradrenaline and serotonin by yet another mechanism.

Thus, depletion of these two neurotransmitters is associated in animals and man with depression, while the drugs that restore their levels and increase their synaptic activity are effective antidepressants.

It is a reasonable inference from the foregoing observations that clinical depression may be the result of an inadequacy of one or both of these neurotransmitters at particular synapses in the brain—and similarly that mania, the obverse of depression, may represent an *overactivity* of such a transmitter. Testing such hypotheses has engaged a number of research groups. There have been some interesting findings, e.g., that in certain types of depression and in mania there is in the urine a decrease or an increase respectively of a particular product of noradrenaline metabolism which appears to be derived largely from the brain. Others have found in cerebrospinal fluid evidence of a decrease in serotonin metabolism in the brain in patients suffering from manic or depressive psychosis. A very effective agent in the treatment of mania and the prophylaxis of manic-depressive illness is *lithium*, a relatively simple substance closely related to sodium, which plays a crucial role in synaptic function. The mechanism by which lithium produces its therapeutic and prophylactic action is as yet unknown.

Similarly, over the past two decades, newly acquired knowledge has begun to unravel the enigma called schizophrenia. This disorder or group of disorders (we may be dealing with a number of different diseases with a common symptomatology) is characterized by disturbances not only in mood but also in thinking and the normal association between them. In the typical severe schizophrenic one sees bizarre behavior, disorders of thinking and speech, impoverishment of feeling, lack of motivation, anhedonia (an inability to experience pleasure), withdrawal from interaction with others, hallucinations, delusions, and educational, occupational, social, and marital disabilities. Such symptoms appear insidiously early in life and become critical in early adulthood. There are such drugs as *mescaline, LSD,* or *dimethyltryptamine*, which are capable of inducing hallucinations and some of the other symptoms of schizophrenia, and have, for some, suggested hypotheses about the nature of schizophrenia itself.

What most hallucinogenic drugs have in common is one or more methyl (CH_3) groups.

It is, therefore, especially interesting that an enzyme has been found in body and brain tissues of animals and man which is capable of adding a methyl group to *normal* metabolites, thus converting them to hallucinogenic substances. To date, however, no such hallucinogenic substance has been clearly identified in schizophrenics. In 1950 a new drug was found to be more effective than any previous treatment in the relief of some of the major symptoms of schizophrenia. That discovery came about in an interesting and unexpected manner. Pharmacologists had been developing and studying drugs that blocked the actions of *histamine,* a substance manufactured within the body, which appears to play an important role in many forms of allergy. The *antihistaminic* drugs thus elaborated have been found to be very beneficial in the treatment of asthma and other types of allergic disorder. One of these drugs was found to combine both antihistaminic and sympatholytic properties—i.e., it also blocked the actions of the sympathetic nervous system.

Henri-Marie Laborit, a French anesthesiologist, was looking for a drug which had such properties as a means of preventing surgical shock, on the hypothesis that both histamine and sympathetic overactivity contributed to its development in surgical operations. He used this drug in preoperative medication, and, because he was a careful observer, he noted in his patients the occurrence of an unwanted and unsearched-for sedation, a kind of sedation different from that which occurs with the barbiturates—a "euphoric quietude." He felt that such a property might be helpful in treating disturbed patients and suggested that to psychiatrists. That drug was the immediate forerunner of *chlorpromazine,* which revolutionized the treatment of schizophrenia. Chlorpromazine was tried in Paris and very quickly in Europe, England, Canada, and the United States. It became the first of a series of "major tranquilizers" or "anti-psychotic" drugs, so named because of their rather specific ability to terminate or ameliorate the psychotic manifestations of schizophrenia, especially the bizarre behavior and thinking, the delusions and hallucinations.

But chlorpromazine had an important side effect—its tendency to produce in some patients the facial and motor disturbances that are seen in Parkinson's disease. Modifications of chlorpromazine were developed in an effort to preserve the therapeutic benefit while avoiding this side effect, but—with very few exceptions—whenever an effective agent appeared it was also found to have the side effect. In addition to the *phenothiazines*, of which chlorpromazine was a member, an entirely new chemical class of drugs appeared, the *butyrophenones*, which were also effective in the treatment of schizophrenia but similarly suffered from the tendency to produce symptoms of Parkinsonism. An explanation of this phenomenon, however, had to await a better understanding of Parkinson's disease. This was not long in coming.

In 1960, a new technique was developed in Sweden for demonstrating certain neurotransmitters within the brain by means of their characteristic fluorescence under appropriate conditions. That technique was quickly applied by neuroanatomists and used within the brain to trace circuits that implied these transmitters. A pathway that used dopamine as its transmitter was discovered in a region of the brain where lesions were known to exist in cases of Parkinsonism. This led to the hypothesis, and the ultimate demonstration, that in Parkinson's disease there was a partial destruction of the dopamine-containing nerve cells. Efforts to replenish the lost dopamine by administration of its precursor *L-dopa* led to marked improvement in the patients and represents one of the major contributions of fundamental neurological research to mental illness in recent times.

It was first suggested by Arvid Carlsson that anti-psychotic drugs must act by blocking the effects of dopamine in the brain, which would explain their tendency to produce the symptoms of Parkinson's disease. On the basis of his studies and more recent observations on dopamine synapses in the brain and components of such synapses studied *in vitro*,

it is now clear that Carlsson's insight was correct and that a major action of both the phenothiazine and the butyrophenone drugs is to diminish the actions of dopamine within the brain.

There is another drug which effects dopamine synapses—*amphetamine*—except that amphetamine exaggerates the effects of dopamine rather than diminishing them. Amphetamine is not at all an anti-psychotic drug— quite the opposite. In animals it produces some of the behavior seen in schizophrenia— i.e., stereotyped movements of various kinds and aimless pacing. When it is abused by human subjects, it produces a psychosis often indistinguishable from schizophrenia. The same drugs that are effective in the treatment of schizophrenia are also practically specific in terminating amphetamine psychosis, and amphetamine is known to exacerbate the psychosis of schizophrenic individuals. Thus drugs that enhance dopamine activity in the brain tend to produce or aggravate schizophrenic symptoms, and those that diminish excessive dopamine activity are capable of relieving these symptoms. That does not mean that the biochemical principles underlying schizophrenia have been found in an abnormal overactivity of dopamine synapses. A therepeutic benefit may sometimes be obtained by an action that only indirectly affects the pathological process. It is nevertheless clear that continued and expanded research on the neurotransmitters in the brain cannot help contributing to our understanding of these illnesses. And with understanding will come more specific treatment and prevention.

What evidence do we have that a continued search for the biochemical factors of mental illness will be rewarding, or that such biochemical disturbances even exist? If there were clear evidence that these illnesses had important genetic bases, that would justify the search for their biochemical principles because genetic factors must express themselves through biochemical processes.

Until quite recently, the evidence for the operation of genetic factors in these major mental illnesses was compelling but not conclusive, because non-genetic factors could account for the observation. Psychiatrists have known for a long time, and every epidemiological study has confirmed their observation, that the major mental illnesses run in families. There is an estimated 10 percent risk for the occurrence of schizophrenia in the parents, siblings, and offspring of schizophrenic individuals, and manic-depressive illness shows a comparable familial tendency. Although this figure is compatible with genetic transmission of these illnesses, it is by no means proof of a fixed pattern. Wealth and poverty run in families but are not genetically transmitted, and the familial occurrence of pellagra was used to support an erroneous genetic concept of what we now know to be a nutritional disorder. A family shares not only its genetic endowments but also its environmental influences, and either or both of these factors may be responsible for familial disorders. Somewhat better evidence came from twin studies; a number of these studies have shown that for both schizophrenia and the affective disorders, a high risk (on the order of 50 percent or more) exists that the illness will appear in the identical twin of an affected person, while the risk for a fraternal twin is of the same order as that for a sibling. Because identical twins are derived from a single fertilized egg and are therefore the same genetically, whereas fraternal twins are no more than siblings conceived at the same time, the high concordance rates for these illnesses in identical twins would be expected in strongly genetic disorders, although that evidence is insufficient, in itself, to establish their genetic nature. Identical twins who look remarkably alike tend to be treated alike by their families and friends. They also share much of their environment and develop a mutual identification. It is those factors, rather than their genetic similarity, that account for the frequency with which they both choose the same occupation or marry similar partners.

During the past 10 years a new approach has been used that appears to have succeeded in separating genetic from environmental factors in the transmission of schizophrenia. This approach consists of the study of adopted individuals who share their genetic endowment with their biological relatives, but their environment with their adoptive relatives. In the several studies that have been completed to date the results are quite consistent. Schizophrenia continues to run in families, but, now, its high prevalence is restricted to the genetic relatives of schizophrenics with whom they have shared few, if any, environmental factors. The adoptive relatives of schizophrenics who reared them and shared their environment show no more tendency to schizophrenia than does the population at large.

In still-incomplete studies of adopted populations compelling evidence that some forms of manic and depressive illness have a genetic basis has recently been discovered; they occur in a number of families, in association with such traits as color blindness and a specific blood group known to reside in the X chromosome. Although this association does not occur in *all* families with manic-depressive illness, when it does occur, it follows a pattern so consistent tht it cannot be explained on a nongenetic basis. One is forced to reach the conclusion that in the majority of severe cases of schizophrenia and in a substantial number of manic-depressive illnesses, genetic factors play a crucial causative role.

There thus exists the basis for a continued and intensified search for the biochemical processes through which these genetic factors operate in the development of the two most important forms of mental illness that confront us. In addition, neurobiology and psychobiology have in recent years provided important clues as to where to look, and powerful techniques have been developed and applied to this search. During this time a cohort of neurobiologists and psychiatrists has been trained, skilled in fundamental research and in clinical investigation. The time has never been more propitious or progress more promising for an understanding of these serious disturbances of the human mind.

SELF TEST: MEASURING COMPREHENSION

"It's Not All In Your Head" By Seymour S. Kety

1. What impact did the contributions of J.W.L. Thudichum have upon the illness perspective as it exists today?

2. Describe the biochemical process by which iproniazid acts as an antidepressant.

3. The street drug "speed" is an amphetamine. Discuss the biochemical implications the use of speed might likely have for a potential schizophrenic.

4. Discuss the reasons why Kety feels that heredity is an important factor in both schizophrenia and manic-depression.

THE PROMISE & PERIL OF PSYCHOSURGERY

from *Saturday Review*

Richard Restak

Psychosurgery refers to the surgical or electrical alteration of the human brain. The issue of whether or not psychosurgery should be performed is one of the most controversial issues in psychiatry today. When psychosurgery is mentioned, many people think of the lobotomy. This is one specific, drastic type of psychosurgery. In the lobotomy, the nerves which connect the frontal lobes of the brain with the thalamus are cut. Lobotomies have the reputation of changing formerly violent, aggressive individuals into human "vegetables". This is the type of operation that left McMurphy in a catatonic state in Ken Kesey's book "One Flew Over the Cuckoo's Nest". Today, professional opinion regarding lobotomies is extremely negative. Currently, less drastic forms of psychosurgery are at the heart of the debate.

Psychosurgery declined in the United States during the 1950's, as it was felt that it would not be needed because of the anti-psychotic drugs developed during that decade. However, as the profession began to realize that the drugs of the fifties were not the cure-alls they were hoped to be, interest in psychosurgery was rekindled. Today, psychosurgery is practiced less than in the postwar years (when at its peak), but in a more discriminate manner.

In the following article, published in 1973, Dr. Richard Restak traces the development of psychosurgery, discusses the pros and cons of it, and makes recommendations for its future. In 1975 the Department of Health, Education, and Welfare published a code of regulations regarding experimentation with humans. These regulations state that no experimentation should be conducted with humans unless the possible benefits to the subject were greater than the potential risks to him. This is very difficult to determine before the fact. Also, legally effective informed consent must be obtained from the subject. The mental patient's capability to make a rational decision regarding informed consent about psychosurgery can be questioned. The brain, the organ that is assumed to be defective, is the organ that must give its permission for the operation to be performed. The issue of whether psychosurgery should be performed or not is a very complex one. It will not likely be resolved in the near future.

Psychosurgery is a term used rather broadly these days to describe surgical, electrical, and other alterations of the brain to change human behavior. An important distinguishing feature of any psychosurgical procedure is irreversibility. Once the brain tissue is altered, it can never be the same again. Since the brain is the essence of what we refer to as personality, it follows that psychosurgery irrevocably alters personality. Even at its best, therefore, psychosurgery is the most hazardous form of psychiatric treatment yet devised and currently the most controversial.

Over the past year experts in medicine, behavior, ethics, and law have clashed over the most fundamental question in the field: Who should designate candidates for psychosurgery and for what symptoms? Should a brain operation to reduce aggression, say, be recommended by a neurologist? A psychiatrist? A social worker? This confusion is inherent in our primitive understanding of the way the brain functions. Since we do not know how it performs "normally," we are even more at a loss to predict how it will perform after surgery. Some examples:

• In San Francisco a fifty-five-year old minister suffering from an incurably painful cancer undergoes "psychosurgery." In three months he returns free of pain to the pulpit after an absence of four years.

• In Jackson, Mississippi, a psychosurgeon operates on a fourteen-year-old boy with explosively violent behavior. After the surgery he is withdrawn and cannot remember his address. After further operations he is described as "deteriorated intellectually."

Last spring the National Institute of Mental Health sponsored a conference on psychosurgery. Appearing by invitation was Dr. O.J. Andy, director of neurosurgery at the University of Mississippi School of Medicine in Jackson. Dr. Andy, perhaps this country's leading proponent of psychosurgery as a solution to the problem of chronic psychiatric disease, explained his position to the conferees:

All abnormal behavior results from structurally abnormal brain tissue. Now, psychiatric techniques are in most instances futile in dealing with these abnormalities. In fact, adequate therapy can be obtained only by techniques, such as surgery, which deal directly with the structurally abnormal brain tissue.

(When pressed on this point, Dr. Andy is willing to admit that no one has demonstrated abnormalities in the structure of brain tissue in psychiatric disease.)

It is unfortunate that our institutions are constantly filled with patients having behavioral disorders which do not respond to psychiatric and medical therapy and which would respond to surgery but are denied appropriate treatment for a variety of rational and irrational reasons. My own clinical interest has been in the realm of controlling aggressive, uncontrollable, violent, and hyperactive behavior which does not respond to medical or psychiatric therapy. I have developed a clinical description of such behavior: the Hyperresponsive Syndrome. This is erratic, aggressive, hyperactive, and emotional instability which in its full-blown expression terminates in attack. These are the patients who need surgical treatment. In addition, there are others: patients who are a detriment to themselves and to society; custodial patients who require constant attention, supervision, and an inordinate amount of institutional care. It should be used in children and adolescents in order to allow their developing brain to mature with as normal a reaction to its environment as possible.

Dr. Andy went on to explain that many of his subjects have been children aged seven and over; at least one was a child of five. The goal in each case is "to reduce the hyperactivity to levels manageable by parents."

The exact number of operations performed by Andy lies between forty and fifty, but he is not sure exactly how many. Moreover, several children have had more than one operation; in at least one case, five different operations were required in order to bring about "behavioral control."

At one point in Dr. Andy's address, he was interrupted by a question regarding the medical ethics of his psychosurgical procedures. He replied:

The ethics involved in the treatment of behavioral disorders is no different from the ethics involved in the treatment of all medical disorders. The medical problems involving behavior have a more direct impact on society than other medical problems such as coronary or kidney disease. Still, if treatment is desired it is neither the moral nor the legal responsibility of society what type of treatment should be administered. The ethics for the diagnosis and treatment of behavioral illness should remain in the hands of the treating physician.

As of this writing, Dr. Andy has returned to Mississippi to continue his highly individual approach to disturbed behavior or, as he prefers to call it, "structurally abnormal brain tissue." What further operations will be performed will be entirely up to Andy and the other psychosurgeons across the country. At this point there are no binding standards of performance by which psychosurgeons can be judged.

The concept of modifying behavior by surgically cutting parts of the brain is not new. First references to such a procedure can be traced to the Roman observation that insanity might be relieved by a sword wound in the head. But all modern psychosurgical methods date from physiologist James Fulton's observation that cutting a specialized group of nerve fibers from the frontal lobes of the brains of two chimpanzees, Becky and Lucy, led to a taming of the animals. The chimps could remember old tricks, even learn new ones, but accepted test situations and frustrations with a "philosophical calm."

In 1936 Egas Moniz, a Portuguese neurologist, applied a similar technique to uncontrollable psychotics. Thirteen years later Moniz won the Nobel Prize and was commended for "the development of prefrontal leucotomy in the treatment of certain psychoses." The number of lobotomies, as this procedure came to be called, performed by Moniz is unknown. Any exact computation is complicated by Moniz's early retirement from neurologic practice several years before a violent death at the hands of a crazed former patient.

In 1942 Walter Freeman, a neurologist, and James Watts, a neurosurgeon, both at George Washington University Hospital, reported that extreme depression and agitation,

even hallucination, could be greatly alleviated by cutting the fibers leading from the frontal lobes of the brain to the neighboring thalamus. The connections between these two structures are normally responsible for a delicate interplay between thought (a frontal lobe function) and emotion (at least partly a thalamic function). After cutting these connections, the doctors reported that exaggerated emotional responses decreased. Although hallucinations might continue, they would be far less terrifying.

The Freeman-Watts treatment spread quickly, and during the 1940s somewhere in the range of 50,000 patients were lobotomized in the United States along. Freeman, a lobotomy zealot, calculated he had personally performed over 4000 operations, using a gold-plated ice pick, which he carried with him in a velvet-lined case. After the local application of a mild pain killer, Freeman would plunge the ice pick through the thin bone of the upper inner angle of the eye socket, severing the frontal nerve connections to the thalamus. No elaborate preparations or precautions preceded this grisly operation, which often took place in the patient's home or in Freeman's office at St. Elizabeth's Hospital. Freeman's enthusiasm for "ice-pick surgery" knew no bounds; several former associates, who prefer to remain unnamed, can recall long lines of patients waiting for treatment outside Freeman's office.

Unfortunately, these lobotomies, especially as practiced by Freeman, often resulted in a zombielike state known as the *frontal lobe syndrome*. Common symptoms included indifference to other people, convulsive seizures, and intellectual impairment. Patients often became self-centered and utterly dependent on others for the simplest routines of day-to-day living.

During the succeeding thirty years, psychosurgeons developed a less crude method of eliminating undesired emotional responses. This involved tampering with the limbic system, or emotional brain—the target of present-day psychosurgery. The limbic system, though still not totally defined, includes such areas as the hippocampus, the amygdala, the cingulum, and the hypothalamus. In lower animals these structures form the basis for emotional reactions. Tampering with the amygdala, for instance, produces in an animal drowsiness, indifference to surroundings, loss of appetite, and a peculiar symptom known as psychic blindness. The animal may stare for hours at food, not realizing it is meant to be eaten. Studies on the human limbic system have established the existence of emotional centers similar in structure, and presumably in function, to lower animals. Proponents argued that operation on these limbic areas produces less "blunting" of the personality than is caused by lobotomies.

With the discovery of tranquilizers in the early Fifties, interest in surgery on both the frontal lobes and the limbic system declined sharply. A drug called Thorazine was widely used as a kind of chemical lobotomy. It soon became apparent, however, that the use of this "miracle drug" carried its own penalties, particularly drug allergies, serious blood abnormalities, paradoxical reactions resulting in further excitement rather than calm, and a bizarre disorder of muscle tone and movement known as tardive dyskinesia. These failures resulted in a resurgence of interest in psychosurgery.

In the last twenty years at least eight different surgical procedures have been developed in which surgical incisions are made in one or more portions of the limbic system. The two commonest operations used today are cingulotomies and amygdalotomies, which involve deep cuts into these two key areas of the emotional brain. According to limbic-system theory, disturbed emotional patterns (violence, deep depressions, suicidal tendencies, etc.) are partly the results of a form of "short circuitry" between the limbic system and the rest of the brain. Cutting of the amygdala or cingulum is intended to interrupt these faulty "connections" in the hope that new "connections" will develop or that the interruption will abolish the disturbed behavior patterns. In actuality, the correlation between behavior patterns and limbic struc-

tures is at best disputable.

Surgical advances in the last fifteen years have led to increasingly precise "targets" within the limbic system. The most innovative development involves stereotactic surgery, a revolutionary treatment for Parkinson's disease in the days before the discovery of the drug L-Dopa. Stereotaxis involves the use of a tiny probe guided externally through a small opening made in the skull. By three-dimensional visualization tiny, accurate cuts can be made in any part of the brain. This procedure markedly reduces the incidence of complications. In many instances ultrasonic beams and radioactive substances have also been used to destroy brain tissue thought to be responsible for emotionally disturbed behavior.

A major advance in the last five years has been the use of small electrodes to stimulate parts of the limbic system. Because the patient is awake, the effects produced by electric stimulation can be described by the patient. If a certain area is found to produce the symptoms for which treatment is sought (rage, depression, etc.), that area can be destroyed. This method has been used for years with good results in the treatment of epilepsy. Its value in treating behavioral disorders, however, has never been established.

Publications regarding psychosurgical operations number many thousands by now. They are, for the most part, contradictory, confusing, and marred by the absence of scientific objectivity. Yet despite the confusion, contradictions, and, occasionally, downright deception, certain accepted facts have emerged. For one thing, tampering with the frontal fibers is almost certain to produce indifference and apathy. Secondly, certain patients have reacted poorly to psychosurgery regardless of the type of operation. Schizophrenics have done worst of all and have been eliminated from the patient pool of even the most enthusiastic of psychosurgeons. So-called psychopaths or sociopaths have not done much better. In fact, the number of patients who stand to gain from psychosurgical procedures turns out to be remarkably small. It includes severe obsessive-compulsives, such as perpetual hand washers, who may excoriate their hands and arms by two or three hundred hand washings a day, and a limited number of severe and unremitting depressives, who, failing to respond to antidepressant medications or even electroconvulsive therapy, gravitate toward inevitable suicide. In addition, psychosurgery may help the terminal cancer patient whose mind is never entirely freed from a totally pain-ridden, drug-addicted existence.

Beyond these few cases, however, lies considerable evidence that the procedure is more often dangerous and even irresponsibly applied. At least one West Coast neurosurgeon, for example, has taken to performing psychosurgery on children as an office procedure. As a result of such abuses, psychosurgery is under challenge as a violation of medical ethics and the individual patient's civil rights.

The most pointed legal objection to psychosurgery revolves on loopholes in the present structure of "informed consent": the extent to which the patient has been informed regarding all possible consequences of psychosurgery. Dr. Harold Edgar, associate professor of law at Columbia University Law Center and author of a forthcoming book on psychosurgery, writes:

> As things stand now, the surgeon is covered as long as he explains to the patient and relatives the uncertainties in the methods and gets them to agree to it without guarantee. It is quite possible that some families would be willing to consent to almost anything to get a troublesome relative off their hands. There must be protection against the collusion of such families with overzealous psychosurgeons. The unwilling patient's right must be safeguarded.

The case of obtaining informed consent from prisoners is even more sensitive. Robert C. Neville, of the Institute of Society, Ethics, and the Life Sciences, Hastings-on-Hudson, New York, cites the case of "Thomas the Engineer" who was asked to submit to a behavior-control experiment:

> When under the influence of calming electrical stimulation, he consented to a psychosurgical procedure to destroy certain brain cells. When the effects of the stimulus wore off, he refused consent. What is informed rational consent in such a setting?

The question came to a court test in July, and the decision clarified the ambiguous legal position of psychosurgery. A Michigan court ruled that state funds could not be used to finance psychosurgery on mental patients despite the patient's willingness—even enthusiasm—for undergoing the procedure. The patient, convicted eighteen years ago for the rape and subsequent slaying of a nurse, was judged criminally insane and committed to Ionia State Hospital in Detroit. His eligibility for discharge notwithstanding, he requested psychosurgery to eliminate the possibility of losing control and killing again. No coercion was brought to bear: the operation was not a precondition to release.

Still, the voluntary nature of the consent was questioned by Att. Charles Halpern of the Center for Law and Social Policy in February at the Society of the Neurosciences in Washington. "There is simply no way," he said, "to ensure that a person in the hospital for eighteen years, with a likelihood of imprisonment for more time, can ever make a voluntary judgment on whether he should have this operation."

During court hearings Dr. Ayub Ommaya, director of the research section of the National Institute of Neurologic Diseases and Stroke, also questioned the scientific premise of the proposed electrode operation. "The role of psychosurgery," Ommaya testified, "has little, if any, applicability for violent behavior."

A similar, federal-level setback for psychosurgery occurred on June 26. The National Institutes of Health rejected a $1.2 million grant proposal by Dr. Vernon Mark of Harvard and other doctors who have pioneered the use of amygdalotomy to treat violent or irrational behavior. The work of the Boston group, in fact, had provided much of the incentive for the Michigan program. Mark and his colleagues had advocated the idea that much crime and other violence have their roots in medical rather than social, causes—a concept that had already won them grant money from the Nixon administration.

According to Dr. Edgar, the definition of psychosurgery as an experimental process could resolve some ambiguities. This would require additional safety and quantitative procedures, such as the maintenance of control groups, which are not currently observed. A bill providing guidelines for all human experimentation has been introduced in Congress by Sen. Edward Kennedy.

The issue of behavior modification is perhaps the century's most compelling medical-social issue. Current fads for ESP and biofeedback reflect our enthusiasm for controlling mental processes with techniques similar to those for controlling our physical environment. Psychosurgery, the most extreme and dramatic form of such modification, involves particularly anguishing decisions that must be made now. Unfortunately, the issue is becoming so politicized that reasoning based on facts is seriously hampered. On December 27, 1972, for example, an open session on psychosurgery and behavioral control at the American Association for the Advance of Science meetings in Washington was disrupted by demonstrators.

In light of such profound disagreements, certain measures seem justified:

1. It is time for a temporary moratorium on all forms of psychosurgery undertaken primarily to modify behavior.

2. We need a clearinghouse of information on the topic of the effects of brain lesions on behavior. As things now stand, the facts are scattered in hundreds of journals. The clearinghouse would enable the evaluation of the data already accumulated from twenty years of various psychosurgical procedures.

3. From here it should be possible to determine national standards of practice concerning (a) when and if psychosurgery is indicated, (b) what procedures offer reasonable hope of result, and (c) most important, what patients are eligible for psychosurgery and under what circumstances.

4. There is an urgent need for measures that will protect the individual patient from having psychosurgical procedures imposed upon him against his will or in a setting in which informed consent or the capacity to choose is impaired.

5. Since the results of psychosurgery have not been established, all psychosurgical procedures should be considered "experimental" and subject to strictly imposed controls. Such operations should be carried out only in a clinical institution able to provide total therapeutic care and follow-up. Non-medical disciplines must have significant influence in the control of psychosurgery.

Some critics have suggested we immediately outlaw psychosurgery altogether. But even this isn't as simple as it seems. What is to be done for tortured compulsives whose senseless rituals defy treatment by any other form? What of the terminal cancer patient whose personality threatens to shatter under the daily strain of unendurable pain? What of the patient who refers himself for a psychosurgical procedure? What are his rights in a possible setting of controlled and reasonably predictable operations? At this point these questions cannot be answered for want of the facts. Only by implementing measures similar to those listed above can we make a good case to abandon—or expand—the use of psychosurgery.

SELF TEST: MEASURING COMPREHENSION
"The Promise and Peril of Psychosurgery" By Richard Restak

1. What evidence is provided in the article to indicate O. J. Andy is a staunch supporter of the illness perspective?

2. Describe the effect that psychosurgery performed on the limbic system has.

3. For what kinds of disorders does psychosurgery seem to have the most beneficial effect?

4. Under what conditions, if any, do you feel psychosurgery should be performed? Why?

Chapter 5
THE PSYCHOANALYTIC PERSPECTIVE

Sigmund Freud, founder of the psychoanalytic perspective, and its primary spokesman until his death in 1939, stands alone as the individual who contributed the most to the development of modern psychiatry and psychology. The beginnings of psychoanalysis can be traced to the 1890's, when Freud, who was a practicing neurologist in Vienna, Austria, began to believe that behavioral abnormality could be motivated by strictly psychological factors. During the nineteenth century the somatic school of thought had been the dominant one. It postulated that behavioral abnormality was caused by organic abnormality. The somatic school was the forerunner of the modern day illness perspective. Thus, Freudian psychoanalysis originated as a revolt against the somatic view of the origin of abnormality, instead postulating psychological origins of behavioral abnormality (Schultz, 1960, pp. 267-268).

Freud, who had earlier learned hypnosis from his associates, began using the technique with his patients. He observed that while in hypnotic states, his patients could recall bits of information from their past that they could not recall in their normal, conscious state of mind. This led him to postulate the existence of the unconscious mind, which he felt harbored the roots of behavioral pathology. Freud felt that if he could bring the deep-rooted unconscious conflicts to the conscious level, they could finally be fully dealt with and laid to rest. He employed the technique of catharsis, or abreaction, in his therapy. Catharsis involved the release of psychological tension that had previously been kept repressed in the unconscious. Freud observed that frequently, when a person catharted, or "cried out", previously repressed, unconscious remembrances, therapeutic change resulted. Freud eventually became disenchanted with hypnosis, and began using free association (saying the first thing that pops into mind), and dream interpretation to unlock the secrets of the unconscious mind.

Freudian theory relies heavily upon the notion that behavior pathology can have its roots in early childhood conflicts of a sexual nature, which had never been completely or successfully resolved. Because of Freud's insistence that unresolved sexual conflicts were an integral part of the pathological picture, psychoanalysis encountered much resistance from the scientific community of conservative, Victorian Europe. Psychoanalysis remains the topic of much controversy today.

Although Freud's life was characterized by tremendous personal accomplishment, it was not without its difficulties. Freud, of Jewish heritage, was deeply troubled by the discriminatory treatment of Jews in Austria. He once commented that Jews were only allowed to make a living as long as they were "willing to step into the gutter to let a Christian pass". He was also troubled by the fact that the scientific community did not immediately accept his theories. One paper Freud presented to a prestigious medical group met with an "icy reception". The chairman of the meeting commented, "It sounds like a scientific fairy tale". Freud's classic, "Studies on Hysteria", which is considered to mark the formal starting point of psychoanalysis, sold only 626 copies in its first thirteen years (a fact I have continually kept in mind as this book was written). Carl Jung and Alfred Adler, two of Freud's staunchest disciples, eventually parted with him to develop their own psychoanalytic theories. Freud, who smoked about twenty cigars daily, developed cancer of the mouth and underwent a series of painful operations. In 1933 the Nazis declared war on psychoanalysis and ordered Freud's books burnt. Despite the Nazi's effort to destroy his works, Freud was still able to sarcastically, yet humorously note, "What progress we are making. In the Middle Ages they would have burned me; nowadays they are content with burning my books." In 1938 he fled to England. He died of cancer a year later (Schultz, 1960, pp 264-277).

Psychoanalysis has not only revolutionized psychiatric practice. It has made an impact on the whole of Western society. Even those therapists who claim they are not Freudian often employ therapeutic techniques originated by him. Few modern figures have been quoted, or misquoted, more than Freud. Innovative theories are often the center of much controversy. Such is the case with psychoanalysis. However, the importance of psychoanalysis cannot be underestimated. It was the first comprehensive theory of personality disorder and its treatment. Today, psychoanalysis remains a vital force within clinical psychology and psychiatry.

The first article I will present in the chapter on psychoanalysis is entitled "Lecture XVIII, Analytic Therapy", by Sigmund Freud. The second article, "The Psychodynamics of Suicide", by Herbert Hendin, offers psychoanalytic insights regarding suicidal motivation. The third article, "Male Supremacy in Freud", by Phil Brown, is an article that is critical of Freudian theory. It criticizes chauvanistic aspects of psychoanalysis.

Reference

Duane P. Schultz, *A History of Modern Psychology* (New York, Academic Press, Inc. 1960)

LECTURE XXVIII
ANALYTIC THERAPY
from *The Complete Introductory Lectures on Psychoanalysis*
Sigmund Freud

Whether we realize it or not, Freudian psychoanalysis has had a great impact upon Western and American culture. Many terms originally used by Freud have today become part of our everyday language. If you have ever viewed an object as a "phallic symbol"; said someone was "repressing" a traumatic experience; referred to someone as being on an "ego trip"; or made a "Freudian slip" in your speech; you have used Freudian terminology.

Although millions of people have strong opinions about Freudian theory, it is likely that many such people have never read any of the original works of Freud. Much of what people know of Freud was learned through secondary sources, or what others have written about Freud. Therefore, I feel that it is important to include some of Freud's own work in this book.

Between 1915 and 1917 Freud delivered a series of 28 lectures on psychoanalysis to the medical students at the University of Vienna. The following selection, "Lecture XXVIII, Analytic Therapy", is the last of this series of lectures, and represents the culmination of his two year's work with his students. James Strachey, translator of this lecture, commented in his introduction to *The Complete Lectures on Psychoanalysis* that ". . . there is no rival to the analysis of the process of psycho-analytic therapy given in the last lecture of all."

In the lecture Freud describes the basic theory of psycho-analysis. He points out how transference, or the patient's perception of the analyst as the reincarnation of significant people from his past, can be used to help the patient's ego gain control over the libido, or sexual instinct, so that the underlying causes of the patient's neurosis can be resolved. He also rebuttles criticisms of psychoanalysis.

Imagine yourself as a student of Freud's. Picture the stern, bearded, cigar-smoking master of psychoanalysis as he delivers his final lecture to his students. Note Freud's modest air, tinged with a sense of confidence in his convictions. The lecture is a beautiful example of the thought, logic, and genius of Sigmund Freud.

Ladies and Gentlemen,—You know what we are going to talk about to-day. You asked me why we do not make use of direct suggestion in psycho-analytic therapy, when we admit that our influence rests essentially on transference—that is, on suggestion; and you added a doubt whether, in view of this predominance of suggestion, we are still able to claim that our psychological discoveries are objective. I promised I would give you a detailed reply.

Direct suggestion is suggestion aimed against the manifestation of the symptoms; it is a struggle between your authority and the motives for the illness. In this you do not concern yourself with these motives; you merely request the patient to suppress their manifestation in symptoms. It makes no difference of principle whether you put the patient under hypnosis or not. Once again Bernheim, with his characteristic perspicacity, maintained that suggestion was the essential element in the phenomena of hypnotism, that hypnosis itself was already a result of suggestion, a suggested state;[2] and he preferred to practise suggestion in a waking state, which can achieve the same effects as suggestion under hypnosis.

Which would you rather hear first on this question—what experience tells us or theoretical considerations?

Let us begin with the former. I was a pupil of Bernheim's, whom I visited at Nancy in 1889 and whose book on suggestion I translated into German.[3] I practised hypnotic treatment for many years, at first by prohibitory suggestion and later in combination with Breuer's method of questioning the patient.[4] I can therefore speak of the results of hypnotic or suggestive therapy on the basis of a wide experience. If, in the words of the old medical aphorism, an ideal therapy should be rapid, reliable and not disagreeable for the patient ['*cito, tuto, jucunde*'], Bernheim's method fulfilled at least two of these requirements. It could be carried through much quicker—or, rather, infinitely quicker—than analytic treatment and it caused the patient neither trouble nor unpleasantness. For the doctor it

became, in the long run, *monotonous*: in each case, in the same way, with the same ceremonial, forbidding the most variegated symptoms to exist, without being able to learn anything of their sense and meaning. It was hackwork and not a scientific activity, and it recalled magic, incantations and hocus-pocus. That could not weigh, however, against the patient's interest. But the third quality was lacking: the procedure was not reliable in any respect. It could be used with one patient; but not with another; it achieved a great deal with one and very little with another, and one never knew why. Worse than the capriciousness of the procedure was the lack of permanence in its successes. If, after a short time, one had news of the patient once more, the old ailment was back again or its place had been taken by a new one. One might hypnotize him again. But in the background there was the warning given by experienced workers against robbing the patient of his self-reliance by frequently repeated hypnosis and so making him an addict to this kind of therapy as though it were a narcotic. Admittedly sometimes things went entirely as one would wish: after a few efforts, success was complete and permanent.[5] But the conditions determining such favorable outcome remained unknown. On one occasion a severe condition in a woman, which I had entirely got rid of by a short hypnotic treatment, returned unchanged after the patient had, through no action on my part, got annoyed with me; after a reconciliation, I removed the trouble again and far more thoroughly; yet it returned once more after she had fallen foul of me a second time. On another occasion a woman patient, whom I had repeatedly helped out of neurotic states by hypnosis, suddenly, during the treatment of a specially obstinate situation, threw her arms round my neck.[6] After this one could scarcely avoid, whether one wanted to or not, investigating the question of the nature and origin of one's authority in suggestive treatment.

So much for experiences. They show us that in renouncing direct suggestion we are not giving up anything of irreplaceable value.

Now let us add a few reflections to this. The practice of hypnotic therapy makes very small demands on either the patient or the doctor. It agrees most beautifully with the estimate in which neuroses are still held by the majority of doctors. The doctor says to the neurotic patient: 'There's nothing wrong with you, it's only a question of nerves; so I can blow away your trouble in two or three minutes with just a few words.' But our views on the laws of energy are offended by the notion of its being possible to move a great weight by a tiny application of force, attacking it directly, without the outside help of any appropriate appliances. In so far as the conditions are comparable, experience shows that this feat is not successfully accomplished in the case of the neuroses either. But I am aware that this argument is not unimpeachable. There is such a thing as a 'trigger-action'.

In the light of the knowledge we have gained from psychoanalysis we can describe the difference between hypnotic and psychoanalytic suggestion as follows. Hypnotic treatment seeks to cover up and gloss over something in mental life; analytic treatment seeks to expose and get rid of something.[7] The former acts like a cosmetic, the latter like surgery. The former makes use of suggestion in order to forbid the symptoms; it strengthens the repressions, but, apart from that, leaves all the processes that have led to the formation of the symptoms unaltered. Analytic treatment makes its impact further back towards the roots, where the conflicts are which give rise to the symptoms, and uses suggestion in order to alter the outcome of those conflicts. Hypnotic treatment leaves the patient inert and unchanged, and for that reason, too, equally unable to resist any fresh occasion for falling ill. An analytic treatment demands from both doctor and patient the accomplishment of serious work, which is employed in lifting internal resistances. Through the overcoming of these resistances the patient's mental life is permanently changed, is raised to a high level of development and remains protected against fresh possibilities of falling ill.[8] This work of overcoming resistances is the essential function of analytic treatment; the patient has to accomplish it and the doctor makes this possible for him with the help of suggestion operating in an *educative* sense. For that reason psychoanalytic treatment has justly been described as a kind of *after-education.*[9]

I hope I have now made it clear to you in what way our method of employing suggestion therapeutically differs from the only method possible in hypnotic treatment. You will understand too, from the fact that suggestion can be traced back to transference, the capriciousness which struck us in hypnotic therapy, while analytic treatment remains calculable within its limits. In using hypnosis we are dependent on the state of the patient's capacity for transference without being able to influence it itself. The transference of a person who is to be hypnotized may be negative or, as most frequently, ambivalent, or he may have protected himself against his transference by adopting special attitudes; of that we learn nothing. In psycho-analysis we act upon the transference itself, resolve what opposes it, adjust the instrument with which we wish to make our impact. Thus it becomes possible for us to derive an entirely fresh advantage from the power of suggestion; we get it into our hands. The patient does not suggest to himself whatever he pleases: we guide his suggestion so far as he is in any way accessible to its influence.

But you will now tell me that, no matter whether we call the motive force of our analysis transference or suggestion, there is a risk that the influencing of our patient may make the objective certainty of our findings doubtful. What is advantageous to our therapy is damaging to our researches. This is the objection that is most often raised against psycho-analysis, and it must be admitted that, though it is groundless, it cannot be rejected as unreasonable. If it were justified, psycho-analysis would be nothing more than a particularly well-disguised and particularly effective form of suggestive treatment and we should have to attach little weight to all that it tells us about what influences our lives, the dynamics of the mind or the unconscious. That is what our opponents believe; and in especial they think that we have 'talked' the patients into everything relating to the importance of sexual experiences—or even into those experiences themselves—after such notions have grown up in our own depraved imagination. These accusations are contradicted more easily by an appeal to experience than by the help of theory. Anyone who has himself carried out psycho-analyses will have been able to convince himself on countless occasions that it is impossible to make suggestions to a patient in that way. The doctor has no difficulty, of course, in making him a supporter of some particular theory and in thus making him share some possible error of his own. In this respect the patient is behaving like anyone else—like a pupil—but this only affects his intelligence, not his illness. After all, his conflicts will only be successfully solved and his resistances overcome if the anticipatory ideas he is given tally with what is real in him. Whatever in the doctor's conjectures is inaccurate drops out in the course of the analysis;[10] it has to be withdrawn and replaced by something more correct. We endeavor by a careful technique to avoid the occurrence of premature successes due to suggestion; but no harm is done even if they do occur, for we are not satisfied by a first success. We do not regard an analysis as at an end until all the obscurities of the case are cleared up, the gaps in the patient's memory filled in, the precipitating causes of the repressions discovered. We look upon successes that set in too soon as obstacles rather than as a help to the work of analysis; and we put an end to such successes by constantly resolving the transference on which they are based. It is this last characteristic which is the fundamental distinction between analytic and purely suggestive therapy, and which frees the results of analysis from the suspicion of being successes due to suggestion. In every other kind of suggestive treatment the transference is carefully preserved and left untouched; in analysis it is itself subjected to treatment and is dissected in all the shapes in which it

appears. At the end of an analytic treatment the transference must itself be cleared away; and if success is then obtained or continues, it rests, not on suggestion, but on the achievement by its means of an overcoming of internal resistances, on the internal change that has been brought about in the patient.

The acceptance of suggestions on individual points is no doubt discouraged by the fact that during the treatment we are struggling unceasingly against resistances which are able to transform themselves into negative (hostile) transferences. Nor must we fail to point out that a large number of the individual findings of analysis, which might otherwise be suspected of being products of suggestion, are confirmed from another and irreproachable source. Our guarantors in this case are the sufferers from dementia praecox and paranoia, who are of course far above any suspicion of being influenced by suggestion. The translations of symbols and the phantasies, which these patients produce for us and which in them have forced their way through into consciousness, coincide faithfully with the results of our investigations into the unconscious of transference neurotics and thus confirm the objective correctness of our interpretations, on which doubt is so often thrown. You will not, I think, be going astray if you trust analysis on these points.

I will now complete my picture of the mechanism of cure by clothing it in the formulas of the libido theory. A neurotic is incapable of enjoyment and of efficiency—the former because his libido is not directed on to any real object and the latter because he is obliged to employ a great deal of his available energy on keeping his libido under repression and on warding off its assaults. He would become healthy if the conflict between his ego and his libido came to an end and if his ego had his libido again at its disposal. The therapeutic task consists, therefore, in freeing the libido from its present attachments, which are withdrawn from the ego, and in making it once more serviceable to the ego. Where, then, is the neurotic's libido situated? It is easily found: it is attached to the symptoms, which yield it the only substitutive satisfaction possible at the time. We must therefore make ourselves masters of the symptoms and resolve them—which is precisely the same thing that the patient requires of us. In order to resolve the symptoms, we must go back as far as their origin, we must renew the conflict from which they arose, and, with the help of motive forces which were not at the patient's disposal in the past, we must guide it to a different outcome. This revision of the process of repression can be accomplished only in part in connection with the memory traces of the processes which led to repression. The decisive part of the work is achieved by creating in the patient's relation to the doctor —in the 'transference'—new editions of the old conflicts; in these the patient would like to behave in the same way as he did in the past, while we, by summoning up every available mental force [in the patient], compel him to come to a fresh decision. Thus the transference becomes the battlefield on which all the mutually struggling forces should meet one another.

All the libido, as well as everything opposing it, is made to converge solely on the relation with the doctor. In this process the symptoms are inevitably divested of libido. In place of the patient's true illness there appears the artificially constructed transference illness, in place of the various unreal objects of his libido there appears a single, and once more imaginary, object in the person of the doctor. But, by the help of the doctor's suggestion, the new struggle around this object is lifted to the highest psychical level: it takes place as a normal mental conflict. Since a fresh repression is avoided, the alienation between ego and libido is brought to an end and the subject's mental unity is restored. When the libido is released once more from its temporary object in the person of the doctor, it cannot return to its earlier objects, but is at the disposal of the ego. The forces against which we have been struggling during our work of therapy are, on the one hand, the ego's antipathy to certain trends of the libido —an antipathy expressed in a tendency to repression—and, on the other hand, the tenacity or adhesiveness of the libido [p. 348], which dislikes leaving objects that it has once cathected.

Thus our therapeutic work falls into two phases. In the first, all the libido is forced from the symptoms into the transference and concentrated there; in the second, the struggle is waged around this new object and the libido is liberated from it. The change which is decisive for a favourable outcome is the elimination of repression in this renewed conflict, so that the libido cannot withdraw once more from the ego by flight into the unconscious. This is made possible by the alteration of the ego which is accomplished under the influence of the doctor's suggestion. By means of the work of interpretation, which transforms what is unconscious into what is conscious, the ego is enlarged at the cost of this unconscious; by means of instruction, it is made conciliatory towards the libido and inclined to grant it some satisfaction, and its repugnance to the claims of the libido is diminished by the possibility of disposing of a portion of it by sublimation. The more closely events in the treatment coincide with this ideal description, the greater will be the success of the psycho-analytic therapy. It finds its limits in the lack of mobility of the libido, which may refuse to leave its objects, and the rigidity of narcissism, which will not allow transference on to objects to increase beyond certain bounds. Further light may perhaps be thrown on the dynamics of the process of cure if I say that we get hold of the whole of the libido which has been withdrawn from the dominance of the ego by attracting a portion of it on to ourselves by means of the transference.

It will not be out of place to give a warning that we can draw no direct conclusion from the distribution of the libido during and resulting from the treatment as to how it was distributed during the illness. Suppose we succeeded in bringing a case to a favourable conclusion by setting up and then resolving a strong father-transference to the doctor. It would not be correct to conclude that the patient had suffered previously from a similar unconscious attachment of his libido to his father. His father-transference was merely the battlefield on which we gained control of his libido; the patient's libido was directed to it from other positions. A battlefield need not necessarily coincide with one of the enemy's key fortresses. The defence of a hostile capital need not take place just in front of its gates. Not until after the transference has once more been resolved can we reconstruct in our thoughts the distribution of libido which had prevailed during the illness.

From the standpoint of the libido theory, too, we may say a last word on dreams. A neurotic's dreams help us, like his parapraxes and his free associations to them, to discover the sense of his symptoms and to reveal the way in which his libido is allocated. They show us, in the form of a wish-fulfilment, what wishful impulses have been subjected to repression and to what objects the libido withdrawn from the ego has become attached. For this reason the interpretation of dreams plays a large part in a psycho-analytic treatment, and in some cases it is over long periods the most important instrument of our work. We already know [p. 218] that the state of sleep in itself leads to a certain relaxation of the repressions. A repressed impulse, owing to this reduction in the pressure weighing down upon it, becomes able to express itself far more clearly in a dream than it can be allowed to be expressed by a symptom during the day. The study of dreams therefore becomes the most convenient means of access to a knowledge of the repressed unconscious, of which the libido withdrawn from the ego forms a part.

But the dreams of neurotics do not differ in any important respect from those of normal people; it is possible, indeed, that they cannot be distinguished from them at all. It would be absurd to give an account of the dreams of neurotics which could not also apply to the dreams of normal people. We must therefore say that the difference between neurosis and health holds only during the day; it is not prolonged into dream-life. We are obliged to carry over to healthy people a number of hypotheses which arise in connection with neurotics as a result of the link between the latter's dreams and their symptoms. We cannot deny that healthy people as well possess in their mental life what alone makes possible the formation both of dreams and of symptoms, and we must conclude that they too have carried out repressions, that they expend a certain amount of energy in order to maintain them, that their unconscious system conceals repressed impulses which are still cathected with energy, and that *a portion of their libido is withdrawn from their ego's disposal.* Thus a healthy person, too, is virtually a neurotic; but dreams appear to be the only symptoms which he is capable of forming. It is true that if one subjects his waking life to a closer examination one discovers something that contradicts this appearance — namely that this ostensibly healthy life is interspersed with a great number of trivial and in practice unimportant symptoms.

The distinction between nervous health and neurosis is thus reduced to a practical question and is decided by the outcome—by whether the subject is left with a sufficient amount of capacity for enjoyment and of efficiency. It probably goes back to the relative sizes of the quota of energy that remains free and of that which is bound by repression, and is of a quantitative not of a qualitative nature. I need not tell you that this discovery is the theoretical justification for our conviction that neuroses are in principle curable in spite of their being based on constitutional disposition.

The identity of the dreams of healthy and neurotic people enables us to infer thus much in regard to defining the characteristics of health. But in regard to dreams themselves we can make a further inference: we must not detach them from their connection with neurotic symptoms, we must not suppose that their essential nature is exhausted by the formula that describes them as a translation of thoughts into an archaic form of expression [p. 199], but we must suppose that they exhibit to us allocations of the libido and object-cathexes that are really present.[11]

We shall soon have reached the end. You are perhaps disappointed that on the topic of the psycho-analytic method of therapy I have only spoken to you about theory and not about the conditions which determine whether a treatment is to be undertaken or about the results it produces. I shall discuss neither: the former because it is not my intention to give you practical instructions on how to carry out a psycho-analysis, and the latter because several reasons deter me from it. At the beginning of our talks [this year, p. 256], I emphasized the fact that under favourable conditions we achieve successes which are second to none of the finest in the field of internal medicine; and I can now add something further—namely that they could not have been achieved by any other procedure. If I were to say more than this I should be suspected of trying to drown the loudly raised voices of depreciation by self-advertisement. The threat has repeatedly been made against psycho-analysts by our medical 'colleagues'— even at public congresses—that a collection of the failures and damaging results of analysis would be published which would open the suffering public's eyes to the worthlessness of this method of treatment. But, apart from the malicious, denunciatory character of such a measure, it would not even be calculated to make it possible to form a correct judgement of the therapeutic effectiveness of analysis. Analytic therapy, as you know, is in its youth; it has taken a long time to establish its technique, and that could only be done in the course of working and under the influence of increasing experience. In consequence of the difficulties in giving instruction, the doctor who is a beginner in psycho-analysis is thrown back to a greater extent than other specialists on his own capacity for further development, and the results of his first years will never make it possible to judge the efficacy of analytic therapy.

Many attempts at treatment miscarried during the early period of analysis because they were undertaken in cases which were altogether unsuited to the procedure and which we should exclude to-day on the basis of our present view of the indications for treatment. But these indications, too, could only be arrived at by experiment. In those days we did not know *a priori* that paranoia and dementia praecox in strongly marked forms are inaccessible, and we had a right to make trial of the method on all kinds of disorders. But most of the failures of those early years were due not to the doctor's fault or an unsuitable choice of patients but to unfavourable external conditions. Here we have only dealt with internal resistances, those of the patient, which are inevitable and can be overcome. The external resistances which arise from the patient's circumstances, from his environment, are of small theoretical interest but of the greatest practical importance. Psycho-analytic treatment may be compared with a surgical operation and may similarly claim to be carried out under arrangements that will be the most favourable for its success. You know the precautionary measures adopted by a surgeon: a suitable room, good lighting, assistants, exclusion of the patient's relatives, and so on. Ask yourselves now how many of these operations would turn out successfully if they had to take place in the presence of all the members of the patient's family, who would stick their noses into the field of the operation and exclaim aloud at every incision. In psycho-analytic treatments the intervention of relatives is a positive danger and a danger one does not know how to meet. One is armed against the patient's internal resistances, which one knows are inevitable, but how can one ward off these external resistances? No kind of explanations make any impression on the patient's relatives; they cannot be induced to keep at a distance from the whole business, and one cannot make common cause with them because of the risk of losing the confidence of the patient, who—quite rightly, moreover—expects the person in whom he has put his trust to take his side. No one who has any experience of the rifts which so often divide a family will, if he is an analyst, be surprised to find that the patient's closest relatives sometimes betray less interest in his recovering than in his remaining as he is. When, as so often, the neurosis is related to conflicts between members of a family, the healthy party will not hesitate long in choosing between his own interest and the sick party's recovery. It is not to be wondered at, indeed, if a husband looks with disfavour on a treatment in which, as he may rightly suspect, the whole catalogue of his sins will be brought to light. Nor do we wonder at it; but we cannot in that case blame ourselves if our efforts remain unsuccessful and the treatment is broken off prematurely because the husband's resistance is added to that of his sick wife. We had in fact undertaken something which in the prevailing circumstances was unrealizable.

Instead of reporting a number of cases, I will tell you the story of a single one, in which, from considerations of medical discretion, I was condemned to play a long-suffering part. I undertook the analytic treatment—it was many years ago—of a girl who had for some time been unable, owing to anxiety, to go out in the street or to stay at home by herself. The patient slowly brought out an admission that her imagination had been seized by chance observations of the affectionate relations between her mother and a well-to-do friend of the family. But she was so clumsy—or so subtle—that she gave her mother a hint of what was being talked about in the analytic sessions. She brought this about by changing her behaviour towards her mother, by insisting on being protected by no one but her mother from her anxiety at being alone and by barring the door to her in her anxiety if she tried to leave the house. Her mother had herself been very neurotic in the past, but had been cured years before in a hydropathic establishment. Or rather, she had there made the acquaintance of the man with whom she was able to enter into a relation that was in every way satisfying to her. The girl's passionate demands took her aback, and she suddenly understood the meaning of her daughter's anxiety: the girl had made herself ill in order to keep her mother prisoner and to rob her of the freedom of movement that her relations with her lover required. The mother quickly made up her mind and brought the obnoxious treatment to an end. The girl was taken to a sanatorium for nervous diseases and was demonstrated for many years as 'a poor victim of psycho-analysis'. All this time, too, I was pursued by the calumny of responsibility for the unhappy end of the treatment. I kept silence, for I thought I was bound by the duty of medical discretion. Long afterwards I learnt from one of my colleagues, who visited the sanatorium and had seen the agoraphobic girl there, that the *liaison* between her mother and the well-to-do friend of the family was common knowledge in the city and that it was probably connived at by the husband and father. Thus it was to this 'secret' that the treatment had been sacrificed.

In the years before the war, when arrivals from many foreign countries made me independent of the favour or disfavour of my own city, I followed a rule of not taking on a patient for treatment unless he was *sui juris*, not dependent on anyone else in the essential relations of his life. This is not possible, however, for every psycho-analyst. Perhaps you may conclude from my warning against relatives that patients designed for psychoanalysis should be removed from their families and that this kind of treatment should accordingly be restricted to inmates of hospitals for nervous diseases. I could not, however, follow you in that. It is much more advantageous for patients (in so far as they are not in a phase of severe exhaustion) to remain during the treatment in the conditions in which they have to struggle with the tasks that face them. But the patients' relatives ought not to cancel out this advantage by their conduct and should not offer any hostile opposition to the doctor's efforts. But how do you propose to influence in that direction factors like these which are inaccessible to us? And you will guess, of course, how much the prospects of a treatment are determined by the patient's social *milieu* and the cultural level of his family.

This presents a gloomy prospect for the

effectiveness of psycho-analysis as a therapy —does it not?—even though we are able to explain the great majority of our failures by attributing them to interfering external factors. Friends of analysis have advised us to meet the threatened publication of our failures with statistics of successes drawn up by ourselves. I did not agree to this. I pointed out that statistics are worthless if the items assembled in them are too heterogeneous; and the cases of neurotic illness which we had taken into treatment were in fact incomparable in a great variety of respects. Moreover, the period of time that could be covered was too short to make it possible to judge the durability of the cures.[12] And it was altogether impossible to report on many of the cases: they concerned people who had kept both their illness and its treatment secret, and their recovery had equally to be kept secret. But the strongest reason for holding back lay in the realization that in matters of therapy people behave highly irrationally, so that one has no prospect of accomplishing anything with them by rational means. A therapeutic novelty is either received with delirious enthusiasm—as, for instance, when Koch introduced his first tuberculin against tuberculosis to the public[13] or it is treated with abysmal distrust—like Jenner's vaccination, which was in fact a blessing and which even to-day has its irreconcilable opponents. There was obviously a prejudice against psycho-analysis. If one had cured a severe case, one might hear people say: 'That proves nothing. He would have recovered on his own account by this time.' And when a woman patient, who had already passed through four cycles of depression and mania, came to be treated by me during an interval after an attack of melancholia and three weeks later started on a phase of mania, all the members of her family—and a high medical authority, too, who was called in for consultation—were convinced that the fresh attack could only be the result of my attempted analysis. Nothing can be done against prejudices. You can see it again to-day in the prejudices which each group of nations at war has developed against

the other. The most sensible thing to do is to wait, and to leave such prejudices to the eroding effects of time. One day the same people begin to think about the same things in quite a different way from before; why they did not think so earlier remains a dark mystery.

It is possible that the prejudice against analytic treatment is already diminishing. The constant spread of analytic teachings, the increasing number of doctors practising analysis in a number of countries seems to vouch for this. When I was a young doctor, I found myself in a similar storm of indignation on the doctors' part against treatment by hypnotic suggestion, which is now held up in contrast to analysis by people of 'moderate' views.[14] Hypnotism, however, has not fulfilled its original promise as a therapeutic agent. We psycho-analysts may claim to be its legitimate heirs and we do not forget how much encouragement and theoretical clarification we owe to it. The damaging results attributed to psycho-analysis are restricted essentially to passing manifestations of increased conflict if an analysis is clumsily carried out or if it is broken off in the middle. You have heard an account of what we do with our patients and can form your own judgement as to whether our efforts are calculated to lead to any lasting damage. Abuse of analysis is possible in various directions; in particular, the transference is a dangerous instrument in the hands of an unconscientious doctor. But no medical instrument or procedure is guaranteed against abuse; if a knife does not cut, it cannot be used for healing either.

I have finished, Ladies and Gentlemen. It is more than a conventional form of words if I admit that I myself am profoundly aware of the many defects in the lectures I have given you. I regret above all that I have so often promised to return later to a topic I have lightly touched on and have then found no opportunity of redeeming my promise. I undertook to give you an account of a subject which is still incomplete and in process of development, and my condensed summary has itself turned out to be an incomplete one.

At some points I have set out the material on which to draw a conclusion and have then myself not drawn it. But I could not pretend to make you into experts; I have only tried to stimulate and enlighten you.

---

[1][This lecture contains Freud's fullest account of the theory of the therapeutic effects of psycho-analysis. His later discussion of the question in his paper on 'Analysis Terminable and Interminable' (1937c) seems in some respects to be at variance with it. Cf. the Editor's Note to that paper. Freud published very little on the details of psychoanalytic technique. See, however, the technical papers in Volume XII of the *Standard Edition*, where a list of his other writings on the subject will be found.]

[2][Freud subsequently expressed his disagreement with this view of Bernheim's. See footnote at the end of Chapter X of *Group Psychology* (1921c).]

[3][In fact Freud translated two of Bernheim's books: *De la suggestion et de ses applications a la therapeutique* (1886, translated 1888-9) and *Hypnotisme, suggestion et psychotherapie* (1891, translated 1892).]

[4][See p. 292 above.]

[5][An instance of this kind was reported by Freud in an early paper, 'A Case of Successful Treatment by Hypnotism' (1892-3).]

[6][Freud described this episode again at the end of Chapter II of his *Autobiographical Study* (1925d), (Norton, 1963).]

[7][This distinction is developed at some length in an early paper of Freud's 'On Psychotherapy' (1905a).]

[8][Cf. footnote, p. 445 above.]

[9][See the paper 'On Psychotherapy' (1905c), where, incidentally, the German word *'Nacherziehung'* ('after-education') is wrongly translated 're-education'.]

[10][Freud gives a small example of this in the 'Wolf Man' case history (1918b).]

[11][Some interesting remarks on the dreams of *psychotic* patients will be found in Section B of 'Some Neurotic Mechanisms' (1922b).]

[12][Freud recurrs to this question in the *New Introductory Lectures,* p. 616, where the therapeutic value of psychoanalysis is again discussed.]

[13][In 1890. Its promise was not fulfilled.]

[14][Some striking evidence of the medical opposition to hypnotism will be found in an early review by Freud of a book on the subject by the well-known Swiss psychiatrist, August Forel (Freud, 1889a).]

SELF TEST: MEASURING COMPREHENSION

"Lecture XXVIII, Analytic Therapy", By Sigmund Freud

1. What were the major reasons why Freud became disenchanted with hypnosis as a therapeutic technique?

2. Describe Freud's ideas regarding how transference can be used to enable the ego to gain control over the libido.

3. Why did Freud feel that the interpretation of a patient's dreams could give important clues toward an understanding of the underlying dynamics of the patient's neurosis?

4. Why did Freud feel that the intervention of the patient's family could be a hindrance to effective psychoanalysis?

5. One major criticism of Freud has been that he failed to provide statistical evidence of the success of psychoanalysis. Why did Freud feel that such evidence was not necessary to validate psychoanalysis?

THE PSYCHODYNAMICS OF SUICIDE
from *Journal of Nervous & Mental Disease*
Herbert Hendin

Although it is estimated that 50,000 Americans commit suicide annually, the actual number of suicides may in reality be much higher. We don't conclusively know how many deaths that are officially classified as accidental are really suicides. It is likely that many one car automobile fatalities, where the driver was going at a ridiculously high rate of speed on a familiar, curving road, are not accidents, but suicides.

Although American women attempt suicide twice as frequently as American men, they are only half as "successful" as men in actually killing themselves. This can be explained by examining the techniques both men and women use in attempting suicide. Men are likely to shoot or hang themselves, and death is likely to result. Women are more likely to use overdoses of drugs, or wrist slitting, which take longer for death to result, giving her an opportunity to change her mind, and allow the possibility of emergency medical treatment to prevent death.

But what motivates a person to take his own life? What thoughts race through his mind when he contemplates suicide? What are his attitudes about death? In the following article, Herbert Hendin offers some insights into the motivations of suicidal individuals. His theoretical orientation is psychoanalytic and he uses Freudian techniques such as hypnosis and dream interpretation to gather his data.

What the suicidal patient wishes to get away from in life is only part of his story. His observed attitudes toward death, dying and afterlife are equally revealing about him and his motivation for suicide. This paper will indicate some psychodynamic patterns of suicide based on differing attitudes toward death on the part of suicidal patients. The case illustrations are taken from patients seen by the writer in New York City at Bellevue Hospital, the New York State Psychiatric Institute and St. Luke's Hospital, as well as from patients observed in three Scandinavian countries (4-8).

Background of the Problem

The first important psychological insight in the literature about suicide came from Freud. He was not working directly with the problem of suicide and in his work described only one patient who actually made a suicide attempt (3). What he did see, however, and in good number, were depressed patients. Freud observed in "Mourning and Melancholia" (1916) that the self-hatred seen in depression originated in anger toward a love object turned back by the individual on himself (1). Freud reasoned that suicide was the ultimate form of this phenomenon and that there would be no suicide without the earlier repressed desire to kill someone else. The concept that suicide can be a kind of inverted murder was extremely important, although unfortunately it became overworked by some in an effort to explain all suicide.

Freud made his observations on depression years before he had concluded that anger or aggression could be non-erotic in origin. At the time he wrote "Mourning and Melancholia," all aggression had to have, in Freud's view, a sexual origin, so that the paper is filled with complicated and undemonstrable discussion of what amounts to retroflexed anger. Ten years later Freud expressed surprise at his having overlooked the "universality of non-erotic aggression" (3). He never rewrote his earlier work so the extraneous libidinal explanations for the existence of anger remain unaltered. This, however, should not lead one to overlook the basic psychological truth contained in the 1916 paper, namely, that anger can become self-directed, can lead to depression and can be a motivating force in suicide.

The current view of depression has also been revised over the years. The significance of both dependency and expiation in depression was made clear by Sandor Rado (10). The idea that retroflexed anger and self-punishment can have atonement or expiation as goals, the individual hoping thus to win back love and affection, does not appear in Mourning and Melancholia, and was primarily Rado's contribution. And just as retroflexed anger can at times be the motivating force in suicidal patients, so, too, can suicide be an act of expiation.

Despite the help that a knowledge of the psychology of depression gives to the understanding of suicide, it is far from the whole picture. A great number of suicidal patients do not manifest the clinical features or classical psychodynamics associated with depression. Most important to keep in mind, however, is the fact that many depressed patients are just not suicidal. This alone would emphasize that the psychodynamics of depression are not sufficient to explain sui-

cide, and thus the study of depressed patients cannot be used as a substitute for directly studying suicidal patients. In investigating suicidal patients one often sees patients who appear to view their death as internalized murder, while others' suicide attempts are acts of expiation, but there is, in addition, a broad range of other attitudes toward death and meanings of the act of suicide.

How To Study The Problem

In first working with the problem of suicide at Bellevue, 100 consecutive admissions of attempted suicides to the hospital were interviewed. They were seen as often as was felt necessary to get a full psychodynamic picture of each case. Patients who had made suicide attempts were later taken into therapy, criteria for selection being as varied a sampling of suicidal motivations and situations as possible. As many as 15 patients who had made suicide attempts were in therapy at one period during this investigation. Currently at St. Luke's Hospital, in addition to the intensive interviewing of the suicidal patients, the writer has also been working with hypnosis, in an attempt to get at the psychodynamics of individual patients and what their motivations for suicide are. In all these approaches, however, as well as in cross-cultural work that the writer has been doing with suicidal patients in Scandinavia, all patients seen have attempted suicide and, obviously, survived. The question often raised—are those who attempted suicide and survived a comparable group in terms of personality and motivation to those who actually died?—bears on any evaluation of the psychodynamics of suicide.

Long ago it proved helpful to rate or evaluate suicidal patients on a scale of one to three with regard to their suicidal intent (1—the patients with minimal intent; 2—with moderate intent; and 3—with maximal suicidal intent [4]). The following two cases illustrate types of patients in the maximal intent group. One was a girl who jumped under a subway train, had two cars pass over her and still lived. This was possible in the particular subway, since there was sufficient room between the wheels and under the train, but this was not known by the girl at the time. A second patient had made a suicide pact with his homosexual partner. They made their attempt in their hotel room on a Saturday night, knowing they would probably not be discovered by the chambermaid until Monday morning. They each took 50 barbiturates of 1/10th gram strength. When found and admitted to the hospital on Monday, they were both comatose and remained so for several days. The initial hospital opinion was that neither would survive. As it turned out, one died and the other lived. The one who lived, however, was placed in the group of those with maximal intent.

It seems reasonable to include the girl under the train and the homosexual man in this group and to assume that in working with them one is working with a situation as close to that resulting in actual suicide as one needs to get. When suicidal patients are divided into intent groups, the group with maximal intent has an age and sex distribution statistically comparable to that of actual suicides, and is quite different from that found when one takes all attempted suicides together (4).

A great deal about suicide can also be learned from the study of patients in the lower intent groups. When, for example, suicide is an act of self-punishment, for one patient only death will be sufficient atonement, while for another the self-damage done in a suicide attempt may suffice. The study of both types, however, throws a light on the psychology of self-punishment and its relation to suicide.

While distinguishing between a patient who is very serious about suicide and one who is not serious at all is not very difficult, the situation is a little more complicated with patients who are in the intermediate group. Patients who have survived taking as many as 25 sleeping pills may say they only wished to sleep and yet admit that they did have the thought that it might be nice never to wake up. They can appear themselves to be unsure whether they wanted to die. One is impressed that there are mixed feelings about the wish to die in most suicidal patients. Menninger, in particular, has stressed and illustrated some of the variations seen in patient's conscious and unconscious wishes with regard to dying (9). Tolstoy describes in *Anna Karenia* the heroine's last feelings and sensations after jumping in front of a train: she feels that she has perhaps made a mistake and struggles unsuccessfully to get up before the train hits her. Tolstoy's sensitive intuition in this regard seems very much borne out by what is learned from actual suicidal patients. One suspects that if a man jumping from a tall building could be interviewed while still in the air three floors down from the top, his feelings about dying would often be already different from what they had been a few seconds before. A recently interviewed patient said she had wished to change her mind right before jumping from a building, but that since she had committed herself in a letter to this action, she was unable to back out.

Hypnosis can be useful in evaluating a patient's suicidal intent as well as his motivation. It is of most obvious use in reconstructing and recovering amnesias connected with suicide attempts. Patients who were under the influence of alcohol at the time and are vague as to the details of the attempt can often recall under hypnosis far more than otherwise. Similarly, one patient who had shot himself with a shotgun and survived was amnestic for all that happened in the minutes prior to pulling the trigger. Under hypnosis his thoughts and feelings during that period as well as the details of his attempt could be recovered.

The most important use of hypnosis as a research tool in studying suicide, however, comes from another direction. As will be more evident in the section below on the psychodynamics of suicide, the dreams of these patients immediately before or after their suicide attempts often deal directly with their death or suicide and are of very great value in getting a psychodynamic picture of the patient. This seems natural enough, for when patients are interviewed soon after their attempts, the dynamics are close to consciousness and apt to be revealed in their dreams. When months have elapsed, these dynamics may be so repressed that a patient may have to be seen in therapy for a long time before the material becomes similarly accessible. Thus, generally it is advisable to see patients within the first days after their attempted suicide. When patients have not been obliging enough to remember dreams during the period of their suicide attempts, hypnosis can be of value. The writer has hypnotized such patients and had them go back in their thoughts to the time of their attempt and to the mood of that time. It was then suggested to them that they would have a dream while under hypnosis, such as they might have had the night they made their suicide attempt, and which would throw some light on their reasons for wanting to kill themselves. While such a technique is productive with only about a third of suicidal patients, from the research standpoint invaluable material can be so learned. In discussing the psychodynamics of suicide some of this material will be considered.

The Psychodynamics Of Suicide

The details, method and circumstances of the suicide attempt often give the first important clue as to the psychodynamics of the particular patient, and they must be carefully established. Often the suicide attempt is a kind of psychological drama and the very way in which it is made is extremely revealing. One woman jumped from a window with a picture of her son in her brassiere and a message on the back of the picture saying, "Timmy knows I love him." Years before, at the time of her divorce, this woman actually had given away her young son to be raised by his paternal grandparents. While she still saw him up to the time of the attempt, she appeared to be tortured by her difficulties in love relationships and her inability to love her son. The picture and message were an attempt to deny the true state of affairs and yet gave the first clue that put one on the right track.

Another older man who made an attempt with barbiturates arranged his attempt so he might be found by his son before succumbing.

The man had been separated from his wife for a year, after 25 years of marriage, and despite the details of the attempt the relationship with his wife first appeared to be the crucial factor. Only when, after three days in the hospital, he reported a dream in which his son fed him poison was it possible for me to reverse my thinking: it became obvious it was the patient's relationship with his son which was the major determinant in this case.

The choice of method involved may very often reveal a good deal about the organization and integration of the personality. Disorganized or multiple suicidal methods, or those carried out in a chaotic manner and lasting over several days, are generally chosen by disorganized, schizoid patients.

It may seem surprising that, in many studies of suicide in the literature, the attitudes of suicidal patients toward death, dying and afterlife have been neglected. In a large measure, this can be attributed to anxiety and inhibition of psychiatrists in relation to suicidal patients. It is reflected right down to the resident on the ward who will ask a patient after ten minutes' acquaintance if he has had homosexual experiences or what he does with regard to masturbation, but will not ask a suicidal patient about his attitude toward death, about what he thinks happens after death, about what he thought of after he turned on the gas and what he might have dreamt of while he was unconscious. These last four questions can elicit invaluable material bearing on the understanding of suicidal patients and their motivation.

The following are some of the varying psychodynamic constellations with regard to death and suicide that have been observed in suicidal patients:

Death as retaliatory abandonment: A homosexual college boy of 18 who was failing in school was seen following a serious suicide attempt with 60 barbiturate pills which he barely survived. During a hypnotic interview it was suggested to the patient that he would have a dream such as he might have had the night of his suicidal attempt. His dream was a simple one. He was working for the United

Nations and had an office that occupied the entire first floor of the UN building in New York. A friend of his was applying for a position and the patient was interviewing him and reviewing his qualifications. He told his friend that he did not qualify and could not have the job. During his waking associations to the dream he revealed his preoccupation with this friend. It appeared that he "had a crush on," but had never tried to become involved sexually with the friend although the friend may have become alarmed at the intensity of the patient's feelings. The friend had been quite obviously backing out of the relationship and several months prior to the attempt had more or less broken off with the patient.

What does the patient accomplish in the dream and by the suicide attempt? He gains an illusory control over the situation that involves rejection. In the dream, if there is any rejecting to be done, he is going to do it; by committing suicide, he is the one who leaves or does the rejecting. The conception that death involves an act of leaving, *i.e.,* an abandonment, is known to derive from childhood. Children's reactions to death most frequently center around its being a violent act inflicted on the dead person or as his having "left" voluntarily. Children who lose or are separated from their mothers invariably react as though the mothers had chosen to leave them. The continuation of this psychological equation is seen in adult life among patients with extreme fears of dying which are usually emotionally linked with the most primitive abandonment fears from childhood.

That this patient also experienced a *feeling of omnipotent mastery through death* is strongly suggested by the important UN position and large office in his dreams. Suicide attempts and the idea of suicide seem to give an illusory feeling of mastery over a situation through the control one has over whether one lives or dies. Another patient who had been a chemistry major in college had struggled through school with a cyanide capsule in his desk, consoling himself with the thought that if he could not manage his work he could always take the cyanide. On graduation he threw it out and never made a suicide attempt. A female patient who eventually did make a very serious suicide attempt had, in the years prior to her attempt, kept a toy pistol in her drawer and had comforted herself through an unhappy love affair with the fantasy that if things got too bad she could always kill herself.

Death as retroflexed murder: A woman of 44 had made a serious suicide attempt with sleeping pills about a year after the breakup of her marriage. Her husband had been unfaithful during their twenty years' marriage and she had alternately managed to deny this to herself or to reassure herself by saying that these affairs were unimportant to him. The last such relationship, however, had gone on for almost two years and, while her husband evidently still did not want to leave her, she precipitated a crisis by barging in on him in the other womean's apartment. He had then begun to live with this woman. About six months later she herself became involved rather unsatisfactorily with a younger man. Her stated attitude immediately following her suicide attempt was that both her children and her husband would be better off with her dead. The children were a boy of 19 and a girl of 15 and she said that they would be better off in a new home. There had been an earlier attempt ten days before: she had gone out to a lake with the intention of drowning herself, "changed her mind" and came home and took fifteen sleeping pills instead. She woke up by herself a day and a half later and the next time took twice that dose. While under the influence of the first pills she had the following dream: she saw a cap belonging to her husband's father floating on the sea and realized that he had drowned. Her husband's father had been a sea captain whom she saw as very much like her husband—extremely domineering, critical and difficult to get along with. At first she saw the dream in terms of her own martyred role, but eventually she related it to her desire to strike back at her husband. She spoke vindictively of the problems with the children that her death would cause him. It soon became evident that her suicide attempt came out of her anger at her husband and was an ineffective attempt at revenge. She was the kind of woman who could do little that was effective with her anger or self-assertion and could not even fight for her children. Her situation illustrates the classical one described by Freud in which the suicide is basically an inverted homicide.

Death as a reunion: One patient made three suicide attempts, scattered over a period of some 20 to 25 years. When seen for the first time, following her third suicide attempt, she was 47 years old. Each attempt had been more serious than the one before; she had been extremely fortunate to survive the last one, with gas. An unfortunate or unhappy love affair was time-related to all three attempts. After two months of treatment following the last attempt, during which the same love affair as had preceded it was continuing unsuccessfully, the patient became acutely suicidal and required admission to the hospital. That night she had the following dream: "I was living in an apartment in Baltimore that I lived in 25 years ago. There were a lot of people around telling me to put on a beautiful wedding dress that was hanging on the wall, and I would not put it on."

Her association was to the apartment in Baltimore where her first romantic liaison had lasted for two years, until one night her lover told her he was going to marry another girl. She thereupon made a suicide attempt. Everything in the dream was the same as it had been in her room at the time of that first attempt. In the wedding ceremonies of her two unhappy marriages she had never worn a wedding dress although she had always wanted to. She felt she had lost the really great love of her life with the end of this first relationship. What impressed her most in the dream was that the wedding dress "looked more like a shroud than like a wedding dress." Union with this first love was to be achieved, apparently, only through her death. This patient recalled that she had had this same dream recurrently before each suicide attempt, an interesting detail.

She was, in her dream, refusing to put on the dress, while struggling, in reality, against suicide. Death was the unpleasant price she must pay for the gratification of her desires for love and affection. For other patients with similar but more masochistic psychodynamics, the act of dying itself can be conceived as pleasurably incorporated into the reunion fantasy. Most frequently the emphasis is not put on the dying but on the gratification to follow; the feeling tone in the reunion dreams of such patients is pleasant. In the overwhelming majority the gratification is of an extremely dependent variety, either directly with parental figures or with wives, husbands or siblings operating as substitute parental figures.

While usually such fantasies are unconscious and have to be elicited from dreams, they can also be conscious. One patient, who was seen following a suicide attempt which eventually proved to be fatal, spent the entire year after his wife's death preoccupied with fantasies about her and with mental pictures of being reunited with her in death.

Death as rebirth: A young woman in her twenties had jumped under a train and lost a leg; this suicide attempt was precipitated by one of the unhappy and impossible love relationships with which her life had been filled. Several years earlier she had been intensely involved with a married Negro man. A few years before that she had been involved with a Communist under investigation by the FBI, who was at that time trying to use his relationship with her to get into the United States. This patient was both extremely bright and well-educated. When she was 13 years old, her father had deserted the family and she had never seen or heard from him again. She had some fascination with death and dying all through adolescence and always remembered by heart death scenes in novels. Under hypnosis and with the suggestion to have a dream about her suicide attempt, she produced the following: She was in a long, narrow tunnel and could see a light at the end of it. She walked toward the light and when she got there, saw a man and woman standing over a manger. In her associations to the dream, the tunnel suggested to her the subway from which she jumped and the way in which the train came out of the tunnel and into the lighted platform area. Coming out of the darkness of the tunnel into light brought to her mind the process of birth. The man and woman she saw as her mother and father. The child in the manger was both the Christ-child and herself. One can see how much she accomplishes in her death fantasy. She is reborn, is a boy, is reunited with her father and is, in addition, omnipotent. It is not hard to imagine that for a patient with such fantasies, dying has a very strong appeal.

Death as self-punishment: A lawyer in his thirties had made a moderately serious suicide attempt stemming from his lack of success in a legal career. It was impossible to hypnotize him during his stay in the hospital following his suicide attempt; he exemplifies one of the difficulties involved if one were tempted to use hypnosis as a routine matter for the evaluation of all psychiatric patients. He was later quite easy to hypnotize when he returned for a second try after hospital discharge, and it became evident that he feared being hypnotized while in the hospital when he was still actively preoccupied with suicide because he felt that if he revealed material related to the suicide attempt, he would not be discharged. His dreams under hypnosis were of the most elemental kind, involving his running to catch a boat and just missing it. His associations revealed that "missing the boat" symbolized the view he took of his entire career. His legal ambitions were very great and he could make no compromise with his grandiose success fantasies. The aggression connected with this grandiosity interfered with his actual performance. This constellation is frequently observed in male patients with extremely high and rigid standards for themselves. What they see as their failure causes an enormous degree of self-hatred, and their suicide can be a self-inflicted punishment for having failed. A high percentage of the male patients in this group have demonstrated a paranoid personality structure in the years prior to their becoming depressed or suicidal (7). A typical example is one stock-broker of 55 who had been depressed to the extent that he was unable to work for several years prior to the suicide attempt which occasioned his being seen by the writer. Before that he had a career spanning thirty years, but changed positions every two or three years. In each he had been the victim, he said, of mistreatment, personal favoritism or corruption. Eventually a combination of these factors and the emotional breakdown of his daughter proved too great for his paranoid defenses, and what was probably always a latent depression made itself evident. He then began blaming himself and his unworthiness for his work failures and bemoaning his misfortune with his daughter. In the course of several months' therapy he became paranoid toward the writer; at the same time, his depression lifted sufficiently so that he could resume work. When his paranoid defenses were activated in relation to his psychiatrist, his depressive symptomatology lessened and he became able to function.

These sorts of suicidal self-punishment reactions with women over failure at work have not been observed, however. A suicidal self-punishment reaction that is often seen in women was illustrated by the case mentioned earlier of the woman who felt herself unable to love her child. When a woman is unable to love her child and this is accompanied by the expectation that she should feel what she is not feeling—strong self-hatred with a consequent need for self-punishment can be the result.

A variation of the view of suicide as a self-punishment seen in patients of both sexes may be illustrated by the following patient. He was a thirty-year-old man from a relatively stable rural family. He was the sixth of eight children and stated that he had felt "superfluous" since childhood. All the other siblings were married and he felt that they were leading responsible lives, and that he was the black sheep of the family. Since the age of 18 he had been a moderately severe alcoholic. He had made an impossible marriage in which he also had felt "superfluous" and which quickly led to divorce. His employment had been mainly as a seaman, but his explosive temper and frequent fights aboard ship had made it impossible for him to continue in this capacity and he was depressed over this. He reported the following dream immediately prior to an impulsive suicide attempt in which he jumped in front of a moving car. "An atom bomb was falling." . . . "I was in hell and about to be burned. My brother was above, saying that I should be burned." The patient said he would end up in hell if he did not lead "a more Christian life." Eight months earlier he had begun attending church in an effort to force himself to live differently, but without success. His mother was extremely religious and opposed to drinking, smoking or any amusement for its own sake. He had never been close to her, but had taken over her religious beliefs, although he felt unable to live up to them. The brother in the dream was the family member the patient had felt most close to although the relationship has been characterized by fights and reconciliations until the time of his brother's death three years earlier.

The patient had made several impulsive suicide attempts during the previous eight years, including one where he jumped in front of a moving jeep and had been severely injured. Suicide was for him an act of atonement, and death a punishment he felt he deserved for his explosiveness, his anger toward his siblings and the world and for the asocial existence he was leading.

Among the most disturbed male and female suicidal patients seen in the mental hospital, feelings of being worthless and no good predominate, and self-punishment is a prominent feature. The original motivation may be centered around failure, guilt over aggression or attempted expiation, but the self-punishment can become dissociated from these goals and become almost an end in itself. Such patients can then become preoccupied with delusional feelings of guilt, sin and unworthiness.

The patient who sees himself as already dead: One man who jumped in front of a train had lost one leg almost to the hip, and an arm. Some months after the attempt he related a dream in which he was shopping for a coffin, and the coffin-maker told him that his coffin was a little over half-finished. Considering that he had lost two limbs in his suicide attempt, the dream seemed a fairly obvious current picture of himself. His associations and elaborations to the dream indicated that he felt that only his physical death was half completed. He considered that he had died emotionally or affectively several years before making any suicide attempt.

One very withdrawn suicidal girl of 18 seen by the writer had a recurrent nightmare in which she saw dry ice coming closer and closer to her and threatening to envelop her, until she woke in panic. She was tormented by her inability to feel for people and she not only felt dead but her physical and motor appearance suggested a kind of walking death. Her dry ice image was a self-image—a self that was seen as permanently frozen, dangerous to others and self-destructive.

These patients were representative of an entire group who are preoccupied with feeling already dead, generally not in a delusional sense but in the sense of being emotionally dead. Strong feelings of detachment, repressed aggression and dampened affectivity are often perceived by the patients as a kind of emotional dying or death. Clinically, they will often appear apathetic rather than depressed, and their suicide attempts do not usually change this mood. Despite the overt apathy, such deadness is experienced by the suicidal patients as extremely torturous and they seem to see suicide both as a release from suffering and as merely carrying out an event which has already happened.

Summary

This article attempts to demonstrate some of the psychodynamic patterns seen in suicidal patients based on different fantasies and attitudes toward death. Seven such patterns are outlined and illustrated: death as abandonment, death as omnipotent mastery, death as retroflexed murder, death as a reunion, death as rebirth, death as self-punishment or atonement, death as a process that in an emotional sense has already taken place.

The death fantasy of the suicidal individual is not simply helpful in revealing his motivation for suicide but is also intriguingly a part of his entire attitude towards life as well as death. The individual who expects his suicide and death to continue a punishment which he deserves is quite different from the individual who hopes for the gratification of dependent desires in a protected reunion with a maternal figure. They reveal quite different character structures and not different suicidal psychodynamics. Death fantasies thus come to serve as a natural aid in distinguishing the various motivations seen in suicide.

[1]1045 Park Avenue, New York City; The Psychoanalytic Clinic for Training and Research, Department of Psychiatry, College of Physicians and Surgeons of Columbia University; St. Luke's Hospital, New York City.

SELF TEST: MEASURING COMPREHENSION

"The Psychodynamics Of Suicide", By Herbert Hendin

1. What did Sigmund Freud feel was the primary motive for suicide?

2. Since it is not possible to interview suicidal individuals after they have killed themselves, what technique did Hendin use to gather his data?

3. What types of motives for suicide was Hendin trying to discover through the use of hypnosis and dream interpretation?

4. Which of the explanations of suicide offered by Hendin seem the most valid to you? Why?

MALE SUPREMACY IN FREUD
from *The Radical Therapist*
Phil Brown

The previous articles on the psychoanalytic perspectives were in support of it. However, the psychoanalytic perspective has been the center of much intense controversy for many years. Psychoanalytic psychology has been criticized as being over speculative, lax in providing definitions of its terminology, unscientific, outdated, and sexually biased against women.

In the following article, Phil Brown strongly condemns psychoanalysis in general, and Freud specifically, for what he feels is an extremely inaccurate and unfair characterization of feminine psychology. On the other hand, staunch psychoanalysts may find the article offensive. Indeed, one psychiatrist, whom I asked to review the article, felt that Dr. Brown's criticisms of psychoanalysis were unfair and unfounded. As we might expect, experts on psychoanalysis also disagree.

After reading the article you will be in a better position to personally evaluate the validity of psychoanalysis regarding feminine psychology.

The article is particularly relevant in a time when the American concept of feminity is undergoing such radical changes.

The intent of this paper is to set forth a critique of Sigmund Freud's ideology of male supremacy, a necessary critique since the Freudian framework has been of tremendous influence in Western culture for the greater part of this century. The context in which I am setting this down is one of attempting to destroy certain mythologies about women. My position as a male makes this task rather difficult, although I am not attempting to create a difinitive work on this subject. Rather, I am working as a man in fighting male supremacy, and this paper is a part of that. I take for granted a basic understanding among readers that male supremacy is a major form of oppression in our nation, and that it is not only a socioeconomic formation. Rather, like most oppression in advanced industrial nations of the West, the oppression of women takes psychological roots within the masses of people by socialization into sex-roles and accompanying lifestyles. Since Freudian theory plays a major role in male supremicist thought, it is imperative that Freudian mythologies be cast aside.

The classical picture of Freud is of an anti-Victorian, struggling against sexual repression. This is, of course, a false picture—Freud codified the prevalent attitudes toward sex rather than oppose them. His work was not part of a "sexual revolution," but of a counterrevolution, as Kate Millett points out,[1] an attempt which succeeded in molding many of the psychological and lay opinions about women which are held to date.

Freud's male supremacist views were more than codification of prevailing beliefs—he also invented new myths, especially penis envy, vaginal orgasm, and masculinity complex. It is amazing that he would not admit to this speculative nature—Freud claimed that his views on women were based on "nothing but observed facts, with hardly any speculative additions."[2] But Freud's patients were mainly adult males, and it is known that a good deal of his theorizing on sexuality is composed of hypothetical thoughts for which his main source was the young son of a patient, and a few admissions by a very small number of female patients. If Freud's theories in general were misinterpretations of clinical observations (they rarely were that close, even), those on women were fabrications with little real basis.

In 1885, Freud's first major work was published, "Studies on Hysteria"[3] with Josef Breuer. It is full of cases of female hysterics (Freud saw hysteria as mainly a female neurosis) who are clearly victims of sexually repressed upbringings with sharply defined sex-typing, but Freud takes this for granted, and it is the women who must adjust to their social conditions. Throughout the book, conversion symptoms are presumed by Freud to be based on sexual fears, traumatically based; and these fears, very real ones, are stated by Freud to be neurotic. Even were Freud's interpretations of the symptoms correct, his approach to the problem as one of adjustment is an implicit statement in support of male-dominated sexuality and patriarchal, capitalist society.

The codification of active and passive human activities, associated by Freud respectively with men and women, is begun in "Hysteria", but is picked up more in *The Interpretation of Dreams*,[4] a book which in fact prefigures much of the later theories on women. There are constant references to the women as the passive sex in her role as housewife, male-seeker, suckler of babies,

and physically clumsy. This is carried on into dream-symbolism:

> All elongated objects, sticks, tree trunks, umbrellas, all sharp and elongated weapons, knives, daggers, and pikes, represent the male member . . . Small boxes, chests, cupboards, and ovens correspond to the female organ; also cavities, ships, and all kinds of vessels.[5]

The basic assumption behind this is the penetration of the male penis into the female vagina as the only acceptable mode of sexuality, but this view is expanded to include all forms of human endeavor; persons in dreams are taken to symbolize the penis, and landscapes to represent the vagina,[6] the logic of this being that men are active persons within an environment, passive women being background for male achievement.

Freud sees dreams as wish-fulfillments, nearly always sexually oriented. Within that framework he attributes women's dreams as desires to be penetrated by men, or as other desires which he equates with passive femininity. Interpreting a woman's dream of putting a candle into a holder, the candle breaking as she tried to perform the task, Freud speaks of the candle as "an object which excited the female genitals" and the breaking of it as representing the woman's frigidity due to masturbation. Similar is the view that when a woman dreams of a man masturbating that is a vicarious act of penetration by him into her.[7] Women's dream symbolism because of Freud's presumed weakness of women, is always representative of the worst: "When a person of the female sex dreams of falling, this almost always has a sexual significance; she becomes a fallen woman." Also due to female weakness, a woman's dream of carrying a man is an infantile fantasy because that is not the proper arrangement of things.[8]

The Oedipus complex, one of psychoanalysis's most warped myths, is mentioned substantially for the first time in "Interpretation of Dreams". It brings with it the fallacy of penis envy. I will take this up at this time, rather than continue chronologically, for most of the basic points of the Freudian psychology of women are at least in embryonic form by this time, to be nearly fully codified five years later in the infamous "Three Contributions to the Theory of Sexuality".

Freud would have us believe that the young girl, upon finding out that little boys have a penis, envies this organ, she feels that she has been castrated, and blames her mother for this. We are further led to believe that the larger part of the female psyche is based on the missing penis and the female wish for it.[10] Freud assumes that the little girl is tremendously threatened by the lack of a penis, feeling "herself at a great disadvantage . . . she clings for a long time to the desire to get something like it . . . "She will then search, through the rest of her life, for surrogates, converting this search into other human activities:

> The desire after all to obtain the penis for which she so much longs may even contribute to the motives that impel a grown-up woman to come to analysis; and what she quite reasonably expects to get from analysis, such as the capacity to pursue an intellectual career, can often be recognized as a sublimated modification of this repressed wish.[11]

The girl's discovery of her "castration" leads to her Oedipal stage, in the opposite order of the male Oedipal situation. Penis envy and its corresponding reverse Oedipal complex will have many consequences for her, including the performance of erroneous acts,[12] seduction fantasies, narcissism, and masochism. These "perversions" are attributed to the female passivity theory of Freud—narcissism since "for them to be loved is a stronger need than to love," and masochism since it is "constitutional" in the weak feminine psyche.[13]

In terms of general development after puberty, the female child has three choices left to her by Freud: ". . . one leads to sexual inhibition or to neurosis, the second to a modification of character in the sense of masculinity complex, and the third to formal femininity."[14] Freud has already dealt with the first alternative to some extent in "Hysteria", but the "masculinity complex" is a new

turn. It involves "clinging" to clitoral activity through masturbation and retaining clitoral sensitivity; Freud sees the clitoris as not good enough for sexual pleasure, and additionally as a male activity since the clitoris is a "stunted penis."[15] In the Freudian view, the woman must transfer sensitivity to the vagina in order to be normal:

> In the transformation to womanhood very much depends upon the early and complete relegation of this sensitivity from the clitoris over to the vaginal orifice. In those women who are sexually anaesthetic, as it is called, the clitoris has stubbornly retained this sensitivity.[16]

This the Freudian biology which is aimed at making the women the property of the man by defining correct sexuality as penetration, thus giving the woman little control or pleasure in sexual intercourse. Vaginal orgasm has, of course, been completely discredited by scientific research and personal experience of women.

The only role that Freud will allow to the clitoris is that of conducting pleasure to the vagina, but even that is minimized. Failure to adjust to this type of sexuality leads, in Freud's view, to neurosis (especially hysteria) and perversions, like foot fetishism.[17]

On hysteria, Freud had this to say:

> One may often observe that it is just those girls who in the years before puberty showed a boyish character and inclinations who had become hysterical at puberty. In a whole series of cases the hysterical neuroses are nothing but an overaccentuation of the typical wave of repression through which the masculine type of sexuality is removed and the woman emerges.[18]

Masculine sexuality in the woman means, for Freud, the refusal to give up the real seat of sexual pleasure.

Another possibility, according to Freud, if the woman does not conform is homosexuality, which he sees as bad,[19] and continued infantile "polymorphous perversity." Freud also sees women as naturally inclined to take part in the so-called perversions at the slightest suggestion by any man.[20]

What, then, is normal female sexuality for Freud? Since clitoral sensitivity is supposed to shift to the vagina, the Freudian view asserts that penetration of the vagina by the penis is the one correct sexual mode. But Freud goes far beyond this, sanctifying this oppression with biological fulfillment: ". . . the achievement of the biological aim is entrusted to the aggressive male, and is to some extent independent of the cooperation of the female."[21] This is related to the male aggressive/female passive approach that exists throughout Freud's writings, based in his eyes at the supposed anal stage where active and passive modes of behavior prefigure what will be the later masculine and feminine sexual modes— Freud sticks to the Victorian idea of sexual activity as correct only for procreation, although he attempts to make it seem otherwise. For him, the culmination of human sexual activity is the discharge of semen by the male into the female.[22] The only attempt at explanation is within the scope of biological determinism:

> The male sexual cell is active and mobile; it seeks out the female one while the latter, the ovum, is stationary, and waits passively. This behavior of the elementary organisms of sex is more or less a model of the behavior of the individual of each sex in sexual intercourse.[23]

It is, by far, a weak analogy, but Freud's procreative bent is not the only fault in this theory. Also important is that for Freud, sexuality precludes anything but penile/vaginal sex, and classifies exceptions as pathological.

Another important part of Freud's male supremacy is found in his theories concerning the nature of families and civilization. He posits the authoritarian father of the primal horde who keeps all the women for himself, and is slain by the sons, who then set up a sexually repressive society to prevent a similar occurence in the future. This is Freud's original Oedipal situation, and agrees with the correctness of the sons setting up a sexually repressive society not only to contain the "aggressive" male sexuality, but also because he sees women as an incitement to sex because of their "peculiar helplessness."[24] The modern parallel to this is the male claim that rape is the fault of the woman for putting out certain psychological feelers and inducements, and certainly shows in what low esteem Freud holds women. The mythical primal horde is the basis for all future male supremacist society, and for Freud this is a positive step in the progress of history.

Based on his conception that sublimation of instincts is necessary for civilization, Freud sees the family as an important nexus of this, although one wonders how much sublimation is required of the male:

> One may suppose that the founding of families was connected with the fact that a moment came when the need for genital satisfaction no longer made its appearance like a guest who drops in suddenly, and after his departure, is heard of no more for a long time, but instead took up its quarter as a permanent lodger. When this happened, the male acquired a motive for keeping the female, or speaking more generally, his sexual object, near him; while the female who did not want to be separated from her helpless young, was obliged in her interests, to remain with the stronger male.[25]

This seems more like legalized rape than "civilization," but Freud consistently equated an oppression of women with the sublimation of instincts and the progress of society:

> The communal life of human beings has, therefore, a two-fold foundation: the compulsion to work, which is created by external necessity, and the power of love, which made the man unwilling to be deprived of his sexual object— the woman—and made the woman unwilling to be deprived of the part of herself which had been separated off from her—her child.[26]

Now we come to the role of the woman in the family—she is no more than one who bears children and then takes care of them; moreover, that is the fulfillment of all her needs, psychologically and socially.[27] The progress of civilization is the enslavement of women:

> Women increasingly represent the interests of the family and of the sexual life. The work of civilization has become increasingly the business of men, it confronts them with the ever more difficult tasks and compels them to carry out instinctual sublimations of which women are little capable.[28]

The only truth that might be hidden here is that the authoritarian sublimation demanded by Freud hits women harder than it does men because of women's socio-sexual subordination. One of the attempts at hiding female sexuality, in Freud's imagination, is the invention by women of weaving and plaiting as an attempt to replicate their pubic hair whose purpose it is to hide their "inferior" genitalia.[29]

Female "weakness," based on the infantile penis envy, is found by Freud in every aspect of human endeavor. Women have weak libido which may be all used up on the first child and thus lead to a bad marriage; but the marriage was fated to fail anyway because all women wish to play the role of mother to their husbands.[30] The woman is damned from the first, and nothing she does will satisfy the Freudian construct of society. But she is again blamed for her own damnation: ". . . the woman finds herself forced into the background by the claims of civilization and she adopts a hostile attitude towards it."[31] If, in fact, all women were engaged in active rebellion against such a society, it would be only the most human reaction to the oppression of such a system.

In the Freudian outlook, women are naturally vain as a "further effect of penis envy,"[32] they have a "conventional reticence and insincerity," and a constitutionally based excessive need for affection.[33] Women's intelligence, like their other Freudian attributes is based on sexual determinism:

> You know, too, that women in general are said to suffer from "physiological feeblemindedness"—that is, from a lesser intelligence than men. The fact itself is disputable and its interpretation doubtful, but one argument in favor of this intellectual atrophy being of a secondary nature is that woman labor under the harshness of an early prohibition against turning their thoughts to what would most have interested them—namely, the problem of sexual life.[34]

Again Freud is blaming women for their oppression in patriarchal, capitalist society, and he posits as the explanation the fact the women are basically only interested in sexuality and nothing more.

Of justice and social interest, Freud has this to say:

> It must be admitted that women have but little sense of justice, and this is no doubt connected with the preponderance of envy in their mental life; for the demands of justice are a modification of envy; they lay down the conditions under which one is willing to part with it. We also say of women that their social interests are weaker than those of men, and that their capacity for the sublimation of their instincts is less.[35]

All in all, there is no hope for women in the psychoanalytic framework. Where Freud sees a thirty-year-old man as youthful with many possibilities ahead, a woman of the same age displays, as he puts it, ". . . psychological rigidity and unchangeability. Her libido has taken up its final positions, and seems powerless to leave them for others.[36] But the classical dehumanizing statement is the last few lines of the lecture on "The Psychology of Women" in the *New Introductory Lectures*, one of his most sexist works:

> You must not forget, however, that we have only described women in so far as their nature is determined by their sexual function. The influence of this factor, is of course, very far-reaching, but we must remember that *an individual woman may be a human being apart from this.* If you want to know more about feminity, you must interrogate your own experience, or turn to the poets, or else wait until Science can give you more profound and more coherent information[37] (my emphasis).

What Freud called the riddle of femininity was a situation for him, as the master of psychoanalysis, to delve into—knowing that he could not understand it; and no one else was to touch the subject, especially the women in the feminist movement whom he reproached for not understanding the immutability of the Oedipal stage and penis envy.[38]

Freudian male supremacy is part of the larger psychoanalytic outlook which even sees private profit as a necessary sublimation of aggression. Freud's essentially conservative social theory derives from the positivism of the Freudian metapsychology which posits an absolute world with definite (and thus unchanging) structures, a universe of immutable human nature. Given this novel form of original sin, people are not to be trusted; and given the mythic Eve, women especially are not to be trusted. There is a real continuity between the oppression of women and the Freudian viewpoint's basic distrust of people in general. This outlook, despite its anticlericalism, is dependent upon Judaeo-Christian traditions of renunciation of pleasure, and of family-based male supremacy. Stripped of its pseudo-biology, much of Freudianism could be found for the greater part, in different language, in the holy books of Western culture.

But Freudianism has taken root in the United States more than in any advanced Western nation. Why is this, given the U.S. as the least religious of these countries? Psychoanalysis, as a new religion, fits into an American framework, for it demands less actual ritual than a traditional religion and required analyst/technicians rather than priest/counselors to administer it, quite a drawing card in a nation so infactuated with technical answers to human problems.

One aspect of religion is the fixation of guilt on a certain group in order to exculpate the mass of believers. This is based on the early church's mythologizing of the "heathens" as the "natural" enemy of the faithful, quite one-sided in light of the conquering stance of the "Church Militant." Women were always a convenient scapegoat; in the Middle Ages, rebellious women—that is, those who distributed contraceptive information, performed abortions, and criticized the church as a repressive and male-dominated authoritarian institution—were called "witches" and burned in order to preserve the sanctity of the rest. Freud pioneered in shifting the blame and guilt of society onto women, and the new religion thus recapitulated its predecessors.

Also, the mystification of sexuality is fitting in a nation where sexuality has been turned around and used in nongential ways to sell consumer products. This holds true to a greater extent in terms of women, for it is their sexuality that is usually thus mystified. Additionally, psychopathology, as the new star

chamber, has been utilized in this country more than anywhere in the interests of social control, and psychoanalysis presents a very comprehensive system of psychopathology which usually sees the cause of problems as intrapsychic rather than social.

For women, this is even more dangerous since in order to keep them tied to societally determined roles, they bear the brunt of psychopathological classiciation—not only in terms of being more relatively diagnosed (and mis-treated) as "mentally ill," but also in terms of special illnesses being invented just for them; e.g., puerperal (childbirth) and menopausal neuroses and psychoses, and, of course, hysteria.

Having earlier mentioned Millett's idea of Freud as a major force in the counterrevolution against the sexual revolution, I would like to pick up on this. Coming as a protest against Victorian moralism (and to some extent emerging from its underground lair inhabited during the Victorian period) a sort of sexual revolution grew up. It protested procreative-oriented sexuality and thus undermined the repressive sexual mores, but it was not complete enough to emancipate the masses, especially the women. Nonetheless, society felt threatened and had to begin a counterattack—Millett clarifies this very well:

> The real cause of the counterrevolution appears to lie in the fact that the sexual revolution had perhaps necessarily, even inevitably, concentrated on the superstructure of patriarchal policy, changing its legal forms, its more flagrant abuses, altering its formal educational patterns, but leaving the socialization processes of temperament and role differentiation intact. Basic attitudes, values, emotions—all that constituted the psychic structure several millennia of patriarchal society had built up—remained insufficiently affected, if not completely untouched. Moreover, the major institutions of the old traditions, patriarchal marriage and the family, were never or rarely challenged.[39]

As to the question of psychoanalytic theory taking root in the U.S. so strongly, Millett states that this nation was the center of the sexual revolution and therefore very much needed Freud.[40]

The rapidly growing women's liberation movement in the country has become very aware of the oppressive Freudian mythology and begun to expose it, not only in scholarly papers and movement periodicals, but in personal understanding and criticism and the development of counterinstitutions as well. Probably one of the most definitive acts by women against Freudianism is leaving therapy which is guided by Freudians and others who believe that women should adjust to sexist society.

And, of course, women's critiques of psychiatric sexism have been accompanied by the creation of alternative theory and practice.[41]

Footnotes

[1]Kate Millett, "Sexual Politics" (New York: Doubleday, 1970).

[2]S. Freud, "New Introductory Lectures on Psychoanalysis", trans. W. J. H. Sprott (New York: Norton, 1933), p. 154.

[3]S. Freud and Josef Breuer, "Studies on Hysteria", trans. James Strachey (New York: Basic Books, 1957).

[4]S. Freud, "The Interpretation of Dreams in Basic Writings of Sigmund Freud, ed. and trans. A. Brill (New York: Random House).

[5]Ibid., p. 371.

[6]Ibid., p. 379.

[7]Ibid., pp. 253-388.

[8]Ibid., pp. 264-327.

[9]S. Freud, "Three Contributions to the Theory of Sexuality", in Brill, *Basic Writings.*

[10]Freud, "Interpretation of Dreams", pp. 306-309, 377-378.

[11]Freud, "New Introductory Lectures", p. 171.

[12]S. Freud, "The Psychopathology of Everyday Life", in Brill, Basic Writings, p. 122.

[13]Freud, "New Introductory Lectures", pp. 158, 164, 180.

[14]Ibid., p. 172.

[15]Ibid., pp. 93, 172, 177.

[16]S. Freud, "A General Introduction of Psychoanalysis", trans. Joan Riviere (New York: Permabook, 1953), p. 327.

[17]Freud, "Three Contributions to the Theory of Sex", p. 592.

[18]S. Freud, "Dora—An Analysis of a Case of "Hysteria", trans. Philip Rieff (New York: Collier, 1963), p. 157.

[19]Freud, *New Introductory Lectures*, p. 177.

[20]Freud, *Three Contributions to the Theory of Sex,* p. 592.

[21]Freud, *New Introductory Lectures*, p. 180.

[22]Freud, *Three Contributions to the Theory of Sex,* pp. 597-598, 604.

[23]Freud, *New Introductory Lectures,* p. 156.

[24]S. Freud, Totem and Taboo, in Brill, *Basic Writings,* pp. 832, 915.

[25]S. Freud, Civilization and Its Discontents, trans. James Strachey (New York: Norton, 1961), p. 46.

[26]Ibid., p. 48.

[27]Freud, Totem and Taboo, p. 818.

[28]Freud, Civilization and Its Discontents, p. 50.

[29]Freud, New Introductory Lectures, p. 181.

[30]Ibid., pp. 182-183.

[31]Freud, Civilization and Its Discontents, p. 50.

[32]Freud, New Introductory Lectures, p. 180.

[33]Freud, Three Contributions, pp. 565-618.

[34]S. Freud, *The Future of an Illusion,* trans. W. D. Robson-Scott (Garden City, NY: Doubleday, 1964), p. 79.

[35]Freud, *New Introductory Lectures,* p. 183.

[36]Ibid., p. 184.

[37]Ibid., p. 184.

[38]Ibid., p. 177.

[39]Millett, Sexual Politics, pp. 176-177.

[40]Ibid., p. 178.

[41]See, for example, Dorothy E. Smith and Sara J. David, eds., *Women Look at Psychiatry* (Vancouver, B.C., Canada: Press Gang Publishers, 1975).

SELF TEST: MEASURING COMPREHENSION

"Male Supremacy In Freud", By Phil Brown

1. For what biological reason did Freud feel that men are naturally aggressive and women naturally passive?

2. Cite evidence of Freud's chauvanistic, negative attitude toward women as presented by Dr. Brown.

3. What is your opinion on the psychoanalytic interpretation of feminine psychology?

Chapter 6
THE LEARNING PERSPECTIVE

During the early part of the twentieth century, a movement to make psychology more scientifically acceptable began. Then, as now, some psychologists felt that their science was not as respectable as the other hard sciences, such as chemistry or physics. At the very end of the nineteenth century, structuralism was becoming very popular. Structuralism argued that if we were to truly understand human consciousness, we must break it down into its smaller parts for analysis. However, consciousness is not directly observable, and therefore could not be scientifically measured. Thus, in the early 1900's a new school of psychology called behaviorism emerged. Its topic of study was overt, observable behavior. Its founder, American John B. Watson, strongly believed that by rejecting untestable notions, such as the existence of consciousness, and dealing only with observable behavior, psychology would become more scientifically valid (Watson, 1913).

If the early behaviorists were skeptical about the untestable nature of structural concepts like consciousness, they were much more suspect of the Freudian notion of the unconscious mind. Did David Berkowitz, convicted "Son of Sam" killer, have an unconscious hatred of women that compelled him to murder innocent young women without any apparent motive? This is an extremely difficult question to answer, as unconscious motives are also not capable of being scientifically measured. Thus, the new school of behaviorism, whose major topic of study was overt, observable behavior, emerged in reaction to the untestable, unobservable, vague nature of structuralism and psychoanalysis.

"Psychology as the behaviorist views it is a purely objective experimental branch of natural science. Its theoretical goal is the prediction and control of behavior" (Watson, 1913). Watsonian behaviorism relied heavily upon the notion that organisms reliably and predictably make specific responses to specific stimuli. Thus, if control over the environment of the organism could be accomplished, so could control over the behavior of the organism. Watson was so strongly convinced of the importance of environmental factors in the control of behavior that in 1925 he stated:

> "Give me a dozen healthy infants, well-informed and my own specified
> world to bring them up in and I'll guarantee to take any one at random
> and train him to become any type of specialist I might select-doctor,
> lawyer, artist, merchant-chief and, yes, even beggar-man and thief, regard-
> less of his talents, penchants, tendencies, abilities, vocations, and race of
> his ancestors" (Watson, 1925 p. 82).

There are no indications that anyone ever gave Watson his dozen healthy infants to experiment with. However, such a statement is indicative of the firmness of Watson's beliefs in the importance of the environment in the development of behavior and personality. One clear distinction now emerges between the orientations of the illness perspective and the behavioristic, or learning perspective. Where the illness perspective postulated organic or genetic origins of behavior pathology, the learning perspective postulates improper environmental conditions as the cause of pathology.

The Freudian view held that emotional disturbances could be traced to childhood experiences of a sexual nature. Watson believed that adult disturbances could be traced to conditioned responses developed earlier in life. Thus, the behaviorist views abnormal behavior as behavior that is learned in much the same manner as any other type of behavior. The behavioral symptoms of the disorder are the disorder, and are not reflective of any deeper, unresolved conflict, as postulated in psychoanalytic theory. Since abnormal behavior is learned, it can also be unlearned. Through the manipulation of the environment of the organism, normal, adaptive behaviors can be learned as substitutes for abnormal, maladaptive behaviors.

The learning perspective postulates that human learning is accomplished through two primary learning models. These models, classical and operant conditioning, will be described in the first article on the learning perspective. The systematic application of these learning models for the therapeutic treatment of behavior pathology is called behavior modification. Behavior modification techniques rely upon the development of some degree of control over the environment of the patient, and the restructuring of the conditions of reinforcement of the patient, to accomplish behavior improvement. Behavior modification is reputed as being very effective in bringing about specific types of behavioral improvement. Although the success of behavior modification is often dependent upon the ability to control the environment of the patient, proponents of the learning perspective argue that the benefits gained through behavior modification outweigh the loss of individual freedom of the patient.

The first article I will present in this chapter on the learning perspective is entitled "Behavior Modification with Children", and was written by Dr. D. G. Brown. It outlines the basic orientation, goals, and principles of behavior modification. The second article, "Behavior Therapy in the Management of Chronic Schizophrenia", by W. Stewart Agras, describes specifically how the principles of behavior modification have been clinically applied to improve the condition of schizophrenics. The third article, "Fall Into Helplessness", by Martin E. P. Seligman, offers a behavioristic explanation for the phenomenon of clinical depression.

References

John B. Watson, *Behaviorism* (New York: Norton, 1925)

John B. Watson, Psychology as the Behaviorist Views It. *Psychological Review.* 1913, v. 20 (2), pp. 158-177.

BEHAVIOR MODIFICATION WITH CHILDREN
from *Mental Hygiene*
Daniel G. Brown, Ph.D.

In the following article, Dr. D. G. Brown provides an excellent overview of the theory, goals, and orientation of behavior therapy. In addition to describing behaviorism's explanation of how abnormal behavior originates, classical and operant conditioning, the two basic learning models upon which behavior therapy is based, are described. The value of behavioristic approaches in the treatment of a wide range of behavioral problems is indicated. Dr. Brown also discusses criticisms that are commonly made of the behavioral model. As you read the article, think of how the goals, orientation, and techniques of behavioral psychology are different from those of psychoanalysis.

There are indications that the establishment of behavioral analysis and the behavior modification approach may, in time, be considered comparable to such milestones in mental health as the reforms in the treatment of the mentally ill by Pinel in France in the last century; the establishment of psychoanalysis and psychodynamic therapy during the first half of the present century; the psychopharmacological advances of the past twenty years; and the current comprehensive community mental health center movement. And as each of these developments has affected the entire field, it may be predicted that developments in behavior modification will also have significant effects in treatment, training, research and prevention in mental health.

What exactly is meant by such terms as behavior therapy, operant and classical conditioning therapy, reinforcement therapy? Basically, the terms involve the *systematic* application of learning theory and principles of conditioning to the modification of deviant or disordered behavior and the strengthening of desired behavior toward the goal of establishing more adaptive behavior in human beings. It has been long recognized that the *present environment* of an individual exerts a strong influence on the response or behavior of that individual. For example, a child may acquire a fear of a small, playful rabbit if the rabbit is presented with a sudden and painfully loud noise—the noise being an unconditioned stimulus. This example illustrates the phenomenon of *classical or Pavlovian or respondent conditioning* and is the basis for many fears, anxieties and phobias as well as other emotional and motivational states in adults as well as in children. The child, however, may gradually lose his fear if the rabbit is presented slowly at a distance and paired with such pleasant activities as eating, playing, etc. Reconditioning is the basis for some of the major therapeutic procedures used in behavior therapy.

Another kind of learning situation is involved when a person acts or responds in some way and a particular *consequence* follows his action or response. If the consequence that follows results in an increase in the probability of the same action or response occurring again, the consequence is referred to as a *reinforcement*. For example, a child cries for a lollipop, is given one by the parent and then stops crying; the crying in an *operant* behavior, i.e., operates on the environment (parent) in such a way to secure a particular outcome or result, namely a lollipop, and it is this reinforcement that makes more likely the occurrence of similar behavior in the future. This example illustrates the phenomenon of *operant or instrumental conditioning*, which is the basis for much human behavior in children and adults, both adaptive and maladaptive. Thus, the deviant behavior of many emotionally disturbed children may be understood as having been learned and supported by contingencies in the present environment, whether in the home, school, hospital, clinic, camp, or wherever. In this connection, a major therapeutic procedure in behavior modification involves changing the environmental conditions or removing the reinforcements that have maintained a child's maladaptive behavior. The conceptualization of behavior in terms of reinforcement learning theory places adaptive and maladaptive behavior on a single continuum, i.e., both kinds of behavior are learned or unlearned on the basis of the same learning process.

Conditioning

The fundamental nature of classical and operant conditioning has been recognized for over half a century, but only with the last several years have systematic applications been made in the modification of various deviant and disordered behaviors in humans. Why has it taken so many years to utilize in practice what has been known for so long a time? Part of the answer would seem to be in the priorities or emphases of traditional approaches to the mentally and emotionally disturbed. In the past, many mental health professionals were primarily concerned with extensive psychodiagnostic appraisals, with protracted psychiatric interviews, with overly detailed case histories, and with focusing on intrapsychic dynamics and conflicts, with undue emphasis on insight as a presumed requirement for meaningful behavioral change, and with an overevaluation of the alleged superiority of long-term, dynamically-oriented, reconstructive therapies. In any event it is a sobering experience to reflect on the fact that now, after a half-century, the systematic, applied use of principles of learning and conditioning in psychotherapeutic work both with children and adults is only now getting underway in substantial numbers of mental health centers, institutions, etc.

Concomitant with demonstrations of the general applicability and efficacy of approaches in behavior modification, it might be predicted that increasing numbers of mental health professionals will begin to focus more on the *present* environment and symptoms of a person than on the past history or the original factors that may have been responsible for the symptoms. In this connection, the following four questions provide a functional frame of reference in mental health work with children based on behavior modification:

1. What is the behavior of the child that should be changed or developed? i.e., specify the behavior. Is it mute, autistic behavior? Acting-out destructive behavior? Fearful, immobilized or phobic behavior? Learning to talk or read? What exactly is the behavior to be developed or modified?
2. What is the rate or frequency of this behavior? When and how often does it occur?
3. What are the current environmental contingencies or conditions that support the child's behavior that is to be modified?
4. How can the child's present environment be changed, contingencies altered, and reinforcements utilized to decrease his maladaptive and increase his adaptive behavior?

Behavioral analysis and modification, then, involves the following systematic procedures: 1) specify or pinpoint the behavior to be modified; 2) record the behavior and establish a baseline of its frequency; 3) determine the contingencies that affect or maintain the behavior; and 4) modify the relevant contingencies to increase adaptive and decrease maladaptive behavior.

There are two major directions or outcomes in work involving operant behavior modification:

1. *Developing, strengthening, accelerating or maintaining desirable behaviors.* For example, a child learns to talk, brush his teeth, dress himself, follow directions, mind his parents better, work or play more cooperatively with others, do more things for himself, increase his vocabulary, become a better swimmer, etc. These are behaviors that may be developed or accelerated through the use of appropriate contingencies involving positive reinforcements.

2. *Weakening, decelerating or eliminating undesirable behaviors.* For example, a child learns *not* to throw tantrums, not to hit his sister, not to suck his thumb, not to bang his head, not to steal from others, not to be late to school, not to disrupt the classroom, etc. These are behaviors that may be decelerated or eliminated through the use of appropriate contingencies involving: 1) *positive reinforcement* for the *non-occurrence* of the undesirable behavior; 2) *negative* or aversive *reinforcement* (e.g., punishment, time-out procedures, etc.) for the *occurrence* of the undesirable behavior; or 3) *no reinforcement of any kind*, positive or negative, for the *occurrence* of the undesirable behavior, e.g., completely ignoring such behavior.

Summed up: behavior is developed, strengthened, weakened, or eliminated by the consequences or effects of the behavior, i.e., behavior is determined by the consequences that follow that behavior, hence, the acceleration or deceleration of a given behavior is based on altering its consequences.

Review of Literature

Now, in order to gain a better understanding of what has been reported in the literature relative to the application of behavior modification as a therapeutic procedure, a content analysis was made of all of the articles that have been published in the two principal journals devoted to work in behavior modification. These are: *Behavior Research and Therapy,* published since 1963, and *The Journal of Applied Behavior Analysis*, published since 1968. As of June 1969, approximately 300 articles had been published in these journals which may be grouped in terms of application to children, adolescents and adults. Among children and adolescents, applications of behavior modification therapy have been made to the following problems, symptoms, deficits, disturbances or developments:

1) autism, psychosis, and schizophrenia; 2) enuresis, encopresis, and related disturbances; 3) tantrums, destructive, anti-social, predelinquent behaviors; 4) school problems, learning deficits and disabilities, failures, disruptive and other maladjustive behaviors in a school setting; 5) phobias, anxieties and fears; 6) psychosomatic disturbances, e.g., anorexia, obesity, etc., 7) speech development and disturbances; 8) sexual disturbances; 9) nervous habits, e.g., nail biting, thumb sucking, nightmares, etc.; 10) mental retardation and other handicapped conditions; 11) self-injurious behaviors; 12) development of social skills, cooperative play, and other socially adaptive behaviors, etc.

While not all of the children and adolescents reported on in these studies responded to behavior modification therapy with 100% improvement, in the majority of instances, substantial gains were made and, in many cases, marked improvement was realized. This was true in a number of cases in which other therapeutic approaches had been used but without success. As the above examples indicate, applications of behavior modification have not been confined to a restricted portion of the population but cover a very wide range of disturbances, deficits and developmental problems in children and youth. An indication of the increasing amount of work and research using a behavioral approach is seen in the fact that four new journals concerned primarily with behavior modification or behavior therapy began publication in 1969-1970.

What are some implications of the behavior modification model for the mental health field as a whole? It is evident that this model represents a departure from the traditional conception of mental illness as a manifestation of disease within a child or adult, hence, as consisting of symptoms of underlying psychopathology. In contrast, the assumption is made in the behavioral model that much that is labeled mental illness consists of nothing more than learned ways of adjusting to the environment. There is, thus, considerable controversy among differing theorists and therapists as to the adequacy or inadequacy of the disease model versus the learning-disorder model of mental illness. And there are significant implications in terms of assumptions and approaches for modifying disturbed behavior. The traditional or psychodynamic therapist essentially views the symptoms of an emotional disturbance as "surface phenomena," as indicative of unconscious processes and unresolved conflicts, and the main task of dynamic psychotherapy, therefore, is to deal with these underlying pathological conditions rather than with the overt symptoms and behaviors themselves. The focus is on the reconstruction and analysis of an individual's *past* history, on the antecedents of his present behavior, on covert behavior, internal states, or subjective processes. On the other hand, the behavior therapist holds that most emotional disorders and neuroses are essentially learned behavior patterns and that there is no underlying illness, but rather the symptoms themselves constitute the disorder. Here the focus is on the construction and analysis of the individual's *existing* life situation, on the *consequences* of his present behavior, on what can be objectively observed and recorded. These two conceptualizations of emotional disorders quite clearly involve a fundamental difference with significant implications in terms of assumptions and approaches for modifying disturbed behavior.

Although the behavioral analysis approach in psychotherapeutic work is a very recent development, about 95% of the literature having been published in the last six or seven years, there are indications that compared to other approaches, it has several important advantages that may be summarized as follows: 1) greater *effectiveness* as a treatment method, i.e., for some of the deviant behaviors previously listed in this paper, the results are often clearly superior; 2) greater *efficiency* as a treatment method, i.e., in general, it may take less time and fewer sessions to bring about desired changes in the patient's life adjustment; 3) greater *specificity* in establishing goals and outcome of therapy, i.e., the specific end result of therapy is specified at the beginning of therapeutic work; 4) greater *applicability* to a wider segment of the population, i.e., the behavioral approach seems to cover the broad spectrum of maladaptive behaviors and is applicable to all social classes, age groups, intellectual and educational levels, etc., rather than, for example, being limited more or less to adult, middle class neurotic patients with above average intelligence, etc.; and 5) greater *utilization* as a treatment method by various groups, i.e., the behavioral approach can be used not only by the core mental health disciplines themselves but by public health nurses, case workers, teachers, etc., and even by parents. In short, there is reason to believe that, compared to traditional therapies, the behavior modification approach may be more effective, more efficient, more specific in therapeutic outcomes, applicable to more people, and may be used by all of the mental health-helping professions and related groups.

Manpower Problems

As suggested above, developments in the use of behavioral procedures have important implications for increasing mental health manpower resources in relation to the mental health needs of children and youth. There are approximately 70 million children and youth under 18 years of age in this country and of this number, between 10% and 22%, depending on the criteria of psychological-psychiatric handicapped conditions, have emotional and behavioral difficulties that require assistance. This involves 7 to 15 million children and youth. To what extent are the manpower resources of the mental health disciplines capable of meeting directly the needs of these millions of children and youth? The answer is: very little. Thus, for each psychiatrist, social worker, nurse and psychologist in mental health programs for children, there are thousands of children with emotional and behavioral difficulties. To be more specific, what about the manpower capability of child psychiatry to cope with the problem? Since there are only about *1,000* child psychiatrists in the United States, this means that for each one, there are between 7 and 15 thousand children and youth who need mental health assistance. These data make dramatically clear a simple fact: that mental health professionals have not, are not, and cannot meet *directly* the needs of overwhelming numbers of children with emotional and behavioral difficulties in this country. When help for mental health problems is sought or needed, for most children, unfortunately, it has not been and is not available. A significant part of the solution to this problem seems obvious: that community care-giving and mental health-related groups such as public health and other nurses, non-psychiatric physicians and social workers, welfare workers, counselors, rehabilitation personnel, clergymen, etc., can and must provide more of the services traditionally considered more or less the exclusive responsibility of the mental health disciplines, i.e., psychiatry, psychology, psychiatric nursing and psychiatric social work. In particular, parents and teachers should be increasingly utilized as mental health resources. Their number, accessibility and availability in relation to the population of children and youth make parents and teachers vital resources both for treatment and prevention in mental health. Thus, while there are thousands of children for every mental health professional who works with children, there are only about 25 children for every school teacher and about 10 or 15 children for every special education teacher and usually one or two parents for each child. Teachers and parents, then, should receive much more attention than they have from the standpoint of the potential contributions they are ca-

pable of making in mental health. Mental health professionals can and must provide more training and consultation for these groups who are the ones actually in contact with the vast majority of children in need of help. A number of references are now available that are specifically concerned with helping parents and teachers manage many kinds of behavior problems in their children and pupils. Fortunately, given proper training, instruction and backup help, these groups can learn to carry out behavior modification procedures. This does not mean that teachers, already overburdened with instructional and other demands, would be expected to become psychotherapists for their disturbed or disturbing pupils. But it does mean that many teachers would be able to reduce the incidence of deviant behaviors and facilitate more effective learning among their pupils. This is in contrast to the more traditional approaches in counseling and psychotherapy in which only professional persons with years of education and advanced training are considered qualified to work with children with disturbed or disordered behavior.

Criticism of Behavioral Conditioning

An attempt has been made in this paper to point up the fact that in very recent years, the development of the behavioral approach has provided the mental health and related professions with new and more effective ways of helping children with various emotional and behavioral problems. There are three remaining observations that may be made relative to this discussion. The first has to do with the fact that there are resistances and misunderstandings, on the part of professionals and laymen alike, concerning the use of behavioral procedures. Like most other major innovations and new conceptualizations in science that were resisted when they first appeared, there have been and will continue to be strong objections to behavior modification. Another example of this in the field of mental health is the initial opposition and rejection of the contributions of Freud and the development of his system for attempting to understand the human mind and modify behavior. The psychoanalytic approach was resisted, misinterpreted, and opposed, but nevertheless survived; and the same outcome may be predicted for the behavior analytic approach despite various attacks that have been made on it. For example, some critics say that behavior modification is "superficial" and not effective with "deep-rooted psychopathological conditions," even though there is now convincing evidence in the literature that shows this approach is capable of bringing about extensive changes in individuals with various behavioral disturbances. Other critics say that the behavioral approach is doomed to failure because "only symptoms" are modified which results in the subsequent development of substitute symptoms, some of which may be worse than the original ones, despite the fact than an increasing number of reports in the literature refute this argument. Still other critics say that behavior modification is "dangerous" and nothing but a form of "brainwashing," despite the fact that, properly used, it may bring about more flexible, adaptive behavior and free a person from fixated or self-defeating patterns. Of course, like any other procedure or tool or treatment in the helping professions, behavior modification should be carried out competently in accordance with high ethical principles and with primary concern for the individual patient or client's welfare. Another criticism of behavior modification is that it is too "mechanical" and "dehumanizing," despite the fact that results in the literature indicate that for the first time in their lives, some children began to make a relatively normal adjustment and some adults, for the first time in many years, were able to resume a relatively normal life after the use of behavior modification therapy. In short, despite considerable opposition and resistance as well as misunderstanding of the basic rationale and application of behavior modification in mental health work, results in the literature suggest that this new development will not only survive but will gradually become an increasingly adopted and respected approach. To paraphrase Charles Kettering, inventor of the electric starter for automobiles, relative to resistance to new ideas and innovations:

First, the critics say that behavior modification is ineffective and they can prove it; failing in this, then they say it may be effective but it is superficial, has very limited application and is insignificant. Finally, the critics acknowledge that behavior modification is both effective and important but they say it is not anything new— they have known about it all along and have been doing "more or less the same thing" for years!

Similarity to Re-Education

The second observation has to do with the fact that behavior modification is entirely compatible with another major advancement in the mental health field, namely the Re-Education Treatment of emotionally disturbed children that has been developed in Tennessee. The Re-Ed approach has demonstrated the effectiveness of a nonclinical program that is essentially a school rather than a hospital and one that provides re-educational and new learning experiences for disturbed children. Such children are seen, not as suffering from "mental disease," but as having learned unproductive and unacceptable behaviors that constitute their emotional disturbance. Behavior modification provides a behavioral management system for the Re-Education approach to child mental health and, as such, can function as an integral component of the total Re-Ed program.

Lack of Training

The third observation has to do with the fact that the mental health disciplines in the past have not included basic course work and experience in behavior modification in their training programs of mental health personnel. This means that the tens of thousands of mental health and related professionals in the field today have been trained in programs that offered no instruction or practicum in the behavioral procedures described in this discussion. Thus, there is a need for staff development and continuing education opportunities that would enable mental health and related personnel to learn and be able to carry out these procedures. A beginning effort in this direction might be to develop a library of basic readings in this area. In this connection Annotated Bibliographies on Behavior Modification have been prepared which provide a representative listing of some of the significant contributions in the professional literature.

In conclusion, it may be predicted that recent, current and continuing developments in behavior modification will bring about substantial advancements in therapeutic work with children and help usher in a new era in the understanding and guidance of children. There is now reason to believe that many emotionally disturbed and mentally handicapped children can be helped more effectively and efficiently than has been possible in the past. As a result the present can be faced with more confidence and the future with more hope.

SELF TEST: MEASURING COMPREHENSION

"Behavior Modification With Children", By D. G. Brown

1. From the behaviorist's point of view, how does abnormal behavior originate?

2. Of the three techniques described by Dr. Brown to weaken undesirable behavior (positive reinforcement for non-occurrence of undesired behavior, aversive reinforcement for occurrence of undesired behavior, or no reinforcement), which do you feel would work best in trying to stop a four year old child from "showing off" in front of relatives? Why?

3. What does Dr. Brown feel are the major advantages of behavior therapy over other types of therapy?

4. What are some of the commonly made criticisms of behavior therapy?

5. What are some of the major differences between the orientations of behavioristic and psychoanalytic psychology?

BEHAVIOR THERAPY IN THE MANAGEMENT OF CHRONIC SCHIZOPHRENIA

from *The American Journal of Psychiatry*

W. Stewart Agras

In the previous article, D. G. Brown outlined the basic theory and orientation of the learning perspective. He indicated that two major outcomes of the application of behavior therapy are the strengthening of desirable behaviors and the weakening of undesirable ones. Thus, behavior therapy endeavors to accomplish specific behavioral objectives through the therapeutic manipulation of the conditions of reinforcement to which the patient is subjected.

The following article, by W. Stewart Agras, provides a precise description of how the principles of behavior therapy have been used in bringing about behavioral improvement in the treatment of chronic schizophrenia. Two cases are presented. In the first, improved eating habits are established in a patient through the removal of reinforcement for non-eating behavior. The second case deals with the use of an aversive technique in eliminating the undesirable behavior of uncontrollable glass breaking.

Critics of the learning perspective often point out that although behavior therapy is successful in bringing about some specific behavioral improvement, it does not improve the overall condition of the patient. Agras does not claim that behavior therapy will "cure" the schizophrenic. He does contend that through specific behavioral improvement in selected aspects of behavior, the overall social adaptation of the patient will be enhanced.

This report attempts to clarify the place of behavior therapy in the management of chronic schizophrenia, reviewing the pertinent literature and illustrating one approach by describing its use in two patients suffering from this illness. The treatment of these patients in a rehabilitation setting had foundered due to one patient's long-standing refusal to eat and the other patient's serious episodes of glass breaking. While such symptoms are often resistant to conventional ther-

apy, conditioning theory provides a suitable framework for their understanding and control.

Most applications of principles and techniques derived from experimental psychology to schizophrenia have been based on the method of operant conditioning. Skinner[12] first described this form of learning as one in which an organism's actions either lead to reward or prevent the onset of, or terminate, aversive stimuli. When a particular behavior is thus reinforced, the probability that the organism will behave in the same way again is increased. Skinner found that desired behavior could be shaped by reinforcing successively closer approximations to the final behavior. Once shaped, the behavior is maintained and varied in a predictable way, depending upon the particular schedule of reinforcement.

Lindsley[8] [9] in a series of investigations used the method of operant conditioning to describe and quantify the behavior of chronic schizophrenic individuals. The patients pulled a vending machine plunger for a reward of either candy or cigarettes. Compared to normal individuals, the majority showed a very low response rate, punctuated by a number of long pauses during which hallucinations occurred. Lindsley found that response rate could be changed by varying the pattern of reinforcement.

This demonstration that the behavior of chronic schizophrenic patients could be shaped and altered, albeit under very specific conditions, was the first step. Following this, Ayllon[1] [2] [3] [4] studied long-standing deviant behaviors such as refusal to eat, food stealing, hoarding, and delusional talk. He found that behavior of this type is often maintained in the hospital by such general factors as the staff paying attention to it. By training ward personnel not to respond in this way, he found that it extinguished quite rapidly. In a series of demonstrations he has shown such behaviors increasing and decreasing in frequency as the reinforcement is altered.

Isaacs and associates[7] were able to reinstate talking in two mute schizophrenic patients by first shaping vocalization and then meaningful communication using chewing gum as a reward. Ayllon[3] and others[11] also demonstrated that delusional talk is contingent upon social reinforcement. When therapist and staff ignored delusional statements and responded only to normal talking, such statements diminished in frequency and finally disappeared.

Other methods based on learning theory have been reported less frequently. Systematic desensitization[5] was reported to be successful in the treatment of a phobia in a schizophrenic patient. A closely related method, that of gradual approach to an anxiety-provoking situation, proved successful in removing rather extensive social inhibitions in another patient.[13]

Procedures and Findings

Case 1. A 34-year-old unmarried man was admitted to the hospital in an emaciated state, weighing 85 pounds. He had suffered from schizophrenia since adolescence and had been treated in a number of institutions with insulin, electroshock therapy, ataractic drugs, and psychotherapy. Despite this he had shown a slow downhill course. He was looked after at home for several years by his mother during which time he led a solitary life, frequenting libraries and museums, making no social contacts.

Following his mother's death three years before admission his condition worsened, he stopped eating regularly, and developed the delusion that he was the Anti-Christ. One year before admission he weighed 87 pounds, and his weight remained at this level despite several hospitalizations. Tube feeding was the only method by which his weight could be increased, only to be lost as soon as the

FIGURE 1

Change in Food Intake in a Patient Undergoing a Conditioning Procedure Designed to Encourage Eating

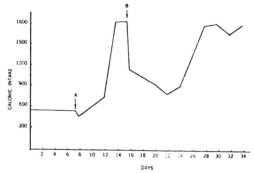

A = start of a conditioning procedure

B = onset of negativistic behavior following a frustrating incident.

feedings were stopped. He was eventually referred to a rehabilitation setting where his continued low weight and poor physical state led to rehospitalization.

During the patient's first days in the hospital it became clear that even with constant urging to eat by the nursing staff very little was to be gained. It appeared that a great deal of attention had been given to the patient both at home and in the hospital when he did not eat. In view of Ayllon's findings it seemed likely that this attention was maintaining the behavior of not eating. It was therefore decided to remove all such reinforcement.

The patient was given a list of times during the day when food would be available to him at his place in the day room. Food was put out for 30 minutes five times daily and then removed. Staff members were instructed to pay no attention to the patient's not eating.

Under these circumstances it was expected that the behavior of not eating would extinguish and a more normal eating pattern would take its place. The changes occurring in food intake are shown in Figure 1. Intake increased remarkably, rapidly reaching a satisfactory level in five days.

After an incident in which the patient was refused permission to buy food at the hospital gift shop by the nurse accompanying him, a period of negativistic behavior ensued in which food intake was somewhat diminished, but did not reach the low level that had obtained before the start of the conditioning procedure.

Following establishment of a stable eating pattern, the patient was discharged, weighing 90 pounds, to the rehabilitation setting in which a similar schedule was followed. At follow-up four months later he weighed 104 pounds, more than he had weighed in two years, and was showing increased general activity. Thus the new eating pattern had apparently generalized to another setting.

Case 2. A 25-year-old man who had been institutionalized with chronic schizophrenia since childhood was referred for investigation and treatment of an uncontrollable urge to break glass. He had been involved in a rehabilitation program for two years in an attempt to overcome his social withdrawal and lack of interest in work. Unfortunately the program had been interrupted on several occasions by his glass-breaking binges which necessitated his being physically restrained and committed.

This habit of glass breaking appeared to have developed from a series of similar behaviors stretching back to childhood. When he was three years old the patient had undergone an eye operation to correct a strabismus. Following the operation the patient's arms were bound to splints to prevent his trying to tear off the bandages. During childhood it was noted that when he was angry he would tear out the pockets of his clothes and also pick at old cuts until they bled. During late childhood and adolescence he developed a habit of breaking spectacles, destroying some 30 pairs over a period of some years and reaching the point where he was not allowed to wear them. Episodes of glass breaking in general followed on this behavior; he would break any and all glass in sight and restraint would be necessary.

Since the problem in this case was to remove or reduce an unwanted behavior, it was decided to use avoidance conditioning. Aversion therapy has been mainly used in alcoholism and the various sexual perversions. Nausea, induced by emetine or apomorphine, is most frequently used as the aversive stimulus.

More recently, however, several workers have used a painful electrical shock as the stimulus. This method has many advantages over drugs since both strength and timing can be accurately controlled. Feldman and MacCulloch[6] describe in detail the technique of avoidance training in homosexuality and discuss the various types of avoidance schedules. No cases of the use of electrical aversion therapy in schizophrenia appear to have been reported.

Four sessions, lasting about 45 minutes each, were held each week. The apparatus used was similar to that described by Mc-

Guire and Vallance,[10] electrodes being placed on the patient's right forearm. The patient was asked to visualize himself breaking a pane of glass in exactly the way he would do it in one of his episodes. When a clear image was obtained he was instructed to raise his finger, at which point a painful shock was administered. One-third of the trials were randomly not accompanied by shock, since partial reinforcement has been found to lead to stronger avoidance behavior, more resistant to extinction, than total reinforcement.

During the third session difficulty in and delay of the visualization of the scene began to occur. By the tenth session there was a delay of between ten and 15 seconds before the patient would visualize the scene, and by the 20th session the delay was some two to three minutes. At this point the patient reported that he had lost all urge to break glass and indeed "could not think of doing so."

Following the patient's discharge from the hospital, sessions were held on a diminishing basis for nine months, a total of 32 sessions being completed. Follow-up at 18 months after discharge revealed that only one brief episode of glass breaking had occurred. The patient broke one pane of glass, but immediately apologized for his behavior. No further episodes have occurred and the patient has worn the same pair of spectacles continually without damaging them. A relapse is of course possible should the avoidance habit be extinguished. However, a useful period of freedom has been gained, and further conditioning sessions could be used to reinstate avoidance behavior.

Discussion

A number of applications of behavior therapy to chronic schizophrenia seem possible. The simplest is that of removing behavior that interferes with ward management and poses a major nursing problem, as described in the first case. The restoration of normal eating behavior saved many hours of staff time that would have been spent in coaxing this man to eat or in tube feeding him.

In addition, both patients were able to continue within a rehabilitation program aimed at eventual return to the community. With the increasing emphasis on rehabilitation of the chronically ill patient, it will become increasingly important to control behavior that interferes with patients' participation in such programs.

More complex applications may be possible since much of the clinical problem posed by the chronic schizophrenic patient is due to deficits in social behavior. New and more adaptive social behavior might be shaped and maintained if the correct environment and reinforcement could be found. Ayllon[2] has found that generalized reinforcers, such as tokens which can be exchanged for money, goods, or privileges, can be used with schizophrenic patients. In this way reinforcement of a particular behavior can be given on exactly determined schedules at exactly the right moment.

Using this technique it seems that social and work behavior of an increasingly complex nature might be shaped and maintained. Whether such behavior can then be transferred to other environments remains to be seen; nevertheless an area of some promise appears to be developing.

Footnotes

[1]Ayllon, T.: Intensive Treatment of Psychotic Behavior by Stimulus Satiation and Food Reinforcement, Behav. Res. Ther. 1:53-61, 1963.

[2]Ayllon, T., and Azrin, N. H.: The Measurement and Reinforcement of Behavior of Psychotics, J. Exp. Anal. Behav. 8:357-383, 1965.

[3]Ayllon, T., and Haughton, E.: Modifications of Symptomatic Verbal Behavior of Mental Patients, Behav. Res. Ther. 2:87-97, 1964.

[4]Ayllon, T., and Michael, J.: The Psychiatric Nurse as a Behavioral Engineer, J. Exp. Anal. Behav. 2:323-334, 1959.

[5]Cowden, R. C., and Ford, L. I.: Systematic Desensitization with Phobic Schizophrenics, Amer. J. Psychiat. 119:241-245, 1962.

[6]Feldman, M. P., and MacCulloch, M. J.: The Application of Anticipatory Avoidance Learning to the Treatment of Homosexuality, Behav. Res. Ther. 2:165-183, 1965.

[7]Isaacs, W., Thomas, J., and Goldiamond, I.: Application of Operant Conditioning to Reinstate Verbal Behavior in Psychotics, J. Speech Hearing Dis. 25:3-12, 1960.

[8]Lindsley, O. R.: Operant Conditioning Methods Applied to Research in Chronic Schizophrenia, Psychiat. Res. Rep. Amer. Psychiat. Ass. 5:118-119, 1956.

[9]Lindsley, O. R.: Characteristics of the Behavior of Chronic Psychotics as Revealed by Free-Operant Conditioning Methods, Dis. Nerv. Syst. 21 (Monogr. Suppl.): 66-78, 1960.

[10]McGuire, R. J., and Vallance, M.: Aversion Therapy by Electric Shock: A Simple Technique, Brit. Med. J. 1:151-153, 1964.

[11]Rickard, H. C., Dignan, P. J., and Horner, R. F.: Verbal Manipulation in a Psychotherapeutic Relationship, J. Clin. Psychol. 16:364-367, 1960.

[12]Skinner, B. F.: The Behavior of Organisms. New York: Appleton-Century, 1938.

[13]Walton, D.: "Strengthening of Incompatible Reactions and the Treatment of a Phobic State in a Schizophrenic Patient," in Eysenck, H. J., ed.: Behavior Therapy and the Neuroses, New York: Pergamon Press, 1960.

SELF TEST: MEASURING COMPREHENSION

"Behavior Therapy In The Management Of Chronic Schizophrenia", By W. Stewart Agras

1. What does the shaping of behavior involve?

2. Describe the technique employed by Agras to improve the eating behavior of the patient.

3. Describe the technique employed by Agras to reduce glass breaking behavior.

4. Is it morally and ethically right to control the times at which a patient is allowed to eat? Why?

5. Is the use of electric shock justified in behavior therapy? Why?

6. Do you feel that the benefits gained through behavior therapy justify the conditions of control to which the patient is subjected to bring about these benefits?

FALL INTO HELPLESSNESS
from *Psychology Today*
Martin E. P. Seligman

"It's Not All In Your Head", by Seymour Kety, an article presented earlier in this book in the chapter on the illness perspective, describes research that has been done in discovering a biochemical basis for depression. Kety describes how antidepressent drugs enhance synaptic reaction in brain cells and serve to improve the condition of depressed patients. The following article, "Fall Into Helplessness", by Martin E. P. Seligman, offers a behavioristic explanation of the phenomenon of depression. Seligman describes the condition of learned helplessness—a phenomenon that results when we learn that no matter what we do, gratification does not occur. If nothing works, we learn to do nothing. Seligman notes many interesting parallels between learned helplessness and clinical depression. Seligman believes that the successful treatment of depression lies in the patient's learning that what he does matters, that he can be successful, and that he is in control of his fate.

Depression is the common cold of psychopathology, at once familiar and mysterious. Most of us have suffered depression in the wake of some traumatic event—some terrible loss—in our lives. Most of these depressions, like the common cold, run their course in time.

Serious forms of depression afflict from four to eight million Americans. Many of these depressive Americans will recover. Some of them won't; they'll just give up, becoming like T.S. Eliot's hollow men, a ". . . shape without form, shade without color. Paralyzed force, gesture without motion. . ." Many of those who are hospitalized will simply turn their heads to the wall. Others, at least one out of 200, will take their own lives. Yet we know there are some individuals who *never* succumb to depression, no matter how great their loss.

The *Wall Street Journal* has called depression the "disease of the '70s," and perhaps it is part of the character of our times. It is not a new malady, however. Physicians have been describing depression since the days of Hippocrates; he called it melancholia. The 2,500 years since Hippocrates have added little to our knowledge of the cure and prevention of depression. Our ignorance is due not to lack of research on the problem, but, I believe, to a lack of clearly defined and focused theory. Without a theory to organize what is known about the symptoms and cause, predictions about the cure and prevention of depression are, at best, haphazard.

A Cogent Theory

I think such a theory is possible, and my belief is based on the phenomenon known as "learned helplessness." [See "For Helplessness: Can We Immunize the Weak?," by Martin E. P. Seligman, PT, June 1969.] There are considerable parallels between the behaviors that define learned helplessness and the major symptoms of depression. In addition, the types of events that set off depression parallel the events that set off learned helplessness. I believe that cure for depression occurs when the individual comes to believe that he is not helpless and that an individual's susceptibility to depression depends on the success or failure of his previous experience with controlling his environment.

So the focus of my theory is that if the symptoms of learned helplessness and depression are equivalent, then what we have learned experimentally about the cause, cure and prevention of learned helplessness can be applied to depression.

Inescapable Shock

A few years ago, Steven F. Maier, J. Bruce Overmier and I stumbled onto the behavioral phenomenon of learned helplessness while we were using dogs and traumatic shock to test a particular learning theory. We had strapped dogs into a Pavlovian harness and given them electric shock—traumatic, but not physically damaging. Later the dogs were put into a two-compartment shuttlebox where they were supposed to learn to escape shock by jumping across the barrier separating the compartments.

A nonshocked, experimentally naive dog, when placed in a shuttlebox, typically behaves in the following way: at the onset of the first electric shock, the dog defecates, urinates, howls, and runs around frantically until it accidentally scrambles over the barrier and escapes the shock. On the next trial, the dog, running and howling, crosses the barrier more quickly. This pattern continues until the dog learns to avoid shock altogether.

But our dogs were not that naive. While in a harness from which they could not escape, they had already experienced shock over which they had no control. That is, nothing

they did or did not do affected their receipt of shock. When placed in the shuttlebox, these dogs reacted at first in much the same manner as a naive dog, but not for long. The dogs soon stopped running and howling, settled down and took the shock, whining quietly. Typically, the dog did not cross the barrier and escape. Instead, it seemed to give up. On succeeding trials, the dog made virtually no attempts to get away. It passively took as much shock as was given.

After testing alternative hypotheses, we developed the theory that it was not trauma per se (electric shock) that interfered with the dog's adaptive responding. Rather, it was the experience of having *no control* over the trauma. We have found that if animals can control shock by any response—be it an active or a passive one—they do not later become helpless. Only those animals who receive uncontrollable shock will later give up. The experience in the harness had taught the dog that its responses did not pay, that his actions did not matter. We concluded that the dogs in our experiments had learned that they were helpless.

Our learned-helplessness hypothesis has been tested and confirmed in many ways with both animal and human subjects. Tests with human beings revealed dramatic parallels between the behavior of subjects who have learned helplessness and the major symptoms exhibited by depressed individuals.

Reactive Depression

Depression, like most clinical labels, embraces a whole family of disorders. As a label it is probably no more discriminating than "disease of the skin," which describes both acne and cancer. The word "depressed" as a behavioral description explicitly denotes a reduction or depression in responding. The reactive depressions, the focus of this article, are most common. As distinguished from process depression, reactive depression is set off by some external event, is probably not hormonally bases, does not cycle regularly in time, and does not have a genetic history. The kind of depression experienced by manic-depressives is process depression.

Some of the events that may set off reactive depression are familiar to each of us: death, loss, rejection by or separation from loved ones, physical disease, failure in work or school, financial setback, and growing old. There are a host of others, of course, but those capture the flavor. I suggest that what all these experiences have in common—what depression is—is the belief in one's own helplessness.

Goodies From the Sky

Many clinicians have reported an increasding pervasiveness of depression among college students. Since this is a generation that has been raised with more reinforcers—more sex, more intellectual stimulation, more buying power, more cars, more music, etc.—than any previous generation, why should they be depressed? Yet the occurrence of reinforcers in our affluent society is so independent of the actions of the children who receive them, the goodies might as well have fallen from the sky. And perhaps that is our answer. Rewards as well as punishments that come independently of one's own effort can be depressing.

We can mention "success" depression in this context. When an individual finally reaches a goal after years of striving, such as getting a Ph.D. or becoming company president, depression often ensues. Even the disciplined astronaut, hero of his nation and the world, can become depressed after he has returned from walking on the Moon.

From a learned helplessness viewpoint, success depression may occur because reinforcers are no longer contingent on present responding. After years of goal-directed activity, a person now gets his reinforcers because of who he *is* rather than because of what he is *doing*. Perhaps this explains the number of beautiful women who become depressed and attempt suicide. They receive abundant positive reinforcers not for what they do but for how they look.

Symptoms in Common

Consider the parallels between depression and learned helplessness: the most prominent symptom of depression, passivity, is also the central symptom of learned helplessness. Joseph Mendels describes the slowdown in responding associated with depression: ". . . Loss of interest, decrease in energy, inability to accomplish tasks, difficulty in concentration and ambition all combine to impair efficient functioning. For many depressives the first signs of illness are in the area of their increasing inability to cope with their work and responsibility. . ." Aaron T. Beck describes "paralysis of the will" as a striking characteristic of depression:

". . . In severe cases, there often is complete paralysis of the will. The patient has no desire to do anything, even those things which are essential to life. Consequently, he may be relatively immobile unless prodded or pushed into activity by others. It is sometimes necessary to pull the patient out of bed, wash, dress and feed him. . ."

Experiments in learned helplessness have produced passivity in many kinds of animals, even the lowly cockroach, and in human subjects. Donald Hiroto subjected college students to loud noise. He used three groups: group one could not escape hearing the loud noise; group two heard the loud noise but could turn it off by pressing a button; group three heard no noise.

In the second part of the experiment, Hiroto presented the students with a finger shuttlebox. Moving one's fingers back and forth across the shuttlebox turned off the loud noise. The students in group two, who had previously learned to silence the noise by pushing a button, and those in group three, who had no experience with the loud noise, readily learned to move their fingers across the shuttlebox to control the noise. But the students in group one, whose previous attempts to turn off the noise had been futile, now merely sat with their hands in the shuttlebox, passively accepting the loud noise. They had learned that they were helpless.

Hiroto also found out that "externals" [see "External Control and Internal Control," by Julian B. Rotter, PT, June 1971] were more susceptible to learned helplessness than "internals." Externals are persons who believe that reinforcement comes from outside themselves; they believe in luck. Internals believe that their own actions control reinforcement.

Born Losers

Depressed patients not only make fewer responses, but they are "set" to interpret their own responses, when they do make them, as failures or as doomed to failure. Each of them bears an invisible tattoo: "I'm a Born Loser." Beck considers this negative cognitive set to be the primary characteristic of depression:

". . . The depressed patient is peculiarly sensitive to any impediments to his goal-directed activity. An obstacle is regarded as an impossible barrier, difficulty in dealing with a problem is interpreted as a total failure. His cognitive response to a problem or difficulty is likely to be an idea such as 'I'm licked,' 'I'll never be able to do this,' or 'I'm blocked no matter what I do' . . ."

This cognitive set crops us repeatedly in experiments with depressives. Alfred S. Friedman observed that although a patient was performing adequately during a test, the patient would occasionally reiterate his original protest of "I can't do it," "I don't know how," etc. This is also our experience in testing depressed patients.

Negative cognitive set crops up in both depression and learned helplessness. When testing students, William Miller, David Klein and I found that depression and learned helplessness produced the same difficulty in seeing that responding is successful. We found that depressed individuals view their skilled actions very much as if they were in a chance situation. Their depression is not a general form of pessimism about the world, but pessimism that is specific to their own actions. In animal behavior this is demonstrated by associative retardation: animals don't catch on even though they make a response that turns off shock; they have difficulty in learning what responses produce relief.

Maier and I found in separate experiments, that normal aggressiveness and competitiveness become deficient in the subjects who have succumbed to learned helplessness. In competition, these animals lose out to animals who have learned that they control the effects of their responses. Further, they do not fight back when attacked.

Depressed individuals, similarly, are usually less aggressive and competitive than nondepressed individuals. The behavior of depressed patients is depleted of hostility and even their dreams are less hostile. This symptom forms the basis for the Freudian view of depression. Freud claimed that the hostility of depressed people was directed inward toward themselves rather than outward. Be this as it may, the *symptom* corresponds to the depleted aggression and competitiveness of helpless dogs and rats.

The Balm of Time

Depression also often dissipates with time. When a man's wife dies he may be depressed for several days, several months, or even several years. But time usually heals. One of the most tragic aspects of suicide is that if the person could have waited for a few weeks, the depression might well have lifted.

Time is also an important variable in learned helplessness. Overmier and I found that the day after they received one session of inescapable shock, dogs behaved helplessly in the shuttlebox. However, if two days elapsed between the inescapable shock and testing, the dogs were not helpless; their helplessness, like the widower's depression, had run its course. Unfortunately, helplessness does not always respond so well to the elixir of time. We found that multiple sessions of inescapable shock made the animals' learned helplessness virtually irreversible. We also found that animals that had been reared from birth in our laboratories with a limited history of controlling reinforcers also failed to recover from learned helplessness over time.

Often when we are depressed we lose our appetites and our zest for life. Jay M. Weiss, Neal E. Miller and their colleagues at Rockefeller University found that rats that had received inescapable shock lost weight and ate less than rats who had been able to escape from shock. In addition, the brains of the rats subjected to inescapable shock are depleted of norepinephrine, an important transmitter substance in the central nervous system. Joseph J. Schildkraut and Seymour S. Kety have suggested that the cause of depression may be a deficiency of norepinephrine at receptor sites in the brain. This is because reserpine, a drug that depletes norepinephrine, among other things, produces depression in man. Moreover, antidepressant drugs increase the brain's supply of norepinephrine. Therefore, there may be a chemical similarity between depression and learned helplessness.

Weiss found that rats subjected to uncontrollable shock got more stomach ulcers than rats receiving no shock or shock they could control.

No one has done a study of ulcers in depression, so we don't know if human experience will correspond to ulceration in helpless rats. However, anxiety and agitation are sometimes seen along with depression. It is my speculation, however, that anxiety persists as long as the depressed person believes there might still be something he can do to extract himself from his dilemma. When he finally comes to believe that no response will work, depression wholly displaces anxiety.

The Chances For Cure

As arrayed above, there are considerable parallels between the behaviors which define learned helplessness and the major symptoms of depression. We have also seen that the cause of learned helplessness and reactive depression is similar: both occur when important events are out of control. Let me now speculate about the possibility of curing both.

In our animal experiments, we knew that only when the dog learned to escape the shock, only when it learned that it could control its environment, would a cure for its learned helplessness be found.

At first, we could not persuade the dog to move to the other side of the box, not even by dropping meat there when the dog was hungry. As a last resort, we forcibly dragged the dog across the barrier on a leash. After much dragging, the dog caught on and eventually was able to escape the shock on its own. Recovery from helplessness was complete and lasting for each animal. We can say with confidence that so far only "directive therapy"—forcing the animal to see that it can succeed by responding—works reliably in curing learned helplessness. However, T.R. Dorworth has recently found that electroconvulsive shock breaks up helplessness in dogs. Electroconvulsive shock is often used as a therapy for depression and it seems to be effective about 60 percent of the time.

Although we do not know how to cure depression, there are therapies that alleviate it, and they are consonant with the learned helplessness approach. Successful therapy occurs when the patient believes that his responses produce gratification, that he is an effective human being.

Against the Grain

In an Alabama hospital, for instance, E.S. Taulbee and H.W. Wright have created an "antidepression room." They seat a severely depressed patient in the room and then abuse him in a simple manner. He is told to sand a block of wood, then is reprimanded because he is sanding against the grain of the wood. After he switches to sanding *with* the grain, he is reprimanded for sanding with the grain. The abuse continues until the depressed patient gets angry. He is then promptly led out of the room with apologies. His outburst, and its immediate effect on the person abusing him, breaks up his depression. From the helplessness viewpoint, the patient is forced to vent his anger, one of the most powerful responses people have for controlling others. When anger is dragged out of him, he is powerfully reinforced.

Other methods reported to be effective against depression involve the patient's relearning that he controls reinforcers.

Expressing strong emotions is a therapy that seems to help depressed patients, as self-assertion does. In assertive training, the patient rehearses asserting himself and then puts into practice the responses he has learned that bring him social reinforcers.

Morita therapy puts patients in bed for about a week to "sensitize them to reinforcement." Then the patients progress from light to heavy to complicated work [see "Morita Therapy," by Takehisa Kora and Kenshiro Ohara, PT, March 1973].

The Lift of Success

Other forms of graded-task assignments also have been effective. Elaine P. Burgess first had her patients perform some simple task, such as making a telephone call. As the task requirements increased, the patient was reinforced by the therapist for successfully completing each task. Burgess emphasized how crucial it is in the graded-task treatment that the patient succeed.

Using a similar form of graded-task assignment, Aaron Beck, Dean Schuyler, Peter Brill and I began by asking patients to read a short paragraph aloud. Finally, we could get severely depressed patients to give extemporaneous speeches, with a noticeable lifting of their depression. What one patient said was illuminating: "You know, I used to be a debater in high school and I had forgotten how good I was."

Finally, there is the age-old strategy adopted by individuals to dispel their own minor depressions: doing work that is difficult but gratifying. There is no better way to see that one's responses are still effective. It is crucial to succeed. Merely starting and giving up only makes things worse.

Dramatic successes in medicine have come more frequently from prevention than from treatment, and I would hazard a guess that inoculation and immunization have saved more lives than cure. Surprisingly, psychotherapy is almost exclusively limited to curative procedures, and preventive procedures rarely play an explicit role.

In studies of dogs and rats we have found that behavioral immunization prevents learned helplessness. Dogs that first receive experience in mastering shock do not become helpless after experiencing subsequent inescapable shock. Dogs that are deprived of natural opportunities to control their own rewards in their development are more vulnerable to helplessness than naturally immunized dogs.

The Masterful Life

Even less is known about the prevention of depression than about its cure. We can only speculate on this, but the data on immunization against learned helplessness guide our speculations. The life histories of those individuals who are particularly resistant to depression or who are resilient from depression may have been filled with mastery. Persons who have had extensive experience in controlling and manipulating the sources of reinforcement in their lives may see the future optimistically. A life without mastery may produce vulnerability to depression. Adults who lost their parents when they were children are unusually susceptible to depression and suicide.

A word of caution is in order. While it may be possible to immunize people against debilitating depression by giving them a history of control over reinforcers, it may be possible to get too much of a good thing. The person who has met only success may be highly susceptible to depression when he faces a loss. One is reminded, for example, of the stock market crash of 1929: it was not the low-income people who jumped to their deaths, but those who had been "super-successful" and suddenly faced gross defeat.

One can also look at successful therapy as preventative. After all, therapy usually does not focus just on undoing past problems. It also should arm the patient against future depressions. Perhaps therapy for depression would be more successful if it explicitly aimed at providing the patient with a wide repertoire of coping responses. He could use these responses in future situations where he finds his usual reactions do not control his reinforcements. Finally, we can speculate about child rearing. What kind of experiences can best protect our children against the debilitat-ing effects of helplessness and depression? A tentative answer follows from the learned helplessness view of depression: to see oneself as an effective human being may require a childhood filled with powerful synchronies between responding and its consequences.

	Learned Helplessness	Depression
SYMPTOMS	1 passivity	1 passivity
	2 difficulty learning that responses produce relief	2 negative cognitive set
	3 lack of aggression	3 introjected hostility
	4 dissipates in time	4 time course
	5 weight loss and undereating, anorexia, sexual deficits (?)	5 loss of libido
	6 norepinephrine depletion	6 norepinephrine depletion
	7 ulcers and stress	7 ulcers (?) and stress
		8 feelings of helplessness
CAUSE	learning that responding and reinforcement are independent	belief that responding is useless
CURE	1 directive therapy: forced exposure to responding producing reinforcement	1 recovery of belief that responding produces reinforcement
	2 electroconvulsive shock	2 electroconvulsive shock (?)
	3 pharmacological agents (?)	3 pharmacological agents (?)
	4 time	4 time
PREVENTION	inoculation with mastery over reinforcement	inoculation (?)

"Fall Into Helplessness", By Martin E. P. Seligman

1. What is learned helplessness?

2. What is the difference between process and reactive depression?

3. What is success depression, and how does Seligman feel it originates?

4. For what reason does Seligman feel there may be a biochemical similarity between depression and learned helplessness?

5. According to the research presented in the article, what is the basic, underlying notion regarding successful treatment of depression?

Chapter 7
THE HUMANISTIC PERSPECTIVE

Adolf Hitler was a skillful behavioral engineer. He was an expert at manipulating the conditions of reinforcement of his subordinates. Obedience to his orders would bring rewards. To disobey him would be unthinkable. He had a personal master plan for what he felt would produce an ideal, utopian society. He was ruthless in exterminating those who did not fit into his master plan. Hitler was proficient in the application of the principles of behavioristic psychology. The point emerges that when in the wrong hands, behavioral technology can be employed for destructive, rather than constructive, purposes.

In the period following World War II it was not surprising that some psychologists would perceive too great a similarity between the techniques of control used by Hitler, and those employed with good intentions within behavioristic psychology. As stated by its founding father, John B. Watson, a major goal of behaviorism is "the prediction and control of behavior" (Watson, 1913). I am not implying that behaviorists would use the principles of behavioral technology for other than beneficial purposes, but it is understandable that some psychologists would object to their employment because of their potential for misuse.

The atrocities committed by Hitler led to much soul searching within psychology during the postwar years. Psychologists sought to understand what Hitler had done, so that it would never happen again. Many Jewish psychologists, strongly influenced by the holocaust, began reflecting upon it. Victor Frankl, who survived the Auschwitz death camp, sought to find some sense of personal significance in the holocaust. Through his own experiences he came to believe that despite all adversity, man still has the capability to be free. No matter what circumstances, man still has choices to make. "Man *can* preserve a vestige of spiritual freedom, of independence of mind, even in such conditions of psychic and physical stress" (Frankl, 1962, p. 65). Other psychologists, such as Kurt Lewin, Frederick Perls, and Abraham Maslow wrote along similar lines. A new psychology began to emerge. This new psychology sought to discover the significance in man's existence. It stressed the innate goodness of mankind. It was optimistic. Because of its concern with the human condition, this new psychology eventually became known as humanism.

Humanism views each individual as unique, and special. Unlike behavioristic psychology, which according to Watson recognizes "no dividing line between man and brute" (Watson, 1913), humans are viewed with upmost regard and respect.

The beginnings of humanism cannot be traced to any one individual or event, such as the founding of psychoanalysis by Freud, or the founding of behaviorism by Watson. Indeed, the personality theories and therapeutic techniques employed by different humanists are many and varied. The client-centered therapy of American humanist Carl Rogers is very different from the therapeutic techniques employed by Scottish humanist-existentialist R. D. Laing.

What binds humanists together are their beliefs in the innate goodness of mankind, the unique quality of the individual, and the ability of man to seek and find significance in his existence.

Humanism is more than specific personality theories and techniques of therapy. For the individual who becomes deeply involved in humanism, it becomes a philosophy of life. The sensitivity and encounter movements of today had their roots in humanistic psychology. Humanism has helped many toward the development of their full potential, and enabled them to find some sense of personal significance in an American society already over-mechanized, computerized, and unconcerned with the individual. The humanistic perspective has emerged as a vital force within psychology today.

To begin the chapter on the humanistic perspective, I will present an article entitled "The Treatment of Autism: A Human Protest", by Dr. Mike Murray. It describes the reaction of one autistic child against being artificially manipulated in a behavior modification program. The second article is entitled "The Third Force in Psychology", by J. F. T. Bugental. This article outlines the basic orientation of humanistic psychology. The third article is entitled "Plight of the Ik and Kaiadilt is seen as a chilling possible end for Man", and was written by John B. Calhoun. It describes how man can cease being human when forced to live in conditions of debasement, degradation and overcrowding. The final selection is taken from humanist Carl Rogers' classic, *On Becoming a Person*. Its title is "Some Hypotheses Regarding the Facilitation of Personal Growth". In this selection Rogers describes the type of therapeutic atmosphere he tries to create in order to enhance the personality growth of his clients.

References

Victor E. Frankl, *Man's Search for Meaning,* (Boston: Beacon Press, 1959).

John B. Watson, Psychology as the Behaviorist Views It. *Psychological Review.* 1913, v. 20 (2), pp. 158-177.

THE TREATMENT OF AUTISM: A HUMAN PROTEST

from *The Journal of Humanistic Psychology*

Mike Murray

The success of behavior therapy often relies upon the ability of the therapist to gain some degree of control over the environment and conditions of reinforcement of the patient. Therefore, as pointed out in D. G. Brown's previous article, "Behavior Modification with Children", behavior therapy is often criticized as being "mechanical" and "dehumanizing". Humanistic psychologists are those who are most likely to make these criticisms. Since the humanist feels that each person has free will, he does not believe that behavioral therapists should be placed in the powerful position of arbitrarily determining what is best for any individual.

Many instances have been reported of psychiatric patients reacting negatively, and sometimes violently, to having their environments and behavior controlled and manipulated through behavior modification programs. In one case in which I was involved, a young woman suffered from anorexia nervosa. Anorexia nervosa, sometimes called the "starving disease", is a disorder that afflicts primarily young women. Sufferers of the disorder systematically starve themselves, and weight loss is dramatic. It is interesting that reports of anorexia nervosa have become more common since the media has more strongly stressed the "thin is in" concept of feminine beauty.

This particular patient, whose normal weight was 105 pounds, denied herself of food until she weighed 65 pounds. She became a patient in a psychiatric hospital that employed strict behavior modification techniques. Reinforcement conditions were designed so that if the girl gained a sufficient amount of weight during the week, she would be rewarded for her weight gain by being allowed to go home for the weekend. She had made some progress for a brief period of time, but one week failed to gain the necessary weight to go home for the weekend. Despite her protests, she was not allowed to leave the hospital. During the weekend she attempted suicide by slashing her wrist. Could this suicide attempt have been the patient's way of protesting her treatment? A humanist would answer yes.

In the following article, Dr. Mike Murray describes the reaction of an autistic child whom he feels was artificially manipulated by the control techniques of behavior therapy. The article implies that therapists must always recognize that every human being, no matter how severe his condition, is still an individual with free will, rights, and personal integrity.

In recent years techniques for treating the behavioral deficits of autistic children have become more refined and effective through the use of behavior modification procedures (Bandura, 1969). This is particularly true regarding the acquisition of imitative language (Lovaas, Berberich, Perloff, & Schaeffer, 1966). Treatment usually involves establishing responsiveness to modeling cues and to attentive behavior, as well as developing the effectiveness of social reinforcements in shaping behavior. Procedures include the use of both aversive and positive consequences, depending on the behavior of the child (Lovaas, 1966; Lovaas, 1967; Risley & Wolf, 1967).

While these procedures have proven useful in establishing basic speech patterns, behavior modification techniques are seen by some critics as dehumanizing and overly mechanistic. Humanistic psychologists have criticized the strictly behavioral approaches for being limited in scope and for failing to encompass the full range of human misery and potential. In order to facilitate more adequate socialization and growth, alternate plans for treating autistic children have been formulated (Bettelheim, 1967). Interestingly, these psychologists are not alone in their criticism of mechanistic treatment. The following case illustrates the human protest against being artificially manipulated, and is a strong reminder of the limitation of our knowledge about psychopathology and personality development.

Case Study

David is a nine-year-old student at a local mental health and retardation center. He has been diagnosed as autistic and shows the typical patterns of avoidance of interpersonal contact and failure to develop meaningful speech. Verbalizations include generally meaningless babbling with an occasional word thrown in that appears meaningless in terms of its context and situation. His parents report that David has never learned to talk or use language effectively.

Recently the staff at the center has been exposed to the theory and use of operant procedures. Having achieved success in teaching another previously nonverbal, autistic child to ask for food through the use of positive reinforcement, the staff decided that David was to be the next candidate.

The modification procedure consisted of asking David if he wanted a cookie each day during snack times. If he responded by saying "yes," he would receive a cookie, and if he made no response, he received nothing. During the first two and a half days of conditioning, David failed to respond and actively engaged in nonattentive and interpersonally disruptive behaviors when asked if he wanted a cookie. On the third day, during afternoon snack time, David's persistent teacher took David's shoulders in order to try to get his attention and asked him if he wanted a cookie. Suddenly, David ceased his struggling and focused his attention on the teacher.

"No," he replied, "and I'm getting tired of this shit!"

Discussion

Several comments seem in order regarding this case study. The psychodynamic interpretation of this incident is based upon the premise that David's response was meaningful, conscious, and goal-directed. It is not unusual for autistic children to make delayed echolalic responses, and occasionally, merely by chance, such a response may appear to be a meaningful statement. However, the the particular situational context and the appropriateness and style of the response are critical to functional interpretation. In the present case report, David's speech is seen as a frustration response to a mechanistic environment.

Upon examination, several aspects of this situation point to the sentence as being a protest rather than echolalia. First, there is the fact that David's response was delayed. It followed the teacher's verbal cue and was not a reaction to being held. Second, the response showed appropriate affect. David focused his attention on the teacher and stated in an assertive and angry manner that he was getting tired of the procedure. This type of statement is, of course, in striking contrast to the normally flat, sing-song sounds of the autistic child's echolalic speech. Finally, David's response did not follow the typical echolalic pattern. As Kanner (1943) states in his original paper, autistic speech is repetitious and parrot-like. There is no conversational give-and-take. The child very rarely answers "yes" or "no," but simply echoes the question. In this vein, personal pronouns are repeated as heard. Thus, the autistic child wrongly refers to himself as "you" and to others as "I." David's response both answered the question with a "no" and correctly used personal pronouns. The appropriateness of the response to the situation, the delayed reaction time, the appropriate affect, and the normal speech pattern strongly argue for this statement's being a very human protest.

References

Bandura, A. *Principles of behavior modification.* New York: Holt, Rinehart and Winston, 1969.

Bettelheim, B. *The empty fortress.* New York: Free Press, 1967.

Kanner, L. Autistic disturbances in affective contact. *Nervous Child,* 1943, 2, 217-250.

Lovaas, O. I. *Reinforcement therapy.* Philadelphia: Smith, Kline, and French Laboratories, 1966. (16 mm. sound film)

Lovaas, O. I. A behavior therapy approach to the treatment of childhood schizophrenia. In J. Hill (Ed.), *Minnesota symposia on child psychology.* Vol. 1. Minneapolis: University of Minnesota Press, 1967.

Lovaas, O. I., Berberich, J., Perloff, B., & Schaeffer, B. Acquisition of imitative speech by schizophrenic children. *Science,* 1966, 151, 705-707.

Risley, T., & Wolf, M. Establishing functional speech in echolalic children. *Behavior Research and Therapy.* 1967, 5, 73-88.

SELF TEST: UNDERSTANDING COMPREHENSION

"The Treatment of Autism: A Human Protest", By Mike Murray

1. What are the characteristics of an autistic child?

2. What are Dr. Murray's criticisms of behavior modification techniques?

3. How do you interpret the verbal response made by David?

4. How might a behavioral therapist defend behavior modification against cirticisms that it is "mechanical" and "dehumanizing"?

THE THIRD FORCE IN PSYCHOLOGY
from *The Journal of Humanistic Psychology*
James Bugental

In the previous article we saw that humanism rejects the behavioral control aspects of the learning perspective. The following article is a concise description of what humanism, or the third force in psychology (the first two forces being psychoanalysis and behaviorism), advocates and what its general orientation is.

In this article, published in 1964, J. F. T. Bugental expresses his enthusiasm over the emergence and blossoming of humanistic psychology. The article is written in a hoping, prophetic manner. However, since the article's publication, the hopes and predictions of Bugental have been largely fulfilled within the humanistic perspective.

Last week, thinking about our meeting here, I was reminded of a kind of peak-experience of the previous winter. Then, I had a fresh look at the familiar scene of professional psychology. As may happen when one catches a new perspective on his usual environment, I recognized with a quickening of feeling that something was importantly different in that scene.

I remember years ago climbing a mountain, endlessly following the trail through forest, through rocky channels. Each point was interesting and had its own beauty, but all sense of where on the path I was in relation to the peak gradually faded as the altitude pulled at my lungs and the demands of each new stretch of hiking pulled at my muscles and mind. Then suddenly — startlingly — I emerged above the timber line on a narrow shoulder and saw ahead of me the summit, and all around the vista spread out for miles. The sense of discovery restored perspective, was as breathtaking as were the altitude and the view. It is an experience such as this that I want to describe to you now.

Much as been happening in our field in the postwar years: the establishment of our new professional life, the battles for legal recognition, the concerns with new topics such as habit strength, ideal image, gestalt therapy, games theory, human factors engineering, and so on. Yet many of us have cried alarm that our concerns are still trivial, that the sciences of man are so badly outdistanced by the sciences of things that the very race of man is in jeopardy. We have hoped for and sought a "breakthrough."

What I recognized quite simply was this: a major breakthrough is occurring right now in psychology. Like many another such major change process—the end of feudalism, the introduction of electricity, the beginnings of the laboratory method in psychology—its presence and potentialities are difficult to recognize for us who are so deep among the tress of daily concerns. Yet I am convinced that the parallels I cite are not vainglorious. I think we are on the verge of a new era in man's concern about man which may—if allowed to run its course—produce as profound changes in the human condition as those we have seen the physical sciences bring about in the past century.

Now I don't mean to tease you unduly by delaying specification of the breakthrough I have in mind. However, I do need to say a few words to prepare you to grasp my meaning. I don't want too many of you to say "Oh, that!" and turn away. You see, I think that we are prisoners of our own involvement with our work. It would be much easier for us to appreciate the report of a breakthrough in historical scholarship or in space physics than in our own familiar domain. Yet I imagine historians and physicists would have the same difficulties in their own provinces. So listen, if you can and will, with the perspective of psychology's whole development in the past 100 years.

Psychology is at last becoming the study of man. Psychology is recognizing that man, as man, has eluded our segmental approaches, out attempts to deal with part-functions, and is beginning to face up to the task of recognizing that no amount of additional findings about parts will ever yield an appreciation or understanding of man in the world.

Now, I'm pretty sure that a majority of you are saying the equivalent of "Oh, that!" I know I would be. Stay with me a bit, and I'll try to show you that this is no small thing I'm trying to depict.

Recall your undergraduate course in the history of psychology: Wundt, Titchner, Watson, Hull; psychophysics, mental elements, conditioned response, factor analysis, habit strength; Stanford-Binet, Kohs Blocks, Porteus Mazes, Wechsler, Iowa Tests.

All along we had had this implicit assumption as foundation: Discover the basic components and from these we can synthesize the whole person. Concurrently, we have rigorously disciplined ourselves to avoid the subjective and the poetic.

Listen to Clark Hull (1943), a near saint of pre-breakthrough psychology (p. 27):

A device much employed by the author has proved itself to be a far more effective prophylaxis. This is to regard, from time to time, the behaving organism as a completely self-maintaining robot, constructed of materials as unlike ourselves as may be.

Contrast this with the following:

A man can understand astronomy only by being an astronomer; he can understand entomology only by being an entomologist (or, perhaps, an insect); but he can understand a great deal of anthropology merely by being a man. He is himself the animal which he studies. Hence arises the fact which strikes the eye everywhere in the records of ethnology and folk-lore—the fact that the same frigid and detached spirit which leads to success in the study of astronomy or botany leads to disaster in the study of mythology or human origins. (G. K. Chesterton, *Science and the Savages,* 1909; quoted in Cantril and Bumstead, 1960, p. 12.)

Or this:

. . . a poem, a painting, or a prayer should be regarded as a psychological datum just as much as the establishment of a sensory threshold in the laboratory of the measurement of an I.Q.

The last quotation is from Cantril and Bumstead's exciting book *Reflections on the Human Venture* (1960), itself an evidence of the change process I am trying to characterize. Other books that are part of this wave have come from Rogers (1961), Maslow (1962), May (1961), Buhler (1962), Cohen (1962), and so on.

Another way of describing what is happening is to say that two great human traditions are converging, and from their convergence we may expect a tremendous outpouring of new awareness about ourselves in our world. One such tradition is that of science; the other is the humanities. It is as though we are suddenly made heirs to a tremendous storehouse of data which has been but little utilized scientifically before or—to use a different analogy—as though a whole new hemisphere of our globe had been discovered by some new Columbus. Certainly much exploration and development must be done, but at last we are reaching its shores.

There is another evidence—a kind of validation—of the significance of the breakthrough I am trying to depict. An ancient and vast body of human experience has for centuries been accumulating in the Eastern countries. Our Western contacts with this have been chiefly to treat it as a curiosity, as pagan error to be destroyed, or as material for ignorant distortion in melodramas. Now we are beginning to appreciate the tremendous amount of wisdom and insight which has been achieved along routes quite different than those we have traveled. Zen and Taoism and other Oriental cultural traditions have much to say to us, much that we can begin to hear now that our separate ways have drawn close in the evolution of men's thoughts about man (Fingarette, 1963; Watts, 1961).

As an aside let me point out that there is tremendous encouragement for the hope of some achievement of an eventual citizenship of humanity in this start on a genuine dialogue between these two great heritages of man's thought, the Oriental and the Occidental.

You will have observed, I am optimistic about our field. A year or two ago, as some of you may recall, I spoke in less hopeful terms to our California State Psychological Association. Then I feared we were on our way to fossilhood (Bugental, 1962). Today this fate seems less likely, I'm pleased to report. Certainly there are still dangers, but I think psychology—or perhaps I should say, humanity—has proven itself hardier than once seemed to me to be the case. I mean by this last to say that I believe the renewed psychology of which I speak is but a phase of an evolutionary process which is arising as a survival response to the biology-threatening forces of nuclear destruction. Just as in a single organism, invasion by disease evokes a counter process of antibody production in defense, so do I think it is with the total evolutionary process.

Basic Postulates and Orientation of Humanistic Psychology

Humanistic psychology is an emerging orientation to the study of man (Bugental, 1963; Cantril, 1955; Maslow, 1956; Rogers, 1963). Sometimes referred to as "the third

force" in psychology, the humanistic orientation endeavors to go beyond the points of view of behaviorism or psychoanalysis, the two most dominant perspectives presently discernable within the broad area of psychology. Humanistic psychology generally does not see itself as competitive with the other two orientations; rather, it attempts to supplement their observations and to introduce further perspectives and insights.

To date it has been hard to designate just what is meant by humanistic psychology, since it is a movement with diverse spokesmen and widely ranging contents and perspectives. The *Journal of Humanistic Psychology*, founded in 1961, has brought together a wide spectrum of papers and a distinguished, through diverse, editorial panel, and it is only through inspection of such publications and of the views of the editorial panel that an implicit definition of the field may be arrived at. Similarly, the American Association for Humanistic Psychology (Sutich, 1962) has found it necessary to use a catalogue type of description of just what it is the Association seeks to represent:

> Humanistic Psychology may be defined as the third main branch of the general field of psychology (the two already in existence being the psychoanalytic and the behaviorist) and as such, is primarily concerned with those human capacities and potentialities that have little or no systematic place, either in positivist or behaviorist theory or in classical psychoanalytic theory: e.g., love, creativity, self, growth, organism, basic need-gratification, self-actualization, higher values, being, becoming, spontaneity, play, humor, affection, naturalness, warmth, ego-transcendence, objectivity, autonomy, responsibility, meaning, fair-play, transcendental experience, psychological health, and related concepts. This approach can also be characterized by the writings of Allport, Angyal, Asch, Buhler, Fromm, Goldstein, Horney, Maslow, May, Moustakas, Rogers, Wertheirmer, etc., as well as by certain aspects of the writings of Jung, Adler, and the psychoanalytic ego-psychologists, existential and phenomenological psychologists.

The present paper will make a beginning on an affirmative statement of the nature of the humanistic orientation in psychology. We will undertake to do this by setting forth five postulates of humanistic psychology which may represent common elements in the perspectives of most writers identifying with this field. We will also attempt to make some defining statements about the humanistic orientation in psychology. These defining statements will be of the nature of process descriptions as opposed to the substantive or content descriptions provided by our postulates. In setting forth these postulates and these characteristics of the humanistic orientation, the writer is well aware of the very tentative nature of these statements. We are only now beginning really to discover the commonalities in the diverse spokesmen in the humanistic perspective. It is probable and highly desirable that the list of postulates that follows be criticised, revised, and supplemented many times.

Five Basic Postulates for Humanistic Psychology

Man, as man, supercedes the sum of his parts

When we speak of "man" in humanistic psychology, we do so with the intent of characterizing a person rather than an "organism." Humanistic psychology is concerned with man at his most human or, to say it differently, with that which most distinguishes man as a unique species.

Our first postulate states the keystone position that man must be recognized as something other than an additive product of various part-functions. Although part-function knowledge is important scientific knowledge, it is not the knowledge of man as man, but knowledge of the functioning of parts of an organism.

Man has his being in a human context

We postulate second that the unique nature of man is expressed through his always being in relationship with his fellows. Humanistic psychology is always concerned with man in his interpersonal potential. This is not to say that humanistic psychology may not

deal with such issues as man's aloneness, but it will be evident that even in so designating it "aloneness," we are speaking of man in his human context. The psychology of part-functions is a psychology which ignores this relatedness (actual or potential) of the human experience.

Man is aware

A central fact of human experience is that man is aware. Awareness is postulated to be continuous and at many levels. By so viewing it, we recognize that all aspects of his experience are not equally available to man, but that, whatever the degree of consciousness, awareness is an essential part of man's being. The continuous nature of awareness is deemed essential to an understanding of human experience. Man does not move from discrete episode to discrete episode, a fact overlooked by experiments of the behavioristic orientation when they treat their subjects as though they had no prior awareness before coming into the experimental situation. Our postulation also provides for unconsciousness as a level of awareness in which there is not direct apprehension, but in which awareness is nevertheless present though denied. This is not the same as the Freudian concept of the unconscious, but it is probably more valid within the humanistic orientation.

Man has choice

There is no desire here to resume the hoary debate regarding free will versus determinism. Phenomenologically, choice is a given of experience. When man is aware, he is aware that his choices make a difference in the flow of his awareness, that he is not a bystander but a participant in experience. From this fact flows man's potential to transcend his creatureliness (Fromm, 1959). Also from this postulation we derive man's capability of change.

Man is intentional

In his experience, man demonstrates his intent. This does not mean "striving," but it does mean orientation. Man intends through having purpose, through valuing, and through creating and recognizing meaning. Man's intentionality is the basis on which he builds his identify, and it distinguishes him from other species.

The characteristics of man's intentionality need to be specified. Man intends both conservation and change. Mechanistic views of man frequently deal only with drive-reduction and homeostatic conceptions. Humanistic psychology recognizes that man seeks rest but concurrently seeks variety and disequilibrium. Thus we may say that man intends multiplely, complexly, and even paradoxically.

The Orientation of Humanistic Psychology

In the following statements we will specify some of the characteristics of the humanistic orientation in psychology, trying to articulate and identify those characteristics which are distinguishing of this point of view.

Humanistic psychology cares about man

Humanistic psychology disavows the sort of scientific detachment pretended to or achieved at great cost by other orientations. Humanistic psychology recognizes that man cannot help but be invested in his study of his own condition. Accepting this as a given, humanistic psychology is founded on man's concern about man and is an expression of that concern.

Humanistic psychology values meaning more than procedure

Although humanistic psychology must find its own methods and must validate those methods as providing dependable knowledge about the human condition, humanistic psychology would be untrue to itself were it to become preoccupied with methodology to the loss of concern with meaningful issues in the human condition.

Humanistic psychology looks for human rather than nonhuman validations

It seems to be a basic tenet of the humanistic position that only that validation which is borne out by human experience can ultimately be counted upon. Humanistic psychology does not disavow the use of statistical methods or of experimental tests. However, it does insist that these are but means and that the ultimate criterion must be that of human experience.

Humanistic psychology accepts the relativism of all knowledge

Humanistic psychology postulates a universe of infinite possibility. Thus it recognizes that all knowledge is relative and subject to change. This tenet does much to free humanistic psychology to use the imaginative and creative potential of its orientation.

Humanistic psychology relies heavily upon the phenomenological orientation

What has been said above about the importance of meaning and about human validation will have indicated the centrality of the phenomenological orientation to the humanistic approach. This is not to deny the merits of other orientations but to insist that the ultimate focus of our concern is in the experience of the human being.

Humanistic psychology does not deny the contributions of other views, but tries to supplement them and give them a setting within a broader conception of the human experience

Let me make a few concluding remarks and then I will welcome your discussion. I have tried to give one man's view of what I think is a tremendously exciting development in our field of psychology. If I see it correctly, we are leaving the state of preoccupation with part-functions and getting back to what psychology seemed to us to mean when we first entered the field. We are returning to what psychology still seems to mean to the average, intelligent layman—that is, the functioning and experience of a whole human being. I have chosen to make my statements in somewhat dogmatic fashion, hoping that you will join me in discussion, hoping that this will prove stimulating to your thinking and observation. I am sure I am not right in all details; I sincerely hope that I do correctly assess the general trend.

This is a bare initial statement for our third force in psychology. We will need much thought, much imagination, much discussion and argument, much creativity—in short, much of being human to bring our perspective to the place it must have as an affirmation of man's respect for man.

References

Bugental, J. F. T. Precognitions of a Fossil, *Journal of Humanistic Psychology,* Vol. 2 (1962), No. 2, pp. 38-46.
_____. Humanistic Psychology: A New Break-Through, *American Psychologist,* Vol. 18 (1963), pp. 563-567.

Buhler, Charlotte. *Values in Psychotherapy.* New York: Free Press of Glencoe, 1962.

Cantril, H. Toward a Humanistic Psychology, *Etc.,* Vol. 12 (1955), pp. 278-298.
_____, and Bumstead, C. H. *Reflections on the Human Venture.* New York: New York University Press, 1960.

Cohen, J. *Humanistic Psychology.* New York: Collier, 1962.

Fingarette, H. *The Self in Transformation.* New York: Basic Books, 1963.

Fromm, E. Value, Psychology, and Human Existence, in A. H. Maslow (ed.), *New Knowledge in Human Values.* New York: Harper, 1959; pp. 151-164.

Hull, C. L. *Principles of Behavior,* New York: Appleton-Century, 1943; p. 27.

Maslow, A. H. Toward a Humanistic Psychology, *Etc.,* Vol. 13 (1956), pp. 10-22.
_____. *Toward a Psychology of Being.* Princeton, N.J.: Van Nostrand, 1962.

May, R. *Existential Psychology.* New York: Random House, 1961.

Rogers, C. R. *On Becoming a Person.* Boston: Houghton Mifflin, 1961.
_____. Toward a Science of the Person, *Journal of Humanistic Psychology,* Vol. 3 (1963), No. 2.

Sutich, A. American Association for Humanistic Psychology: Progress Report. Palo Alto, California, November 1, 1962; mimeographed.

Watts, A. *Psychotherapy East and West.* New York: Pantheon, 1961.

SELF TEST: MEASURING COMPREHENSION

"The Third Force In Psychology", By J. F. T. Bugental

1. What does Bugental mean when he states that "Psychology is at last becoming the study of man"?

2. Bugental states that man is intentional and his behavior is motivated to both conservation (staying the same) and change. Examine your own life. In what ways are you conserving? In what ways are you changing?

3. Describe the general orientation of humanism, indicating that you have a personal understanding of what it is.

4. How does the overall orientation of the humanistic perspective differ from that of the learning perspective?

PLIGHT OF THE IK AND KAIADILT IS SEEN AS A CHILLING POSSIBLE END FOR MAN

from *Smithsonian Magazine*
John B. Calhoun

In June of 1979, 18 year old Renee Katz, a gifted flutist, was maliciously, and without provocation or motive, pushed in front of a moving New York City subway train. Her hand was severed in the incident, but has since been miraculously reattached. A man charged with the crime was acquitted in January of 1980. Unfortunately, such cases of wanton violence seem to be occurring more frequently in American society. Whenever we hear of events such as this, we puzzle over what could possibly motivate such cruel, heinous behavior. Perhaps an examination of the nature of contemporary American society can provide us with an answer.

Humanistic psychologists have stressed that man needs to perceive purpose, significance, and meaning in his existence in order to be well adjusted and fulfilled as a human being. Abraham Maslow considered the opportunity to develop one's full potential, be creative and productive, and be engaged in work that is personally meaningful, as crucial for the self-actualization of the individual. Carl Rogers has long maintained that people need to be valued and prized as unique, inherently good individuals in order to develop positive self-concepts.

Neo-Freudian Erik Erikson has added to our understanding of the emotional and adjustment problems of people who have suffered existential crises. Through his research involving American Indians on reservations and disabled war veterans in a rehabilitation hospital, he came to believe that these peoples' problems were related to the fact that they had been uprooted from their normal life style and cut off from what was meaningful in their lives. They had lost the sense of who and what they were. They had been robbed of their sense of identity.

Humanist Rollo May has warned that the human costs of life in a technological, automated, computerized society can be great. While we may benefit materially by living in the technological society, our lives may become emotional and spiritual vacuums. We may feel insignificant, alienated from our fellow man, powerless, lonely, and lost.

What happens to man when he is deprived of those things that make him most human: when he lives under conditions that make self-actualization and the development of a positive self-concept impossible, when he is stripped of his sense of identity, and when he cannot experience a sense of personal significance and purpose because of the impersonal, overcrowded, technological society in which he lives? The unfortunate answer to this question is that man may cease to be human. He may lose the ability to enjoy living. He may lose the capacity to love, share with, and care for others. As opposed to being self-actualized, he becomes self-absorbed. He may learn that he can gain some sense of personal significance through cruelty to others. Certainly this sense of significance is a perverted one, but at least his cruel behavior will receive recognition.

The following article, by John B. Calhoun, describes the pathological conditions that resulted when groups of people were uprooted from their normal environments, stripped of their identity, and forced to live in conditions of debasement and overcrowding. Calhoun indicates that similar pathology results within colonies of mice when they are experimentally subjected to similar conditions. After reading the article you should have a better understanding of the kind of environmental conditions that can lead to senseless, cruel, violence, such as the assault suffered by Renee Katz. The article is a grim prophesy of pathology that may become more common, particularly in our large cities, should conditions of overcrowding, unemployment, dehumanization, and debasement persist.

The Mountain—how pervasive in the history of man. A still small voice on Horeb, mount of God, guided Elijah. There, earlier, Moses standing before God received the Word. And Zion: "I am the Lord your God dwelling in Zion, my holy mountain."

Then there was Atum, mountain, God and first man, one and all together. The mountain rose out of a primordial sea of nothingness—Nun. Atum, the spirit of life, existed within Nun. In creating himself, Atum became the evolving ancestor of the human race. So goes the Egyptian mythology of creation, in which the Judaic Adam has his roots.

And there is a last Atum, united in his youth with another mountain of God, Mt. Morungole in northeasternmost Uganda. His people are the Ik, pronounced eek. They are the subject of an important new book, *The Mountain People,* by Colin M. Turnbull (Simon and Schuster, $6.95). They still speak Middle-Kingdom Egyptian, a language thought to be dead. But perhaps their persistence is not so strange. Egyptian mythology held that the waters of the life-giving Nile had

their origin in Nun. Could this Nun have been the much more extensive Lake Victoria of 10 to 50 millenia ago when, near its borders, man groped upward to cloak his biological self with culture?

Well might the Ik have preserved the essence of this ancient tradition that affirms human beginnings. Isolated as they have been in their jagged mountain fastness, near the upper tributaries of the White Nile, the Ik have been protected from cultural evolution.

What a Shangri-la, this land of the Ik. In its center, the Kidepo valley, 35 miles across, home of abundant game; to the south, mist-topped Mt. Morungole; to the west the Niangea range; to the north, bordering the Sudan, the Didinga range; to the east on the Kenya border, a sheer drop of 2,000 feet into the Turkanaland of cattle herdsmen. Through ages of dawning history few people must have been interested in encroaching on this rugged land. Until 1964 anthropologists knew little of the Ik's existence. Their very name, much less their language, remained a mystery until, quite by chance, anthropologist Colin M.

Turnbull found himself among them. What an opportunity to study pristine man! Here one should encounter the basic qualities of humanity unmarred by war, technology, pollution, over-population.

Turnbull rested in his bright red Land Rover at an 8,000-foot-high pass. A bit beyond this only "navigable" pass into the Kidepo Valley, lay Pirre, a police outpost watching over a cluster of Ik villages. There to welcome him cam Atum of the warm, open smile and gentle voice. Gray-haired at 40, appearing 65, he was the senior elder of the Ik, senior in authority if not quite so in age. Nattily attired in shorts and woolen sweater—in contrast to his mostly naked colleagues—Atum bounced forward with his ebony walking stick, greeted Turnbull in Swahili, and from that moment on took command as best he could of Turnbull's life. At Atum's village a plaintive woman's voice called out. Atum remarked that that was his wife—sick, too weak to work in the fields. Turnbull offered to bring her food and medicine. Atum suggested he handle Turnbull's gifts. As the weeks wore on Atum picked up the parcels that Turnbull was supplying for Atum's wife.

One day Atum's brother-in-law, Lomongin, laughingly asked Turnbull if he didn't know that Atum's wife had been dead for weeks. She had received no food or medicine. Atum had sold it. So she just died. All of this was revealed with no embarrassment. Atum joined the laughter over the joke played on Turnbull.

Another time Atum and Lojieri were guiding Turnbull over the mountains, and at one point induced him to push ahead through high grass until he broke through into a clearing. The clearing was a sheer 1,500-foot drop. The two Iks rolled on the ground, nearly bursting with laughter because Turnbull just managed to catch himself. What a lovable cherub this Atum! His laughter never ended.

New Meaning of Laughter

Laughter, hallmark of mankind, not shared with any other animal, not even primates, was an outstanding trait of the Ik. A whole village rushed to the edge of a low cliff and joined in communal laughter at blind old Lo'ono who lay thrashing on her back, near death after stumbling over. One evening Iks around a fire watched a child as it crawled toward the flames, then writhed back screaming after it grasped a gleaming coal. Laughter erupted. Quiet came to the child as its mother cuddled it in a kind of respect for the merriment it had caused. Then there was the laughter of innocent childhood as boys and girls gathered around a grandfather, too weak to walk, and drummed upon his head with sticks or pelted him with stones until he cried. There was the laughter that binds families tobether: Kimat, shrieking for joy as she dashed off with the mug of tea she had snatched from her dying brother Lomeja's hand an instant after Turnbull had given it to him as a last token of their friendship.

Laughter there had always been. A few old people remembered times, 25 to 30 years ago, when laughter mirrored love and joy and fullness of life, times when beliefs and rituals and traditions kept a bond with the "millions of years" ago when time began for the Ik. That was when their god, Didigwari, let the Ik down from heaven on a vine, one at a time. He gave them the digging stick with the instruction that they could not kill one another. He let down other people. To the Dodos and Turkana he gave cattle and spears to kill with. But the Ik remained true to their instruction and did not kill one another or neighboring tribesmen.

For them the bow, the net and the pitfall were for capturing game. For them the greatest sin was to over-hunt. Mobility and cooperation ever were part of them. Often the netting of game required the collaboration of a whole band of 100 or more, some to hold the net and some to drive game into it. Between the big hunts, bands broke up into smaller groups to spread over their domain, then to gather again. The several bands would each settle for the best part of the year along the edge of the Kidepo Valley in the foothills of Mt. Morungole. There they were once again fully one with the mountain. "The Ik, without their mountains, would no longer be the Ik and similarly, they say, the mountains without the Ik would no longer be the same mountains, if indeed they continued to exist at all."

In this unity of people and place, rituals, traditions, beliefs and values molded and preserved a continuity of life. All rites of passage were marked by ceremony. Of these, the rituals surrounding death gave greatest meaning to life. Folded in a fetal position, the body was buried with favorite possessions, facing the rising sun to mark celestial rebirth. All accompanying rituals of fasting and feasting, of libations of beer sprinkled over the grave, of seeds of favorite foods planted on the grave to draw life from the dust of the dead, showed that death is merely another form of life, and reminded the living of the good things of life and of the good way to live. In so honoring the dead by creating goodness the Ik helped speed the soul, content, on its journey.

Such were the Ik until wildlife conservation intruded into their homeland. Uganda decided to make a national park out of the Kidepo Valley, the main hunting ground of the Ik. What then happened stands as an indictment of the myopia that science can generate. No one looked to the Ik to note that their hunter-gatherer way of life marked the epitome of conservation, that the continuance of their way of life would have added to the success of the park. Instead they were forbidden to hunt any longer in the Kidepo Valley. They were herded to the periphery of the park and encouraged to become farmers on dry mountain slopes so steep as to test the poise of a goat. As an example to more remote villages, a number of villages were brought together in a tight little cluster below the southwest pass into the valley. Here the police post, which formed this settlement of Pirre, could watch over the Ik to see that they didn't revert to hunting.

These events contained two of the three strikes that knocked out the spirit of the Ik. *Strike No. 1:* The shift from a mobile hunter-gatherer way of life to a sedentary farming way of life made irrelevant the Ik's entire repertoire of beliefs, habits and traditions. Their guidelines for life were inappropriate to farming. They seemed to adapt, but at heart they remained hunters and gatherers. Their cultural templates fitted them for that one way of life.

Strike No. 2: They were suddenly crowded together at a density, intimacy and frequency of contact far greater than they had ever before been required to experience. Throughout their long past each band of 100 or so individuals only temporarily coalesced into a whole. The intervening breaking up into smaller groups permitted realignment of relationships that tempered conflicts from earlier associations. But at the resettlement, more than 450 individuals were forced to form a permanent cluster of villages within shouting distance of each other. Suppose the seven million or so inhabitants of Los Angeles County were forced to move and join the more than one million inhabitants of the more arid San Diego County. Then after they arrived all water, land and air communication to the rest of the world was cut off abruptly and completely. These eight million people would then have to seek survival completely on local resources without any communication with others. It would be a test of the ability of human beings to remain human.

Such a test is what Dr. Turnbull's book on the Mountain People is all about. The Ik failed to remain human. I have put mice to the same test and they failed to remain mice. Those of you who have been following *Smithsonian* may recall from the April 1970 and the January 1971 issues something about the projected demise of a mouse population experiencing the same two strikes against it as did the Ik.

Fate Of a Mouse Population

Last summer I spoke in London behind the lectern where Charles Darwin and Alfred Wallace had presented their papers on evolution—which during the next century caused a complete revision of our insight into what life is all about and what man is and may become. In summing up that session of 1858 the president remarked that nothing of importance had been presented before the Linnean Society at that year's meeting! I spoke behind this same lectern to a session of the Royal Society of Medicine during its symposium on "Man in His Place." At the end of my paper, "Death Squared: The Explosive Growth and Demise of a Mouse Population," the chairman admonished me to stick to my mice: the insights I had presented could have no implication for man. Wonderful if the chairman could be correct—but now I have read about the Mountain People, and I have a hollow feeling that perhaps we, too, are close to losing our "mountain."

Turnbull lived for 18 months as a member of the Ik tribe. His identity transfer became so strong that he acquired the Ik laughter. He laughed at seeing Atum suffer as they were completing an extremely arduous journey on foot back across the mountains and the Kidepo Valley from the Sudan. He felt pleasure at seeing Lokwam, local "Lord of the Flies," cry in agony from the beating given him by his two beautiful sisters.

Well, for five years I have identified with my mice, as they lived in their own "Kidepo Valley"—their contrived Utopia where resources are always abundant and all mortality factors except aging eliminated. I watched their population grow rapidly from the first few colonizers. I watched them fill their metal "universe" with organized social groups. I watched them bring up a host of young with loving maternal care and paternal territorial protection—all of these young well educated for mouse society. But then there were too many of these young mice, ready to become involved in all that mice can become, with nowhere to go, no physical escape from their closed environment, no opportunity to gain a niche where they could play a meaningful role. They tried, but being younger and less experienced they were nearly always rejected.

Rejecting so many of these probing youngsters overtaxed the territorial males. So de-

fense then fell to lactating females. They became aggressive. They turned against their own young and ejected them before normal weaning and before adequate social bonds between mother and young had developed. During this time of social tension, rate of growth of the population was only one third of that during the earlier, more favorable phase.

Strike No. 1 against these mice: They lost the opportunity to express the capacities developed by older mice born during the rapid population growth. After a while they became so rejected that they were treated as so many sticks and stones by their still relatively well-adjusted elders. These rejected mice withdrew, physically and psychologically, to live packed tightly together in large pools. Amongst themselves they became vicious, lashing out and biting each other now and then with hardly any provocation.

Strike No. 2 against the mice: They reached great numbers despite reduced conceptions and increased deaths of newborn young resulting from the dissolution of maternal care. Many had early been rejected by their mothers and knew little about social bonds. Often their later attempts at interaction were interrupted by some other mouse intervening unintentionally as it passed between two potential actors.

I came to call such mice the "Beautiful Ones." They never learned such effective social interactions as courtship, mating and aggressive defense of territory. Never copulating, never fighting, they were unstressed and essentially unaware of their associates. They spent their time grooming themselves, eating and sleeping, totally individualistic, totally isolated socially except for a peculiar acquired need for simple proximity to others. This produced what I have called the "behavioral sink," the continual accentuation of aggregations to the point that much available space was unused despite a population increase to nearly 15 times the optimum.

All true "mousity" was lost. Though physically they still appeared to be mice, they had no essential capacities for survival and continuation of mouse society. Suddenly, population growth ceased. In what seemed an instant they passed over a threshold beyond which there was no likelihood of their ever recouping the capacity to become real mice again. No more young were born. From a peak population of 2,200 mice nearly three years ago, aging has gradually taken its toll until now there are only 46 sluggish near-cadavers comparable to people more than 100 years old.

It was just such a fading universe Colin Turnbull found in 1961. Just before he arrived, *Strike No. 3* had set in: starvation. Any such crisis could have added the coup de grace after the other two strikes. Normally the Ik could count on only making three crops every four years. At this time a two-year drought set in and destroyed almost all crops. Neighboring tribes survived with their cultures intact. Turkana herdsmen, facing starvation and death, kept their societies in contact with each other and continued to sing songs of praise to God for the goodness of life.

By the beginning of the long drought, "goodness" to the Ik simply meant to have food—to have food for one's self alone. Collaborative hunts were a thing of the past, long since stopped by the police and probably no longer possible as a social effort, anyway. Solitary hunting, now designated as poaching, became a necessity for sheer survival. But the solitary hunter took every precaution not to let others know of his success. He would gorge himself far off in the bush and bring the surplus back to sell to the police, who were not above profiting from this traffic. Withholding food from wife, children and aging parents became an accomplishment to brag and laugh about. It became a way of life, continuing after the government began providing famine relief. Those strong enough to go to the police station to get rations for themselves and their families would stop halfway home and gorge all the food, even though it caused them to vomit.

Village of Mutual Hatred

The village reflected this reversal of hu-

manity. Instead of open courtyards around each group of huts within the large compound, there was a maze of walls and tunnels booby trapped with spears to ward off intrusion by neighbors.

In Atum's village a whole band of more than 100 individuals was crowded together in mutual hostility and aloneness. They would gather at their sitting place and sit for hours in a kind of suspended animation, not looking directly at each other, yet scanning slowly all others who might be engaged in some solitary task, watching for someone to make a mistake that would elicit the symbolic violence of laughter and derision. They resembled my pools of rejected withdrawn mice. Homemaking deteriorated, feces littered doorsteps and courtyard. Universal adultery and incest replaced the old taboo. The beaded virgins' aprons of eight-to-twelve-year-old girls became symbols that these were proficient whores accustomed to selling their wares to passing herdsmen.

One ray of humanity left in this cesspool was 12-year-old, retarded Adupa. Because she believed that food was for sharing and savoring, her playmates beat her. She still believed that parents were for loving and to be loved by. They cured her madness by locking her in her hut until she died and decayed.

The six other villages were smaller and their people could retain a few glimmers of the goodness and fullness of life. There was Kuaur, devoted to Turnbull, hiking four days to deliver mail, taunted for bringing food home to share with his wife and child. There was Losike, the potter, regarded as a witch. She offered water to visitors and made pots for others. When the famine got so bad that there was no need for pots to cook in, her husband left her. She was no longer bringing in any income. And then there was old Nangoli, still capable of mourning when her husband died. She went with her family and village across Kidepo and into the Sudan where their village life turned for a while back to normality. But it was not normal enough to keep them. Back to Pirre, to death, they returned.

All goodness was gone from the Ik, leaving merely emptiness, valuelessness, nothingness, the chaos of Nun. They reentered the womb of beginning time from which there is no return. Urination beside the partial graves of the dead marked the death of God, the final fading of Mount Morungole.

My poor words give only a shadowy image of the cold coffin of Ik humanity that Turnbull describes. His two years with the Ik left him in a slough of despondency from which he only extricated himself with difficulty, never wanting to see them again. Time and distance brought him comfort. He did return for a brief visit some months later. Rain had come in abundance. Gardens had sprung up untended from hidden seeds in the earth. Each Ik gleaned only for his immediate needs. Granaries stood empty, not refilled for inevitable scarcities ahead. The future had ceased to exist. Individual and social decay continued on its downward spiral. Sadly Turnbull departed again from this land of lost hope and faith.

Last summer in London I knew nothing about the Ik when I was so publicly and thoroughly chastised for having the temerity to suspect that the behavioral and spiritual death my mice had exhibited might also befall man. But a psychiatrist in the audience arose in defense of my suspicion. Dr. Geoffrey N. Bianchi remarked that an isolated tribe of Australian Aborigines mirrored the changes and kinds of pathology I had seen among mice. I did not know that Dr. Bianchi was a member of the team that had studied these people, the Kaiadilt, and that a book about them was in preparation, *Cruel, Poor and Brutal Nations* by John Cawte (The University Press of Hawaii). In galley proof I have read about the Kaiadilt and find it so shattering to my faith in humanity that I now sometimes wish I had never heard of it. Yet there is some glimmer of hope that the Kaiadilt may recover—not what they were but possibly some new life.

A frail, tenacious people, the Kaiadilt never numbered more than 150 souls where they lived on Bentinck Island in the Gulf of Carpentaria. So isolated were they that not even their nearest Aboriginal neighbors, 20 miles away, had any knowledge of their existence until in this century; so isolated were the Kaiadilt from their nearest neighbors that they differ from them in such heredity markers as blood type and fingerprints. Not until the early years of this century did an occasional visitor from the Queensland Government even note their existence.

For all practical purposes the first real contact the Kaiadilt had with Western "culture" came in 1916 when a man by the name of McKenzie came to Bentinck with a group of male mainland Aborigines to try to establish a lime kiln. McKenzie's favorite sport was to ride about shooting Kaiadilt. His helpers' sport was to commandeer as many women as they could, and take them to their headquarters on a neighboring island. In 1948 a tidal wave poisoned most of the fresh-water sources. Small groups of Kaiadilt were rounded up and transported to larger Mornington Island where they were placed under the supervision of a Presbyterian mission. They were crowded into a dense cluster settlement just as the Ik had been at Pirre.

Here they still existed when the psychiatric field team came into their midst 15 years later. They were much like the Ik: dissolution of family life, total valuelessness, apathy. I could find no mention of laughter, normal or pathological. Perhaps the Kaiadilt didn't laugh. They had essentially ceased the singing that had been so much a part of their traditional way.

The spiritual decay of the Kaiadilt was marked by withdrawal, depression, suicide and tendency to engage in such self-mutilation as ripping out one's testes or chopping off one's nose. In their passiveness some of the anxiety ridden children are accepting the new mold of life forced upon them by a benevolent culture they do not understand. Survival with a new mold totally obliterating all past seems their only hope.

So the lesson comes clear, and Colin Turnbull sums it up in the final paragraph of his book: "The Ik teach us that our much vaunted human values are not inherent in humanity at all, but are associated only with a particular form of survival called society, and that all, even society itself, are luxuries that can be dispensed with. That does not make them any the less wonderful or desirable, and if man has any greatness it is surely in his ability to maintain these values, clinging to them to an often very bitter end, even shortening an already pitifully short life rather than sacrifice his humanity. But that too involves choice, and the Ik teaches us that man can lose the will to make it."

Blind Lo'ono almost died in a fall on the mountain, to the glee of Ik neighbors. They abandoned her.

SELF TEST: MEASURING COMPREHENSION

"Plight of the Ik and Kaiadilt is seen as a chilling possible end for Man", By John B. Calhoun

1. List some examples of the pathological humor of the Ik.

2. Describe the cultural, religious, and occupational identity of the Ik prior to their uprooting.

3. What were the "Three Strikes" suffered by the Ik that made them cease to be human?

4. Describe the similarities between the behavior of the Ik following their uprooting and Dr. Calhoun's mice.

5. In contemporary American society, what kind of environmental conditions could influence a person to push an innocent girl in front of a subway train?

SOME HYPOTHESES REGARDING THE FACILITATION OF PERSONAL GROWTH
from *On Becoming a Person*
Carl Rogers

Carl Rogers has been a prominent spokesman of the humanistic perspective since its beginning. Rogers refers to his particular type of psychotherapy as client-centered therapy. The very title indicates the essence of his therapy. Unlike the doctor-patient terminology used by the illness, behavioristic, and psychoanalytic perspectives, Rogers views the person with whom he is involved in therapy as his client. In much the same way that a person in need of legal assitance becomes the client of a lawyer, a person in need of psychological help enters therapy with Rogers and becomes his client.

Rogers feels that the success of therapy depends upon the therapeutic atmosphere he creates and the relationship he develops with his client. Under proper conditions Rogers feels that the relationship between the client and therapist can be used by the client to enhance his personality growth. In the following selection from *On Becoming a Person*, Rogers describes the conditions under which maximum beneficial therapeutic change can occur.

As you read the article you may get the impression that Rogers is overly optimistic. Some consider his naive. However, optimism is a key characteristic of the true humanist.

To be faced by a troubled, conflicted person who is seeking and expecting help, has always constituted a great challenge to me. Do I have the knowledge, the resources, the psychological strength, the skill—do I have whatever it takes to be of help to such an individual?

For more than twenty-five years I have been trying to meet this kind of challenge. It has caused me to draw upon every element of my professional background: the rigorous methods of personality measurement which I first learned at Teachers' College, Columbia; the Freudian psychoanalytic insights and methods of the Institute for Child Guidance where I worked as interne; the continuing developments in the field of clinical psychology, with which I have been closely associated; the briefer exposure to the work of Otto Rank, to the methods of psychiatric social work, and other resources too numerous to mention. But most of all it has meant a continual learning from my own experience and that of my colleagues at the Counseling Center as we have endeavored to discover for ourselves effective means of working with people in distress. Gradually I have developed a way of working which grows out of that experience, and which can be tested, refined, and reshaped by further experience and by research.

A General Hypothesis

One brief way of describing the change which has taken place in me is to say that in my early professional years I was asking the question, How can I treat, or cure, or change this person? Now I would phrase the question in this way: How can I provide a relationship which this person may use for his own personal growth?

It is as I have come to put the question in this second way that I realize that whatever I have learned is applicable to all of my human relationships, not just to working with clients with problems. It is for this reason that I feel it is possible that the learnings which have had meaning for me in my experience may have some meaning for you in your experience, since all of us are involved in human relationships.

Perhaps I should start with a negative learning. It has gradually been driven home to me that I cannot be of help to this troubled person by means of any intellectual or training procedure. No approach which relies upon knowledge, upon training, upon the acceptance of something that is *taught,* is of any use. These approaches seem so tempting and direct that I have, in the past, tried a great many of them. It is possible to explain a person to himself, to prescribe steps which should lead him forward, to train him in knowledge about a more satisfying mode of life. But such methods are, in my experience, futile and inconsequential. The most they can accomplish is some temporary change, which soon disappears, leaving the individual more than every convinced of his inadequacy.

The failure of any such approach through the intellect has forced me to recognize that change appears to come about through experience in a relationship. So I am going to try to state very briefly and informally, some of the essential hypotheses regarding a helping relationship which have seemed to gain in-creasing confirmation both from experience and research.

I can state the overall hypothesis in one sentence, as follows. If I can provide a certain type of relationship, the other person will discover within himself the capacity to use that relationship for growth, and change and personal development will occur.

The Relationship

But what meaning do these terms have? Let me take separately the three major phrases in this sentence and indicate something of the meaning they have for me. What is this certain type of relationship I would like to provide?

I have found that the more that I can be genuine in the relationship, the more helpful it will be. This means that I need to be aware of my own feelings, in so far as possible, rather than presenting an outward facade of one attitude, while actually holding another attitude at a deeper or unconscious level. Being genuine also involves the willingness to be and to express, in my words and my behavior, the various feelings and attitudes which exist in me. It is only in this way that the relationship can have *reality,* and reality seems deeply important as a first condition. It is only by providing the genuine reality which is in me, that the other person can successfully seek for the reality in him. I have found this to be true even when the attitudes I feel are not attitudes with which I am pleased, or attitudes which seem conducive to a good relationship. It seems extremely important to be *real.*

As a second condition, I find that the more acceptance and liking I feel toward this individual, the more I will be creating a relationship which he can use. By acceptance I mean a warm regard for him as a person of unconditional self-worth—of value no matter what his condition, his behavior, or his feelings. It means a respect and liking for him as a separate person, a willingness for him to possess his own feelings in his own way. It means an acceptance of and regard for his attitudes of the moment, no matter how negative or positive, no matter how much they may contradict other attitudes he has held in the past. This acceptance of each fluctuating aspect of this other person makes it for him a relationship of warmth and safety, and the safety of being liked and prized as a person seems a highly important element in a helping relationship.

I also find that the relationship is significant to the extent that I feel a continuing desire to understand—a sensitive empathy with each of the client's feelings and communications as they seem to him at that moment. Acceptance does not mean much until it involves understanding. It is only as I *understand* the feelings and thoughts which seem so horrible to you, or so weak, or so sentimental, or so bizarre—it is only as I see them as you see them, and accept them and you, that you feel really free to explore all the hidden nooks and frightening crannies of your inner and often buried experience. This *freedom* is an important condition of the relationship. There is implied here a freedom to explore oneself at both conscious and unconscious levels, as rapidly as one can dare to embark on this dangerous quest. There is also a complete freedom from any type of moral or diagnostic evaluation, since all such evaluations are, I believe, always threatening.

Thus the relationship which I have found helpful is characterized by a sort of transparency on my part, in which my real feelings are evident; by an acceptance of this other person as a separate person with value in his own right; and by a deep empathic understanding which enables me to see his private world through his eyes. When these conditions are achieved, I become a companion to my client, accompanying him in the frightening search for himself, which he now feels free to undertake.

I am by no means always able to achieve this kind of relationship with another, and sometimes, even when I feel I have achieved it in myself, he may be too frightened to perceive what is being offered to him. But I would say that when I hold in myself the kind of attitudes I have described, and when the other person can to some degree experience these attitudes, then I believe that change and constructive personal development will *invariably* occur—and I include the word "invariably" only after long and careful consideration.

The Motivation For Change

So much for the relationship. The second phrase in my overall hypothesis was that the individual will discover within himself the capacity to use this relationship for growth. I will try to indicate something of the meaning which that phrase has for me. Gradually my experience has forced me to conclude that the individual has within himself the capacity and the tendency, latent if not evident, to move forward toward maturity. In a suitable psychological climate this tendency is released, and becomes actual rather than potential. It is evident in the capacity of the individual to understand those aspects of his life and of himself which are causing him pain and dissatisfaction, an understanding which probes beneath his conscious knowledge of himself into those experiences which he has hidden from himself because of their threatening nature. It shows itself in the tendency to reorganize his personality and his relationship to life in ways which are regarded as more mature. Whether one calls it a growth tendency, a drive toward self-actualization, or a forward-moving directional tendency, it is the mainspring of life, and is, in the last analysis, the tendency upon which all psychotherapy depends. It is the urge which is evident in all organic and human life—to expand, extend, become autonomous, develop, mature—the tendency to express and activate all the capacities of the organism, to the extent that such activation enhances the organism or the self. This tendency may become deeply buried under layer after layer of encrusted psychological defenses; it may be hidden behind elaborate facades which deny its existence; but it is my belief that it exists in every individual, and awaits only the proper conditions to be released and expressed.

The Outcomes

I have attempted to describe the relationship which is basic to constructive personality change. I have tried to put into works the type of capacity which the individual brings to such a relationship. The third phrase of my general statement was that change and personal development would occur. It is my hopothesis that in such a relationship the individual will reorganize himself at both the conscious and deeper levels of his personality in such a manner as to cope with life more constructively, more intelligently, and in a more socialized as well as a more satisfying way.

Here I can depart from speculation and bring in the steadily increasing body of solid knowledge which is accumulating. We know now that individuals who live in such a relationship even for a relatively limited number of hours show profound and significant changes in personality, attitudes, and behavior, changes that do not occur in matched control groups. In such a relationship the individual becomes more integrated, more effective. He shows fewer of the characteristics which are usually termed neurotic or psychotic, and more of the characteristics of the healthy, well-functioning person. He changes his perception of himself, becoming more realistic in his views of self. He becomes more like the person he wishes to be. He values himself more highly. He is more self-confident and self-directing. He has a better understanding of himself, becomes more open to his experience, denies or represses less of his experience. He becomes more accepting in his attitudes toward others, seeing others as more similar to himself.

In his behavior he shows similar changes. He is less frustrated by stress, and recovers from stress more quickly. He becomes more mature in his everyday behavior as this is observed by friends. He is less defensive, more adaptive, more able to meet situations creatively.

These are some of the changes which we now know come about in individuals who have completed a series of counseling interviews in which the psychological atmosphere approximates the relationship I described. Each of the statements made is based upon objective evidence. Much more research needs to be done, but there can no longer be any doubt as to the effectiveness of such a relationship in producing personality change.

A Broad Hypothesis of Human Relationships

To me, the exciting thing about these research findings is not simply the fact that they give evidence of the efficacy of one form of psychotherapy, though that is by no means unimportant. The excitement comes from the fact that these findings justify an even broader hypothesis regarding all human relationships. There seems every reason to suppose that the therapeutic relationship is only one instance of interpersonal relations, and that the same lawfulness governs all such relationships. Thus it seems reasonable to hypothesize that if the parent creates with his child a psychological climate such as we have described, then the child will become more self-directing, socialized, and mature. To the extent that the teacher creates such a relationship with his class, the student will become a self-initiated learner, more original, more self-disciplined, less anxious and other-directed. If the administrator, or military or industrial leader, creates such a climate within his organization, then his staff will become more self-responsible, more creative, better able to adapt to new problems, more basically cooperative. It appears possible to me that we are seeing the emergence of a new field of human relationships, in which we may specify that if certain attitudinal conditions exist, then certain definable changes will occur.

Conclusion

Let me conclude by returning to a personal statement. I have tried to share with you something of what I have learned in trying to be of help to troubled, unhappy, maladjusted individuals. I have formulated the hypothesis which has gradually come to have meaning for me—not only in my relationship to clients in distress, but in all my human relationships.

I have indicated that such research knowledge as we have supports this hypothesis, but that there is much more investigation needed. I should like now to pull together into one statement the conditions of this general hypothesis, and the effects which are specified.

If I can create a relationship characterized on my part:

> by a genuineness and transparency, in which I am my real feelings:
>
> by a warm acceptance of and prizing of the other person as a separate individual;
>
> by a sensitive ability to see his world and himself as he sees them;

Then the other individual in the relationship:

> will experience and understand aspects of himself which previously he has repressed;
>
> will find himself becoming better integrated, more able to function effectively;
>
> will become more similar to the person he would like to be;
>
> will be more self-directing and self-confident;
>
> will become more of a person, more unique and more self-expressive;
>
> will be more understanding, more acceptant of others;
>
> will be able to cope with the problems of life more adequately and more comfortably.

I believe that this statement holds whether I am speaking of my relationship with a client, with a group of students or staff members, with my family or children. It seems to me that we have here a general hypothesis which offers exciting possibilities for the development of creative, adaptive, autonomous persons.

SELF TEST: MEASURING COMPREHENSION

"Some Hypotheses Regarding the Facilitation of Personal Growth" By Carl Rogers

1. What are the specific elements of the client-therapist relationship that Rogers feels are important for successful therapy?

2. Rogers feels that if he can create the proper therapeutic atmosphere the client will be better able to move toward maturity. What does he feel are the characteristics of the mature individual?

3. What specific changes occur in clients as the result of successful Rogerian therapy?

4. What evidence of psychoanalytic influence can you find in the writing of Rogers?

Chapter 8
THE SOCIAL PERSPECTIVE

The final perspective we will cover is the social perspective. Unlike the other perspectives, which had their roots in either psychology or medicine, the beginnings of the social perspective can be traced to sociology. Two of the perspective's dominant spokesmen, Erving Goffman and Thomas J. Scheff, are primarily sociologists. A basic premise of the social perspective is that abnormality is the result of complex social factors, and not the result of medical or strictly psychological etiologies, as proposed by other perspectives.

During the past two decades an antipsychiatry movement has begun. While the social perspective and the antipsychiatry movement are not synonymous, they are similar in that both are extremely critical of conventional psychiatry, and the illness perspective in particular. Psychiatrist Thomas Szasz has long been critical of the term mental illness as it is used by the mental health profession. He points out that since there is little evidence to indicate organic etiologies in "mental illness", the employment of the concept of illness is inappropriate in the description of behavioral abnormality. Rather than saying that a person is "mentally ill", it would be more accurate to say that the person is having "problems in living" (Szasz, 1960). Erving Goffman has also condemned the notion of viewing emotional problems in the same way we view medical ones (Brown, 1973, p. 5).

Another major cirticism of conventional psychiatry made by the social perspective involves the imprecise, inconsistent and ambiguous classification system employed in making clinical diagnoses. In physical medicine, if a person has nasal congestion, a sore throat, and a cough, the diagnosis is obvious—the person has a cold. However, accurate diagnoses are more difficult to obtain when dealing with psychiatric disorders. It may be understandable if two clinicians differed in their diagnosis of a patient's condition as either phobic neurosis or anxiety neurosis. However, Maurice Temerlin (1968) has shown that the problem of accurate and consistent psychiatric diagnosis is indeed a very serious problem. Temerlin showed a group of 95 clinicians a recorded interview of a professional actor portraying the part of a perfectly normal, healthy, man. The clinicians were 25 psychiatrists, 25 clinical psychologists, and 45 graduate students in clinical psychology. Before the subjects witnessed the interview, a professional person of high prestige, a confederate in the study, told the group that the individual to be diagnosed was "a very interesting man because he looked quite neurotic but was actually quite psychotic."

Although the man in the film behaved normally, Temerlin found that 27 of the clinicians diagnosed him as psychotic, 60 as neurotic, and only 8 as mentally healthy. Even more astounding was that the psychiatrists were the least accurate in their diagnoses, and the graduate students most accurate. Apparently, if mental illness exists, clinicians are quite confused about its diagnosis. At times, my personal observations tend to verify Temerlin's observations.

Psychiatrist E. Fuller Torrey, one of his own profession's most vicious critics, has stated:

> "Psychiatry is an emperor standing naked in his new clothes. It has worked
> and striven for 70 years to become an emperor, a full brother with the

other medical specialities. And now it stands there resplendent in its finery. But it does not have any clothes on; and even worse, nobody has told it so" (Torrey, 1974, preface).

The social perspective has assumed the responsibility for informing the psychiatric profession that "it does not have any clothes on". However, the role of the social perspective is not merely one of a tattletale. It has offered concrete suggestions to the psychiatric profession and provided realistic alternatives to the long term institutionalization of mental patients. It has also provided us with a better understanding of the role that social factors play in determining abnormality.

To begin the chapter on the social perspective, I will present a Penthouse interview of Dr. Thomas Szasz, previously described as critic of conventional psychiatry. The second article is Thomas J Scheff's "Schizophrenia as Ideology". The selection articulates Scheff's contention that a diagnosis of schizophrenia is likely to result when an individual consistently violates subtle, unwritten codes of societal conduct. The third article, "The Art of Being Schizophrenic", by Jay Haley, investigates complex social factors that operate in families and contribute to the likelihood of an individual's becoming schizophrenic. The final article is entitled "The Principle of Normalization and Its Implications to Psychiatric Services". It was written by Wolf Wolfensberger. The article describes the principle of normalization as it relates to the deinstitutionalization movement now progressing in America.

References

Phil Brown, editor, *Radical Psychology*, (New York: Harper and Row, 1973).

Thomas Szasz, The Myth of Mental Illness. *American Psychologist.* 1960, 15, 113-118.

Maurice K. Temerlin, Suggestion Effects in Psychiatric Diagnosis. *The Journal of Nervous and Mental Disease.* (Baltimore, the Williams and Wilkens Company, 1968).

E. Fuller Torrey, *The Death of Psychiatry.* (Radnor, Pennsylvania, Chilton Book Company, 1974).

AN INTERVIEW WITH DR. THOMAS SZASZ
from *Penthouse Magazine*
Richard Ballad

The following interview of psychiatrist Thomas Szasz appeared in the October 1973 edition of Penthouse magazine. It was conducted by Richard Ballad.

In the introduction to this chapter, I referred to an antipsychiatry movement that has emerged in this country during the past two decades. Although Szasz is commonly associated with this movement, he denies that he is against all psychiatry. His major complaints are against psychiatric treatment forced upon individuals, and a psychiatric vocabulary that protrays personal problems (mental illness) as disease, prisons as mental "hospitals", and conversation (psychotherapy) as treatment.

In the interview Szasz makes some poignant remarks concerning the symbiotic, or mutually beneficial, relationship between the medical profession and the government. Other issues discussed include confidentiality in psychiatry, individual rights to psychiatric treatment, and responsibility for criminal acts committed while temporarily insane.

The comments of Szasz clarify some of the major reasons why a significant number of mental health professionals have become so disenchanted with conventional psychiatry that a new perspective, the social perspective, has emerged.

Dr. Thomas Szasz sent shock and rage through the psychiatric fraternity in 1961 with his book *The Myth of Mental Illness*. He has remained the most stinging gadfly of his profession. He acknowledges brain disease, brain damage, brain defects, but not *mental* illness. "Disease," he says, "cannot be cured by conversation." What so many doctors call mental disease, Szasz calls human conflict expressed in ways society can't live with. He has become this country's leading spokesman for the newest trend in behavioral science— the belief that science belongs on the side of the people it studies, rather than aligning itself with a society that wants to control differentness. Szasz is opposed to all involuntary hospitalization, and he has wakened America's conscience to many "crimes" committed in the name of "mental health," from abuses in private practice to our system of criminal justice.

Within a year after *The Myth of Mental Illness* appeared, the New York State Commissioner of Mental Hygiene called for Szasz's resignation as a professor at the state university's Upstate Medical Center at Syracuse a position Szasz has held since 1956. After great turmoil, including the resignation of the chairman of the department of psychiatry, the rebellious Szasz emerged secure in his job. He is still there.

Yesterday's shock artist is today's authority. Many of Szasz's aphorisms have become slogans for Young Turks in medicine who stand with the patient rather than the hospitals and the jails. The following are excerpts from his book *The Second Sin,* published in 1973:

- "If a man says he is talking to God we say he is praying. If he says God is talking to him we say he is a schizophrenic."
- "Treating addiction to heroin with methadone is like treating addiction to Scotch with bourbon."
- "Mental hospitals are the POW camps of our undeclared and unarticulated civil wars."

Szasz pours them out, and they inspire retaliation. The late Dr. Manfred Guttmacher, a distinguished forensic psychiatrist, wrote: "A bird that fouls its nest courts criticism. Dr. Szasz doubtless enjoys the contentions he is creating."

Dr. Guttmacher was right: Szasz gets a huge kick out of twisting tails. He criticized Dr. Bernard Diamond, chief psychiatrist for Sirhan B. Sirhan, who assassinated Robert F. Kennedy. He ridiculed the idea of Sirhan's being portrayed as unaware of what he'd done because he was presumably insane at the time. Dr. Diamond, in turn, called some of Szasz's ideas on psychiatry and the law "irresponsible, reprehensible, and dangerous."

But now Szasz has many defenders. Some have joined the American Association for the Abolition of Involuntary Mental Hospitalization, of which Szasz is co-founder and chairman of the board. The American Humanist Association named him the 1973 Humanist of the Year. Far-out admirers have talked of forming "The Insane Liberation Front" in his honor.

Szasz was born in Hungary in an upper-middle-class Jewish family. His father had a law degree and was overseer of several estates. In 1938, young Szasz came to the U.S. to avoid the impending Nazi take-over. He was an honors graduate of the University of Cincinnati in 1941, with a major in physics, and three years later he was graduated at the top of his class from that university's medical school. He interned at Boston City Hospital, took his residence in psychiatry at the University of Chicago Clinics, and his analytic training at the Chicago Institute for Psychoanalysis. He has maintained a private psychiatric practice since that time.

Dr. Szasz has written more than two hundred articles and eight books and has recently edited an anthology called *The Age of Madness* (1973).

Some of his better-known works are *Psychiatric Justice* (1965), *The Ethics of Psychoanalysis* (1965), *The Manufacture of Madness* (1970) and *Idealogy and Insanity* (1970).

Penthouse: What do psychiatrists do when they are said to be treating mental illness?

Szasz: In my view, when psychiatrists "treat" so-called mental illness, they actually intervene, in one way or another, in a conflict. Now, in the face of a conflict, there are three alternatives: you side with one party, side with the other, or try to remain neutral and act as an arbitrator or judge. Psychiatric interventions—which is the term I prefer to "psychiatric treatments"—are actually a confused and confusing mixture of these three kinds of social actions.

Penthouse: Give us some examples.

Szasz: Let's first take the case of a person who goes of his own accord to a private psychiatrist—say, someone like Dr. Daniel Ellsberg. Such a person hires the psychiatrist to help him with whatever he, the so-called patient, considers to be his problem, and to help him deal with it the way he, the client, wants to deal with it. Such a person is likely to have secrets—from his wife, his employer, the government—which he may share with his psychiatrist, but which the psychiatrist is expected to keep confidential. In Ellsberg's case, for example, the psychiatrist may have come into the possession of information which the U.S. government wanted to have. In short, in the conflict between Ellsberg and the American government, Ellsberg's psychiatrist acted as an agent of his client—protecting his client's interests, even where these might have been in conflict with the interests of the government.

Penthouse: But, isn't this an exceptional case?

Szasz: Only insofar as government agents burglarized the psychiatrist's office—which, I assume, is not yet common practice. For the principle it illustrates, however, it is not unusual at all; it is typical. In the less sensational case, the patient may confide secrets to the therapist that have to do with his conflicts with his wife, or a wife may confide her conflicts with her husband; the therapist will then be acting for the interests of one marital partner and against those of the other.

Penthouse: Give us some examples of other things psychiatrists do.

Szasz: In my first example, the psychiatrist did something *for* the patient. In the case of the husband and wife—which is economically and statistically more important than the first—the psychiatrist does something *to* the patient: for example, a husband contacts a psychiatrist, tells him that his wife has delusions or is depressed, and the psychiatrist then commits the wife to a mental hospital. The wife, the ostensible patient, does not want to be in the hospital; she wants to be left alone. Here then, the psychiatrist acts not as the patient's agent, but as his or her adversary. Finally, when a psychiatrist is hired and paid to "evaluate" individuals—for example, for a court, a draft board, the Peace Corps, an insurance company, and so forth—he acts as an arbitrator or judge. He is, in principle, neither the patient's agent nor his adversary; he is the agent of whoever hires him and pays him—assuming that he does his job honestly.

Penthouse: How can people tell what sort of thing a psychiatrist will do; whether he will act for or against what you call the patient's "self-defined interests?"

Szasz: They often can't. That's why I have gone to such great pains, in several books, to try to show that there are a minimum of two very different kinds of psychiatry—voluntary and involuntary, and that the difference is at least as important as the difference between, say, psychotherapy and organic therapy.

Penthouse: Are you opposed to involuntary psychiatry?

Szasz: Indeed I am.

Penthouse: Why?

Szasz: Because I consider all involuntary psychiatric interventions to be punishments. Because I believe that physicians should be healers, not jailers. And because I believe that no one should be punished who did not break the law and who was not duly tried and convicted in court for it.

Penthouse: Not many psychiatrists share your idea that involuntary psychiatry is punishment.

Szasz: Not many psychiatrists. But many writers do. James Thurber described this in *The Unicorn in the Garden.* Of course, the victims of involuntary psychiatry think it's punishment, but their opinion doesn't count; they are considered "crazy." I suspect it's the main reason people are afraid of psychiatrists. After all, dermatologists and gynecologists are not in the business of locking people up, but psychiatrists are. And people know this. So what I am saying is at once shockingly novel, because it is the exact opposite of what medical and psychiatric orthodoxy says; and yet it is terribly obvious, because no one wants to be locked up in an insane asylum. That's why we have committment laws and closed wards in mental hospitals.

Penthouse: You often complain that psychiatrists do not keep their patients' confidences. You mention, for example, the psychiatrist who released reports on a man who shot and killed several people from a tower at the University of Texas. Why do psychiatrists do that?

Szasz: Because they are no more honest than politicians. They often comply with popular expectations and pressures. There are countless such cases. For example, there was Lee Harvey Oswald, the man who supposedly killed President Kennedy. A psychiatrist saw him when he was in his teens. After Oswald was apprehended and killed—perhaps even before he was killed, I don't remember the exact timing—this psychiatrist gave out the whole story on Oswald; that is, when he saw him, and what he thought was wrong with him, and Oswald's mother, and so forth. An utter breach of confidence, in my opinion.

Penthouse: What about President Nixon's psychiatric record? Didn't he see a psychiatrist in the 1950's?

Szasz: He saw a physician who at the time was said to have specialized in psychosomatic medicine. He subsequently became a psychotherapist. This doctor also talked—perhaps blabbered would be a better term. The very fact that he acknowledged that Mr. Nixon had been his patient was in my opinion a breach of confidence. But that wasn't all; he also published a story in one of the mass magazines in which he went on at length about how mentally healthy Mr. Nixon was. This too was improper. He shouldn't have said anything.

Penthouse: Doesn't the ethics committee of the American Psychiatric Association do anything about this?

Szasz: You must be joking! Ethics committee! You know what such committees are for? To protect the *profession*—not the patient or the public. This is the whole problem with professions, especially when they manage to instill awe and fear in the public. George Bernard Shaw said that "every profession is a conspiracy against the public." Nowhere is this now more true than with respect to psychiatry.

Penthouse: In your writings, you cite the names of many public figures who have been "psychiatrized against their will." Can you mention some of them and just what happened?

Szasz: The list is a mile long. Ernest Hemingway was involuntarily hospitalized and given electric shock treatment. Secretary of Defense James V. Forrestal was apprehended, supposedly because he was suicidal. He was taken to the Bethesda Naval Hospital and was placed in a room on the top floor—the eleventh, I believe. A few weeks later he was found dead on the pavement in front of his window. Earl Long, the former governor of Louisiana, was incarcerated in a psychiatric hospital in Texas. When he was returned to a Louisiana mental hospital, he freed himself by firing the head psychiatrist of the Louisiana state mental health system. Long was a smart man. He understood psychiatric gangsterism better than most politicians do.

Finally, I want to mention the Goldwater case. During the 1964 presidential race, Senator Goldwater was, as you may recall, called crazy by about one thousand psychiatrists. Now, the interesting thing—and to me the terrible thing—about the aftermath of that affair was that Senator Goldwater sued Ralph Ginzburg, the publisher of *Fact* magazine, where this psychiatric defamation was published. Ginzburg was found guilty of libel and had to pay a substantial sum to Goldwater for damages. But, interestingly, Goldwater didn't sue any of the psychiatrists, even though they were the ones who produced and supplied the libelous material to Ginzburg. This shows, I think, how afraid politicians are of psychiatrists, of the psychiatric profession as a whole, and that they consider psychiatrists more sacrosanct than Presidents or White House candidates. It's a dangerous situation.

Penthouse: You have criticized the symbiotic relationship between medicine—especially psychiatry—and the state. How did this symbiosis develop?

Szasz: This is a complicated matter, but in a nutshell, as the prestige and popularity of organized religion diminished, following the Enlightenment, medicine took over many of the functions formerly performed by the churches. Physicians became the new priesthood and it has been the psychiatrists especially who have played the roles of priests. They are our secular and "scientific" priests.

In a theocratic society the religious values, as interpreted by the priest, are enforced by the government; for example, you must close your shop on Sunday, or Saturday. In a therapeutic society, the medical values, as interpreted by the physician, are enforced by the government; for example, you must be vaccinated against smallpox and you cannot buy a hypodermic syringe.

Penthouse: If you are so critical of psychiatry, why do you teach and practice it?

Szasz: I am not critical of *all* of psychiatry. I am no more against psychiatry than a 16th-century priest who opposed the Inquisition was against Catholicism. Of course, many orthodox Catholics in the 16th century would have said such a priest was against Catholicism, and many orthodox psychiatrists would now say that I am against psychiatry. This proves only that there is a conflict between me and orthodox psychiatrists, which is obvious. It does not prove that I am "against" psychiatry and that they are "for" it. The situation is a lot more complicated than that.

I object to only two things. First, I object to any and all *involuntary* psychiatry; to any kind of psychiatric measure that's imposed on a person against his will. Second, I object to the widespread mislabeling in psychiatry, whether it is voluntary or involuntary psychiatry; that is, calling personal problems "diseases," calling prisons "hospitals," calling conversation "treatment," and so forth.

Penthouse: What do you approve of?

Szasz: I approve of any kind of psychiatry that's voluntary and to which the so-called patient consents, and which is correctly labeled—or at least approximately so. If people want to do it, they should have the right to use all the existing psychiatric measures and any others that anyone wants to add—you name them: psychoanalysis, psychotherapy, group therapy, drugs, hospitalization, electroshock. They are all okay for those who *want* them. If someone like Senator Eagleton wants to go to a hospital and hire a doctor to give him electrically induced convulsions, why shouldn't he? I think he is making a bad mistake in doing so, but that's only my opinion. He is entitled to have his opinion and to act upon it.

Penthouse: You are personally opposed to electroshock. Why?

Szasz: It's a barbarity. I have never used it and never would. I wouldn't dream of recommending it. If someone asked me about it, I would point out that neurologists go to great lengths trying to prevent seizures in persons who have epilepsy, because every time a person has a grand mal seizure, his brain gets damaged. Nevertheless, psychiatrists claim that giving someone a seizure is a form of treatment. But then the history of medicine is full of instances of so-called cures that were actually harmful. You know the old saying, "The cure is worse than the disease." It applies to a lot of things psychiatrists do—electroshock, lobotomy, often the use of drugs, and sometimes even psychotherapy or psychoanalysis.

Penthouse: Despite this you would not want to see these things abolished.

Szasz: Certainly not! In my view of life, the foremost value is individual freedom and responsibility. People should have a chance to make their own choices. I am willing to state my views—for example, that I think that anyone who has electroshock is an idiot, but I would not want to impose my views on anyone. For one thing, I *could* by wrong. But even being right should not give one the right to impose his views or will on others. I view all this on the model of religion and religious freedom. It isn't only electroshock and lobotomy that I don't think much of. I don't think much of being a Jehovah's Witness or a Christian Scientist; but I certainly think people should have a right to these religious beliefs and the practices they entail. And I think the same way about medical beliefs and practices.

Penthouse: Then you are not an antipsychiatrist, as so many seem to think?

Szasz: Of course not. I am against psychiatric coercion and deception, but I'm not antipsychiatry! There is now a whole literature on what is called "antipsychiatry," and I am supposed to be one of the originators of this whole movement. Words are very important, especially in psychiatry. So I reject the term "antipsychiatry." It's a bad term. It's misleading. It fails to make the distinction between voluntary and involuntary psychiatry. If one values individual freedom and dignity, then one must, of course, oppose involuntary psychiatry; at the same time, one must *not* oppose voluntary psychiatry, not try to prevent people from choosing psychiatric interventions that one personally dislikes or disapproves of.

Penthouse: You often refer to religion. Are you religious?

Szasz: Not in any formal sense. In the sense that I hold some values dear, yes. In a sense, everyone is religious. Man is fundamentally a religious being.

Penthouse: What do you think about death? What happens when we die? As a scientist, aren't you curious about it?

Szasz: Not really. This may sound foolish, but I think I know what happens when we die.

Penthouse: What?

Szasz: We are dead. That's it.

Penthouse: But do you accept the *possibility* that you might not know *everything* that happens when we die?

Szasz: Well, of course. All I am saying is that I don't believe in a life after death—whatever that phrase means. I have just never had the usual hang-ups about death. Life is very precious. But when one dies, one dies. That's the way it is, I think.

Penthouse: You often refer to John Stuart Mill and Ralph Waldo Emerson. What other men do you admire? Who influenced you?

Szasz: The great writers and playwrights— Shakespeare, Moliere, Dostoevski, Camus, and countless others. Among contemporaries, people like Wittgenstein, Bertrand Russell, Karl Popper.

Penthouse: How about psychoanalysts?

Szasz: I admire all three of the great founders of psychoanalysis; not uncritically, though. Freud, Jung, and Adler were, all three of them, immensely gifted and creative and important people. It's too bad people no longer read them very much—read their original works. They are better than 99 percent of the current stuff.

Penthouse: What do you admire about these men or their work?

Szasz: I admire Freud's brilliance and his systematic style of work; Jung's humaneness and sensitivity to man's moral and religious nature; and Adler's common sense and directness. It seems to me, too, that Jung and Adler must have been superb psychotherapists, which Freud clearly was not.

Penthouse: In your new book, *The Second Sin,* you say that, "The narcotics laws are our dietary laws." Why don't you consider the addict a sick person?

Szasz: Because a bad habit is not a disease. In fact, I maintain that not only is the addict not sick, but that there is no such thing as "addiction" and no such person as an "addict." There are, to be sure, people who take some drugs which some other people do not want them to take; and if the latter have more power than the former, then they can and sometimes do call the former "addicts."

Penthouse: Do you say this for effect or do you really believe it?

Szasz: Both. But look at the similarities between this drug situation and the situation as it was not so long ago with religion. A few hundred years ago, if a person was not a Christian, or was not a Christian in just the right way, he was considered a heretic. Today we know there are no heretics. Heretics were simply people whose religious habits offended those who defined the true faith. I hold that, in the same way, addiction is a sort of pharmacological heresy.

Penthouse: I presume you don't think much of methadone?

Szasz: It's as good a narcotic as another. It's much like heroin—just as Orthodox Judaism is much like fundamentalist Christianity, which is why they make such perfect antagonists.

Penthouse: Isn't methadone a treatment?

Szasz: Of course it's a "treatment." It must be. The United States government says so. The American Medical Association says so. The American Psychiatric Association says so. So most people are likely to go along and believe this. I don't. But I don't expect most people to agree with me on a thing like this, which is almost entirely a matter of fashion, of fast-changing definition.

Penthouse: At one time heroin was used as a treatment for morphone addiction. You think the same thing may happen to methadone?

Szasz: Yes, I think there is an excellent chance for that. As methadone is used more widely and over a longer period, more and more people will be "abusing" it, and then the medical profession and the government will decide one nice day that it's no longer a "treatment" but a disease!

Penthouse: You are opposed to prescriptions. Wouldn't a lot of people hurt themselves and perhaps hurt others if anyone could buy any drug he wanted?

Szasz: If people buy drugs and hurt themselves, that's their problem. If they hurt somebody else, they should be punished especially hard instead of it being an extenuating circumstance calling for mercy. Under Roman law, a person who committed a crime while intoxicated was punished especially hard. That was two thousand years ago. What we need is a little catching up. But you don't penalize people by stopping them from buying and taking drugs. That is not a crime.

Penthouse: Give us some other examples of this alliance between medicine and the state.

Szasz: There are so many, and we are so embedded in them, that we are unaware of them, as people are unaware of the air they breathe—until they get asthma. A few years ago, abortion was a crime. Now it's a treatment—and Blue Cross pays for it! Pimping is a crime, but when a so-called sex therapist like Dr. Masters gets you a prostitute and calls her a "surrogate wife," then pimping becomes a form of treatment, which you can take off your income tax. Sending your son or daughter through college is not tax-deductible, but "sex-therapy" is. If that doesn't drive home the truth about the alliance between medicine and state, the politicalization of illness and treatment, I certainly don't know what would.

Penthouse: You don't believe there is such a thing as "mental illness." Well, how does schizophrenia develop, and other behavior conventionally called "mental illness?"

Szasz: I don't want to be difficult, but I must insist that schizophrenia doesn't develop. A certain kind of behavior develops, and that may be called "schizophrenia." Assuming

that, and assuming we have the same sort of behavior in mind, this would be my answer. There are two basic ways of being badly screwed up in childhood: by being neglected too much or by being interfered with too much. Being left alone, being left unoccupied, unstimulated—or, on the other hand, being overprotected, intruded upon, overstimulated —both are pretty nearly intolerable for children—as well as for adults. To develop what we in our culture call "properly," we must be able to grow up and live in some middle range between too much aloneness and too much togetherness.

Penthouse: Some researchers claim that diet—and especially some vitamins—can affect schizophrenia and may be used to treat it. Could you comment on this?

Szasz: I can't comment on the biology of this matter, because I don't know what dietary influences or vitamins do for whatever may be physiologically the matter with some "schizophrenics"—if anything. But I do want to emphasize that if schizophrenia is a disease, like diabetes, to which medically oriented psychiatrists often compare it, then the "schizophrenic" patient should have the same rights as those of the diabetic patient. Foremost among these are the right to reject treatment, the right to reject being diagnosed —indeed, the right to reject being a "patient" at all, in the sense of having the right to refuse to submit to medical ministrations. At the same time, as I said before, people should have the right to whatever treatment they want—vitamins, electroshock, even lobotomy; but *only* if they want it.

Penthouse: Why do you emphasize the right to reject treatment?

Szasz: Because psychiatrists and medically oriented psychiatric researchers make constant claims about this or that being physiologically wrong with "mental patients"—as if establishing the presence of an objectively identifiable disease would legitimize treating such patients. It wouldn't. Syphilis is an objectively identifiable disease. But there is no law, in New York State, authorizing a physician to treat a person for syphilis who does not want to be treated. In other words, what makes treatment legitimate in medicine is that the patient wants it; whereas what makes it legitimate in psychiatry is that the physician *claims* that the "patient" is "sick." I insist on distinguishing between illness as a biological condition and the act of treating a person—with or without his consent—which is a political event.

Penthouse: Your objective to involuntary mental hospitalization and treatment leaves open the problem of what to do with people who are dangerous, those who commit crimes.

Szasz: Here I must refer you to my two books, *Law, Liberty and Psychiatry* and *Psychiatric Justice*, where I discuss this subject in detail. Briefly, my position is that in a free society, no one should be deprived of liberty without due process of law. And to me, due process implies that the only justification for loss of liberty is the commission of an illegal act. Mental illness can never justify it, just as heresy can't—just as being too fat or too thin can't. In other words, if someone is suspected of breaking the law, he should be accused, tried, and if convicted, sentenced. If the sentence calls for loss of liberty, then the offender should be confined in an institution that's penal, not medical, in character. Of course, in many cases where such sentences are imposed, they really should *not* be imposed if we are to be truly concerned with the protection of public safety and the maintenance of human dignity. In any event, I don't want doctors to be jailers or torturers. We have already forgotten what doctors did in Nazi Germany, and we don't *want* to know what they do in Communist Russia.

Penthouse: All right, so we send criminals to jail without considering insanity as an extenuating circumstance. But our jails are very bad. Very few people come out of them fit for society. What does does it do to send them there unless you hold everybody for life terms?

Szasz: Of course our prisons are bad. I didn't say they were good. Nor did I promise to solve all social problems. I am only trying to clarify

what psychiatrists do and to identify what I think is good or bad among the things they do, and why. If prisons are bad, and if we want to do something about this, the remedies are obvious enough. We should send fewer people to prison and we should make the prisons better. Placing lawbreakers or suspected lawbreakers—and indeed, innocent persons suspected of being "dangerous," whatever that term might mean—in mental hospitals, which are themselves horrible prisons, is not my idea of prison reform.

Penthouse: You say that committing suicide should be a human right. But suppose I tried to jump out of that window? Wouldn't your impulse be to restrain me?

Szasz: Yes, of course, I would try to stop you, partly because I would assume that that's what you would want me to do; otherwise you wouldn't be trying to kill yourself right in front of me. But the point is that I would *not* call the police; I would *not* commit you to a mental hospital; I would *not* even try to persuade you to see a psychiatrist. What I might say is, "Look, you are insulting me. You call me on the telephone. You say you want to talk to me, to do an interview. You come and we talk. And then you want to jump out of *my* window. How can you do this to me? Why did you deceive me?"

Penthouse: Suppose I then told you: "All right, I'm going to get a room of my own, check in, and jump out of *my* window." Then what?

Szasz: I would offer to talk about it with you. That's all. The rest would be up to you. Perhaps I would also ask you why you tell me that you are going to kill yourself. Why don't you keep it to yourself?

Penthouse: You seem reluctant to say much about the possibilities of altering behavior chemically. Why is that?

Szasz: Because I do not consider myself particularly knowledgeable about biochemistry or pharmacology. Of course, I recognize that it is possible to alter behavior chemically. But I try to focus on the ethical and political aspects of how such alteration is brought about rather than on the alteration itself.

Penthouse: I'm sorry. You'll have to clarify that.

Szasz: I know that chemical substances alter behavior. That's not in dispute. Right now, we are drinking vodka tonics. If we drink enough of the stuff, we shall produce an alteration in our behavior due to alcohol. That's the model. The idea is simple enough; alcohol, nicotine, opium, methadone, barbiturates, amphetamines—it's a long list. All those drugs alter behavior. So I am not denying any of this or that drugs may be useful for what is now called psychiatric treatment.

Penthouse: But shouldn't medical men, chemists, biologists, be working full speed on this? Aren't you excited about the possibilities?

Szasz: I am not particularly excited about this area simply because I happen to believe—and, of course, I could be wrong about this—that most of the things we call "mental diseases" are personal problems, human problems; and there isn't much you can do about human problems by drugging the person who has them. Second, I am not too excited about this area because it seems to me that, by and large, drugs affect mood and behavior in one of two ways: they stimulate or they depress—that is, they make you feel more energetic and awake (at least for a while) or they make you feel less energetic and more sleepy. Now, each of these effects may be useful. In fact, I happen to believe that we have too many restrictions on drugs that have these effects. They should be freely available. And this carries me to my third point, which is the moral and political one. Who now controls, and who will control in the future, the use of these drugs? The government? The medical profession? The free citizen of a free society? It may be foolish to plunge ahead and develop more and more psychopharmacological agents when we can't seem to decide how to use the agents we now have. After all, opium has been around for thousands of years; and we now consider it "progress" to prohibit its use and to replace it with synthetic drugs. And last but not least, I think we should grapple—and I mean politicians, lawyers, civil libertarians and people in general—with the basic question of whether such drugs should ever be used involuntarily, and if so, when, how, by whom, on whom, and what sort of protections will the citizen have against being drug-controlled by physicians and politicians? It's not enough to write science fiction about this. It's necessary to confront it as the political—not medical—problem that it is.

Penthouse: One last question: In many of your books you are concerned with the dangers of medical oppression, or a kind of therapeutic tyranny. You have coined the term "therapeutic state." Could you clarify what you mean?

Szasz: For nearly twenty years now I have been writing about the fundamental similarities between the persecution of heretics and witches in former days and the persecution of madmen and mental patients in ours. Briefly, my view is that just as a theological state is characterized by the preoccupation of the people with religion and religious matters, and especially with the religious deviance called heresy, so a therapeutic state is characterized by the preoccupation of the people with medicine and medical matters, and especially with the medical deviance called illness. The aim of a therapeutic state is not to provide favorable conditions for the pursuit of life, liberty, and happiness, but to repair the defective mental health of the subject-patients. The officials of such a state parody the roles of physician and psychotherapist. This arrangement gives meaning to the lives of countless bureaucrats, physicians, and mental health workers by robbing the so-called patients of the meaning of *their* lives. We thus persecute millions—as drug addicts, homosexuals, suicide risks and so forth—all the while congratulating ourselves that we are great healers curing them of mental illness. We have, in short, managed to repackage the Inquisition and are selling it as a new scientific cure-all.

"Dr. Thomas Szasz: Penthouse Interview", By Richard Ballad

1. According to Szasz, what do psychiatrists do when they are said to be treating mental illness?

2. What is the major reason why people are likely to be afraid of psychiatrists and not other types of doctors?

3. For what reasons is Szasz against electroshock therapy?

4. Cite examples of what Szasz feels is evidence of an alliance between medicine and the state.

5. Do you feel that his criticisms regarding the alliance between medicine and the state are justified? Why or why not?

6. What does Szasz believe regarding responsibility for criminal acts committed under extenuating circumstances, such as temporary insanity?

SCHIZOPHRENIA AS IDEOLOGY
from *Schizophrenia Bulletin*
Thomas J. Scheff

Thomas J. Scheff is a leading spokesman for the social per-spective and another ardent critic of conventional psychiatry. In the following article, Scheff points out that cultures develop unwritten codes of conduct that govern social behavior and serve to maintain the social order and protect the status quo. Most people obey these subtle, unwritten rules of social conduct, which Scheff calls residual rules. Residual rules "go without saying", and their violation would be unthinkable. For example, in our culture a residual rule prohibits an individual from talking aloud to himself as he sits alone in a crowded restaurant. There is no written law prohibiting this, but most people would just not do so.

Scheff distinguishes between two different types of philosophy. Ideological philosophy clings to the existing social status quo and attempts to maintain existing social and economic interests. Hold-ers of an ideological philosophy are likely to be those who currently control social and economic policy. Since they are already in a position of power, they would stand to lose the most should social and economic revolution occur. They are conservative.

Utopian philosophy challenges the values of ideological philos-ophy. It deals more with "how things should be" rather than "how things are". Utopian philosophers do not generally have much control over existing social and economic conditions. They would stand to gain through revolution. The utopian philosopher might be considered as "radical" by the ideological. Thus, a continual struggle exists between the ideological and utopian philosophies.

As Szasz indicated in the previous selection, the church was once the major source of social authority. The priest interpreted religious beliefs for the public, and his dictates were then put into laws which were enforced by the government. The church was ideological. It had power and wished to maintain it. Ultimately, the church developed rules which served to maintain its strength. For example, by ruling that stores must be closed on Sunday, it was eliminating competition for church attendance. The merchant who opened his store on Sunday could be considered as utopian. He threatened the existing social order. The priest, however, had the power to label such a merchant as a heretic who deserved punishment. In other instances utopians were assumed to be "possessed by the devil" and burned at the stake.

Today, to a large extent, the medical profession has replaced the church as our major source of social authority. Many people who once turned to religious leaders for guidance new turn to doctors, psychiatrists, and psychologists. Thus, the medical profession and the doctor have assumed the positions of authority once held by the church and the priest. Although progress has been made since the time of burning witches at the stake, modern doctors still have the power to label the utopian who threatens the social order. For example, a person's talking aloud to himself while alone in a restaurant can be considered as symptomatic of a "mental illness", such as schizophrenia, and may be used to justify his committment to a mental hospital. In essence, the doctor has the same power to label and stigmatize the utopian as did the priest.

In the article, Scheff articulates his contention that a diagnosis of schizophrenia is likely to result when an individual violates numerous residual rules, and probably unintentionally threatens the social order. He describes a sequence of events that occurs as a person becomes labeled and stigmatized as a schizophrenic.

Proponents of the illness perspective may find the notions of Scheff offensive. Hopefully, however, the article will allow you to perceive, understand, and appreciate schizophrenia from a different perspective.

In lieu of beginning this paper with a (necessarily) abstract discussion of a concept, *the public order,* I shall invite the reader to consider a *gedanken* experiment that will illustrate its meaning. Suppose in your next conversation with a stranger, instead of looking at his eyes or mouth, you scrutinize his ear. Although the deviation from ordinary behavior is slight (involving only a shifting of the direction of gaze a few degrees, from the eyes to an ear), its effects are explosive. The conversation is disrupted almost instantaneously. In some cases, the subject of this experiment will seek to save the situation by rotating to bring his eyes into your line of gaze; if you continue to gaze at his ear, he may rotate through a full 360 degrees. Most often, however, the conversation is irretrievably damaged. Shock, anger, and vertigo are experienced not only by the "victim" but, oddly enough, by the experimenter himself. It is virtually impossible for either party to sustain the conversation, or even to think coherently, as long as the experiment continues.

The point of this experiment is to suggest the presence of a public order that is all-pervasive, yet taken almost completely for granted. During the simplest kinds of public encounter, there are myriad understandings about comportment that govern the participants' behavior—understandings governing posture, facial expression, and gestures, as well as the content and form of the language used. In speech itself, the types of conformity are extremely diverse and include pronunciation; grammar and syntax; loudness, pitch, and phrasing; and aspiration. Almost all of these elements are so taken for granted that they "go without saying" and are more or less invisible, not only to the speakers but to society at large. These understandings constitute part of our society's assumptive world, the world that is thought of as normal, decent, and possible.

The probability that these understandings are, for the most part, arbitrary to a particular historical culture (is shaking hands or rubbing noses a better form of greeting?) is immaterial to the individual member of society whose attitude of everyday life is, *whatever is, is right.* There is a social, cultural, and interpersonal status quo whose existence is felt only when abrogated. Since violations occur infrequently, and since the culture provides no very adequate vocabulary for talking about either the presence or abuse of its invisible understandings, such deviations are considered disruptive and disturbing. The society member's loyalty to his culture's unstated conventions is unthinking but extremely intense.

The sociologist Mannheim referred to such intense and unconscious loyalty to the status quo as *ideological*. Ideology, in this sense, refers not only to the defense of explicit political or economic interests but, much more broadly, to a whole world view or perspective on what reality is. As a contrast to the ideological view, Mannheim cited the *utopian* outlook, which tends "to shatter, either partially or wholly, the order of things prevailing at the time".[7] The attitude of everyday life, which is ideological, is transfixed by the past and the present; the possibility of a radically different scheme of things, or revolutionary changes in custom and outlook, is thereby rejected. The utopian perspective, by contrast, is fixed on the future; it rejects the status quo with abrupt finality. *Social change* arises out of the clash of the ideological and utopian perspectives.

Residual Rule Violations

It is the thesis of this paper that the concepts of mental illness in general—and schizophrenia in particular—are not neutral, value-free, scientifically precise terms but, for the most part, the leading edge of an ideology embedded in the historical and cultural present of the white middle class of Western societies. The concept of illness and its associated vocabulary—symptoms, therapies, patients, and physicians—reify and legitimate the prevailing public order at the expense of other possible worlds. The medical model of disease refers to culture-free processes that are independent of the public order; a case of pneumonia or syphilis is pretty much the same in New York or New Caledonia. (For criticism of the medical model from psychiatric, psychological, and sociological perspectives, see [3 4 6 8 11 13].)

Most of the "symptoms" of mental illness, however, are of an entirely different nature. Far from being culture-free, such "symptoms" are themselves offenses against implicit understandings of particular cultures. Every society provides its members with a set of explicit norms—understandings governing conduct with regard to such central institutions as the state, the family, and private property. Offenses against these norms have conventional names: for example, an offense against property is called "theft," and an offense against sexual propriety is called "perversion." As we have seen above, however, the public order also is made up of countless unnamed understandings. "Everyone knows," for example, that during a conversation one looks at the other's eyes or mouth, but not at his ear. For the convenience of the society, offenses against these unnamed residual understandings are usually lumped together in a miscellaneous, catchall category. If people reacting to an offense exhaust the conventional categories that might define it (e.g., theft, prostitution, and drunkenness), yet are certain that an offense has been committed, they may resort to this residual category. In earlier societies, the residual category was witchcraft, spirit possession, or possession by the devil; today, it is mental illness. The symptoms of mental illness are, therefore, violations of residual rules.

To be sure, some residual-rule violations are expressions of underlying physiological processes: the hallucinations of the toxic psychoses and the delusions associated with general paresis, for example. Perhaps future research will identify further physiological processes that lead to violations of residual rules. For the present, however, the key attributes of the medical model have yet to be established and verified for the major mental illnesses. There has been no scientific verification of the cause, course, site of pathology, uniform and invariant signs and symptoms, and treatment of choice for almost all of the conventional, "functional" diagnostic categories. Psychiatric knowledge in these matters rests almost entirely on unsystematic clinical impressions and professional lore. It is quite possible, therefore, that many psychiatrists' and other mental-health workers' "absolute certainty" about the cause, site, course, symptoms, and treatment of mental illness represents an ideological reflex, a spirited defense of the present social order.

Residue of Residues

Viewed as offenses against the public order, the symptoms of schizophrenia are particularly interesting. Of all the major diagnostic categories, the concept of schizophrenia (although widely used by psychiatrists in the United States and in those countries influenced by American psychiatric nomenclature) is the vaguest and least clearly defined. Such categories as obsession, depression, and mania at least have a vernacular meaning. Schizophrenia, however, is a broad gloss; it involves, in no very clear relationship, ideas such as "inappropriateness of affect," "impoverishment of thought," "inability to be involved in meaningful human relationships," "bizarre behavior" (e.g., delusions and hallucinations), "disorder of speech and communication," and "withdrawal."

These very broadly-defined symptoms can be redefined as offenses against implicit social understandings. The appropriateness of emotional expression is, after all, a cultural judgment. Grief is deemed appropriate in our society at a funeral, but not at a party. In other cultures, however, such judgments of propriety may be reversed. With regard to thought disorder, cultural anthropologists have long been at pains to point out that ways of thought are fundamentally different in different societies. What constitutes a meaningful human relationships, anthropologists also report, is basically different in other times and places. Likewise, behavior that is bizarre in one culture is deemed tolerable or even necessary in another. Disorders of speech and communication, again, can be seen as offenses against culturally prescribed rules of language and expression. Finally, the notion of "withdrawal" assumes a cultural standard concerning the degree of involvement and the amount of distance between the individual and those around him.

The broadness and vagueness of the concept of schizophrenia suggest that it may serve as the residue of residues. As diagnostic categories such as hysteria and depression have become conventionalized names for residual rule breaking, a need seems to have developed for a still more generalized, miscellaneous diagnostic category. If this is true, the schizophrenic explores not only "inner space" (Ronald Laing's phrase) but also the normative boundaries of his society.

These remarks should not be taken to suggest that there is no internal experience associated with "symptomatic" behavior; the individual with symptoms *does* experience distress and suffering, or under some conditions, exhilaration and freedom. The point is, however, that public, consensual "knowledge" of mental illness is based, by and large, on knowledge not of these internal states but of their overt manifestations. When a person goes running down the street naked and screaming, lay and professional diagnosticians alike assume the existence of mental illness within that person—even though they have not investigated his internal state. Mental-health procedure and the conceptual apparatus of the medical model posit internal states, but the events actually observed are external.

Labeling Theory

A point of view which is an alternative to the medical model, and which acknowledges the culture-bound nature of mental illness, is afforded by labeling theory in sociology. (For a general statement of this theory, see[2].) Like the evidence supporting the medical model, which is uneven and in large measure unreliable, the body of knowledge in support of the labeling theory of mental illness is by no means weighty or complete enough to prove its correctness. (Useful supporting material can be found in[1 5 6 9 10].) But even though labeling theory is hypothetical, its use may afford perspective—if only because it offers a viewpoint that, along a number of different dimensions, is diametrically opposed to the medical model.

The labeling theory of deviance, when applied to mental illness, may be presented as a series of nine hypotheses:

1. Residual rule breaking arises from fundamentally diverse sources (i.e., organic, psychological, situations of stress, volitional acts of innovation or defiance).

2. Relative to the rate of treated mental illness the rate of unrecorded residual rule breaking is extremely high.

3. Most residual rule breaking is "denied" and is of transitory significance.

4. Stereotyped imagery of mental disorder is learned in early childhood.

5. The stereotypes of insanity are continually reaffirmed, inadvertently, in ordinary social interaction.

6. Labeled deviants may be rewarded for playing the stereotyped deviant role.

7. Labeled deviants are punished when they attempt the return to conventional roles.

8. In the crisis occurring when a residual rule breaker is publicly labeled, the deviant is highly suggestible and may accept the lable.

9. Among residual rule breakers, labeling is the single most important cause of careers of residual deviance.

The evidence relevant to these hypotheses is reviewed in the author's *Being Mentally Ill.*[8]

According to labeling theory, the societal reaction is the key process that determines outcome in most cases of residual rule breaking. That reaction may be either denial (the most frequent reaction) or labeling. Denial is to "normalize" the rule breaking by ignoring or rationalizing it ("boys will be boys"). The key hypothesis in labeling theory is that, when residual rule breaking is denied, the rule breaking will generally be transitory (as when the stress causing rule breaking is removed; e.g., the cessation of sleep deprivation), compensated for, or channeled into some socially acceptable form. If, however, labeling occurs (i.e., the rule breaker is segregated as a stigmatized deviant), the rule breaking which would otherwise have been terminated, compensated for, or channeled may be stabilized; thus, the offender, through the agency of labeling, is launched on a career of "chronic mental illness." Crucial to the production of chronicity, therefore, are the contingencies (often external to the deviants) that give rise to labeling rather than denial; e.g., the visibility of the rule breaking, the power of the rule breaker relative to persons reacting to his behavior, the tolerance level of the community, and the availability in the culture of alternative channels of response other than labeling (among Indian tribes, for example, involuntary trance states may be seen as qualification for a desirable position in the society, such as that of shaman).

"Schizophrenia—A Label

On the basis of the foregoing discussion, it would seem likely that labeling theory would prove particularly strategic for facilitating the investigation of schizophrenia. Schizophrenia is the single most widely used diagnosis for mental illness in the United States, yet the cause, site, course, and treatment of choice are unknown, or the subject of heated and voluminous controversy. Moreover, there is some evidence that the reliability of diagnosis of schizophrenia is quite low. Finally, there is little agreement on whether a disease entity of schizophrenia even exists, what constitutes schizophrenia's basic signs and symptoms if it *does* exist, and how these symptoms are to be reliably and positively identified in the diagnostic process. Because of the all but overwhelming uncertainties and ambiguities inherent in its definition, "schizophrenia" is an appellation, or "label," which may be easily applied to those residual rule breakers whose deviant behavior is difficult to classify.

In this connection, it is interesting to note the perfectly enormous anomaly of classification procedures in most schizophrenia research. The hypothetical cause of schizophrenia, the independent variable in the research design—whether it is a physiological, biochemical, or psychological attribute— is measured with considerable attention to reliability, validity, and precision. I have seen reports of biochemical research in which the independent variable is measured to two decimal places. Yet the measurement of the dependent variable, the diagnosis of schizophrenia, is virtually ignored. The precision of the measurement, obviously, is virtually nil, since it represents at best an ordinal scale, or, much more likely, a nominal scale. In most studies, the reliability and validity of the diagnosis receives no attention at all: An experimental group is assembled by virtue of hospital diagnoses—leaving the measurement of the dependent variable to the mercy of the obscure vagaries of the process of psychiatric screening and diagnosis. Labeling theory should serve at least to make this anomaly visible to researchers in the field of schizophrenia.

More broadly, the clash between labeling theory and the medical and psychological models of mental illness may serve to alert researchers to some of the fundamental assumptions that they may be making in setting up their research. Particular reference should be made to the question of whether they are unknowingly aligning themselves with the social status quo; for example, by accepting unexamined the diagnosis of schizophrenia, they may be inadvertently providing the legitimacy of science to what is basically a social value judgment. For the remainder of this paper, I wish to pursue this point—the part that medical science may be playing in legitimating the status quo.

As was earlier indicated, there is a public order which is continually reaffirmed in social interaction. Each time a member of the society conforms to the stated or unstated cultural expectations of that society, as when he gazes at the eyes of the person with whom he is in conversation, he is helping to maintain the social status quo. Any deviation from these expectations, however small and regardless of its motivation, may be a threat to the status quo, since most social change occurs through the gradual erosion of custom.

Since all social orders are, as far as we know, basically arbitrary, a threat to society's fundamental customs impels its conforming members to look to extrasocial sources of legitimacy for the status quo. In societies completely under the sway of a single, monolithic religion, the source of legitimacy is always supernatural. Thus, during the Middle Ages, the legitimacy of the social order was maintained by reference to God's commands, as found in the Bible and interpreted by the Catholic Church. The Pope was God's deputy, the kings ruled by divine right, the particular cultural form that the family happened to take at the time—the patrilocal, monogamous, nuclear family—was sanctified by the church, and so on.

In modern societies, however, it is increasingly difficult to base legitimacy upon appeals to supernatural sources. As complete, unquestioning religious faith has weakened, one very important new source of legitimacy has emerged: In the eyes of laymen, modern science offers the kind of absolute certainty once provided by the church. The institution of medicine is in a particularly strategic position in this regard, since the physician is the only representative of science with whom the average man associates. To the extent that medical science lends its name to the labeling of nonconformity as mental illness, it is giving legitimacy to the social status quo. The mental-health researcher may protest that he is interested not in the preservation of the status quo but in a scientific question: "What are the causes of mental illness?" According to the argument given here, however, his question is loaded—like, "When did you stop beating your wife?" or, more to the point, "What are the causes of witchcraft?" (For a comparison of the treatment of witches and the mentally ill, see[12].) Thus, a question about causality may also be ideological, in Mannheim's sense, in that it reaffirms current social beliefs, if only inadvertently.

Footnotes

[1]Balint, M. *The Doctor, the Patient, and the Illness.* New York: International Universities Press, Inc., 1957.
[2]Becker, H. *Outsiders.* New York: Free Press, 1963.
[3]Goffman, E. *Asylums.* New York: Doubleday-Anchor, 1961.
[4]Laing, R. *The Politics of Experience.* New York: Pantheon Book, 1967.

[5]Laing, R., and Esterson, A. *Sanity, Madness and the Family*. London: Tavistock, 1964.

[6]Lemert, E. M. *Social Pathology*. New York: McGraw-Hill, Inc., 1951.

[7]Mannheim, K. *Ideology and Utopia*. London: Routledge and Kegan Paul, Ltd., 1936.

[8]Scheff, T. J. *Being Mentally Ill: A Sociological Theory*. Chicago: Aldine Publishing Company, 1966.

[9]Scheff, T. J. *Mental Illness and Social Processes*. New York: Harper & Row, Publishers, 1967.

[10]Spitzer, S. P., and Denzin, N. K. *The Mental Patient: Studies in the Sociology of Deviance*. New York: McGraw-Hill, Inc., 1968.

[11]Szasz, T. S. *The Myth of Mental Illness*. New York: Hoeber-Harper, 1961.

[12]Szasz, T. S. *The Manufacture of Madness*. New York: Harper & Row, Publishers, 1970.

[13]Ullman, L. P., and Krasner, L. *A Psychological Approach to Abnormal Behavior*. Englewood Cliffs, N.J.: Prentice-Hall, Inc., 1969.

Thomas J. Scheff, Ph.D., is Chairman, Department of Sociology, University of California at Santa Barbara.

SELF TEST: MEASURING COMPREHENSION

"Schizophrenia As Ideology", By Thomas J. Scheff

1. As used by Scheff, what do the terms "ideological" and "utopian" mean?

2. Scheff points out that the schizophrenic is a person who chronically violates residual rules. What is a residual rule?

3. Give specific examples of behavior that would violate residual rules in our culture, but wouldn't in other cultures.

4. Scheff describes a labeling theory of mental illness. Hypothesis 6 states that "Labeled deviants may be rewarded for playing the stereotyped deviant role." Specifically, how might the deviant be rewarded for playing the deviant role?

THE ART OF BEING SCHIZOPHRENIC
from *Voices*
Jay Haley

Proponents of the social perspective deny that a disease entity, schizophrenia, exists. According to R. D. Laing, a Scottish psychiatrist commonly associated with the antipsychiatry movement,

> ". . . . behavior that gets labelled schizophrenic is a special sort of strategy that a person invents in order to live in an unlivable situation. In his life situation the person has come to be placed in an untenable position. He cannot make a move or make no move, without being beset by contradictory pressures both internally, from himself, and externally, from those around him. He is, as it were, in a position of checkmate. I must make it clear that this state of affairs may not be perceived as such by any of the people in it. The man at the bottom of the heap may be being crushed and suffocated to death without anyone noticing . . . . (Laing, 1964)."

The double bind theory of schizophrenia was originally published by Bateson, Jackson, Haley, and Weakland in 1956. Simply stated, it postulates that schizophrenia results from confusing, complicated, and threatening social situations consistently encountered by an individual. Children, who eventually become schizophrenic, are often placed in "no win" situations by their parents. The language used within the family is ambiguous. The child learns to be remote, evasive, and withdrawn in order to avoid conflict and criticism in this confused and confusing home environment. Remoteness, evasion, and withdrawal are considered to be common symptoms of schizophrenia. Thus, schizophrenia is the result of complex social factors.

In the following article, Jay Haley, one of the original authors of the double bind hypothesis, elaborates on some of its basic tenets. He describes the dynamics of the family situation encountered by the potential schizophrenic. He notes parallels between the struggles faced by the schizophrenic when at home and those he faces when in the mental hospital. As previously stated, the social perspective is critical of the illness perspective and psychiatry. Haley seizes the opportunity to criticize them.

The article may be difficult to understand. No one writes quite like Jay Haley. Much of the article is written in a tongue-in-cheek manner. However, "The Art of Being Schizophrenic" is a beautiful account of schizophrenia as it is viewed by the social perspective.

It is common today to hear complaints that standards are falling in every field of endeavor. Like most generalizations, this one may not be true, but certainly standards are dropping in the field of psychiatric diagnosis. Where there was once neatness and rigor, one now finds a slipshod, lackadaisical, devil-may-care lumping together of the most diverse maladies as if the need for diagnostic precision no longer existed. The most shocking example is the diagnosis of schizophrenia. At one time it was clear that a man was either schizophrenic or he was not, and the several species were neatly catalogued and appreciated. Today we find that the label of schizophrenia is likely to be applied to just about anyone. A passing temper tantrum by an adolescent can earn a diagnosis of schizophrenia without providing the youth any opportunity to show his true nature and abilities in this line of endeavor. Not only are the wrong sort of people included in this category, but we also find ourselves drowning in the attempts to water down the diagnosis so that just about anyone can be classed in this way. Let us face facts: what on earth is a schizoid, or worse yet a schizo-affective state? Are not such labels merely absurd compromises showing an unwillingness to keep the diagnosis clean and pure in the European, particularly the German, tradition? At this time we should review what is required of a person who truly merits this diagnosis so that we can ruthlessly eliminate the false contenders and draw a sharp line between this and other maladies. To use the term "schizophrenic" loosely for anyone who wanders in the hospital door looking befuddled betrays those individuals who have worked long and hard to achieve the disease.

The Right Sort of Family

To say that not everyone can achieve schizophrenia is to say a great deal. Today any competent diagnostician who is sifting the true schizophrenic from the chaff will include in his observation the environment of the patient. After all, to be schizophrenic it is essential that one be born into the right sort of family and if one can manage that all else may follow. However, we cannot choose our parents, they are a gift of heaven. People who have attempted schizophrenia without the correct family background have universally failed. They can erupt into psychotic-like behavior in combat or when caught in some other mad and difficult situation, but they are unable to sustain that behavior when the environment seems to right itself. The same point applies to the variety of fascinating drugs which are falsely said to induce psychosis. Not only does the drug influence miss the essence of the experience, but the effect wears rapidly off. The occasional goat who manages to be a schizophrenic after the drug has left his system is easily separated from the sheep who go back to normal—he has come from the right sort of family and probably would have achieved schizophrenia even without the benefit of medical research.

The type of family one must come from to become schizophrenic has been extensively described in the professional journals. One can summarize these scientific reports by saying that as individuals the family members are unrecognizable on the street but bring them together and the outstanding feature is immediately apparent—a kind of formless, bizarre despair overlaid with a veneer of glossy hope and good intentions concealing a power-struggle-to-the-death coated with a quality of continual confusion.

Observing such a family one is struck by the central figure, the mother, and notes at once that the schizophrenic owes to her his flexibility and his exasperating skill in frustrating people who attempt to influence him. Just as the child in a circus family learns from his parents how to maneuver on the slack wire, so does the schizophrenic learn from his mother how to maneuver acrobatically in interpersonal relations. To achieve schizophrenia a man must have experienced a mother who has a range of behavior unequalled except by the most accomplished of actresses. She is capable when stung (which occurs when any suggestion is made to her) of weeping, promising violence, expressing condescending concern, threatening to go mad and fall apart, being kind and pious, and offering to flee the country if another word is said. At the minimum, and on an off day, this type of mother is able to reply to an accusation about her alcoholism by saying, "I never drink, at least not often, and then only because it makes me more cheerful for the family's sake." When faced with the dreadful child she has raised, she is able to reply innocently that the fault lies elsewhere since she has done nothing in life for herself but everything for her child. This halo-effect is apparent in the comment of a mother who said, "A mother sacrifices, if you would be a mother yourself you would know this, like even Jesus with his mother, a mother sacrifices everything for her child."

It should be obvious that such mothers are not easy to find and probably don't represent more than twenty percent of the females born. Yet for the true flowering of schizophrenia, even such a mother is not enough. To balance the flexibility provided by mother, the schizophrenic must have a father who will teach him to remain immovable. The father of the schizophrenic has a stubbornness unequalled among men (as well as the skill to keep a woman in the state of exasperated despair which helps mother make use of her full range of behavior). On occasions when present and sober such a father can easily say, "I am right, God in heaven knows I cannot be proven wrong, black is not white and you know it too in your heart of hearts." This sort of father is not easily found in the general population, largely because he is rarely home.

When one considers the odds that this type of uncommon man will find such an uncommon woman, and the even more astonishing odds that two such people could copulate, it is clear at once that the incidence of true schizophrenia could not be high. (Often such parents report that the copulation only occurred when one or both was asleep and that is why they had to get married, but even granting this possibility the odds against schizophrenia being common do not change appreciably.)

Finally, it is important, although not essential, that a schizophrenic have as part of his environment a certain type of brother or sister. This sibling must be the kind of person who is hated on contact—a do-gooder, a good-in-schooler, a sweet, weak, kind bastard of a sibling who can provide the contrast for the future schizophrenic by showing him up to be the complete idiot his family expects him to be.

Given this array of talent around him, one might think the individual raised in such a family constellation would inevitably achieve schizophrenia. However, this is obviously not true since all children in such families do not go clearly mad. The schizophrenic must not only have such a family, but he must hold a certain position in it and serve certain vital functions over an extended period of time. Like any artist, several hours a day of practice over many years are necessary.

Regarding his position, he must be the child the parents choose to focus upon—that special child the parents expect to be remarkable for reasons related to their own dark pasts. Whatever this particular child does is of exaggerated importance to the parents, and he soon learns that touching his nose can set off an earthquake in the family. This parental focus is sufficiently intense that when it is turned from the schizophrenic to the sibling, the sibling begins to disintegrate like a match head placed under a burning glass.

It is the primary function of the schizophrenic to be the representative failure in the family, and in that sense be remarkable. The parents feel themselves to be insignificant wretches, lost souls incapable of any human accomplishment (although many of them make rather good scientists). Therefore for their survival they must have before their eyes the schizophrenic child as an example of a worse failure so they can stand a little higher in the world by that fact. The child can fulfill this function rather easily since he need only fail at whatever he attempts. The average schizophrenic shows his artistry by achieving more than usual ability along this line, while also indicating at regular intervals that he could do quite a good job at succeeding if he wanted to, thus shining in the light of his parents' admiration while giving them sufficient cause for disappointment.

The schizophrenic is not only the focus of his parents' life, but he serves a key position in the wider morass that is the total family network. One is reminded of the vast array of tumblers who stand upon each other's shoulders, all constructed upon one man standing at the bottom holding up the entire edifice. Just as the child is caught up in the conflict between his parents, so is he in the middle of the triangular struggle between his mother and her mother, his father and his mother, and the many other cross-generational conflicts in this type of family. (When the schizophrenic sides with his mother against father, father can only protest weakly since he is joining *his* mother against his wife.)

The average schizophrenic has had a lifetime balancing conflicting family triangles, each one focussed upon his every action, so that whatever he says and does in one triangle has repercussions in another. If he should please his grandparents, he will displease his parents, and should he agree with any one person he is certain to antagonize several others. Therefore the schizophrenic must learn to communicate in a way that satisfies everyone by saying one thing and disqualifying it with a conflicting statement and then indicating he didn't mean any of it anyhow. This complicated mode of adaptation makes his behavior appear rather peculiar.

The schizophrenic soon learns, of course, that he has a position of extreme power in manipulating triangles to his advantage. The importance of his skill in this essential game cannot be overemphasized. For example, one teenage schizophrenic, precocious as most schizophrenics are, said, "My parents and I are involved in the eternal triangle," and she showed her skill in this game by climbing into bed between her parents and kicking her mother out (while her father protested weakly that mother should have locked the bedroom door). The schizophrenic also takes for granted what social scientists are only beginning to realize—the true disturbance in human life comes when secret coalitions occur across generations or other power hierarchies (this is The Second Law of Human Relations). The schizophrenic is, of course, the master at cross-generation coalitions. He may decline to join his peers, but he will join a parent or a grandparent, and he has even been known to provoke a great grandfather to intrude into the parental conflict.

The primary responsibility of the schizophrenic is to hold the family together. Although social scientists, even family therapists, have not yet the vaguest idea how to prevent a family from disintegrating the schizophrenic child accomplishes this with ease. It is his duty to use his keen perception and interpersonal skill to maintain the family system in a stable state, even if that state is a mood of constant despair. His importance in this function appears on those rare occasions when the schizophrenic abandons his disease and becomes normal, succeeding in life and leaving his family. His parents at once individually collapse, losing their sense of purpose in life, and they set about to divorce (weakly apologizing to *their* parents for being more successful as parents than they were).

The schizophrenic child prevents divorce and family dissolution in a rather simple way; he provides the parents an excuse for staying together by offering himself as a problem. With minor threats of separation, he merely looks unhappy to provide mother and father with an excuse to stay together. When the parents are constantly on the verge of leaving one another, the child must present himself as a more severe problem. Such children learn quickly how to behave; a few odd mannerisms and grimaces in inappropriate moments are helpful, as well as muteness and a kind of twisting, weird waving of the hands accompanied by an occasional idiotic squeal. If of school age, the child must show that he is incapable of existing outside the family and therefore his parents must stay together and comfort him since they are his only source of life. By becoming the family problem, the child requires his parents to stay together to save him, offers himself as an excuse for their misery with each other, and he also challenges them. These parents feel they must be perfect parents and when their child behaves oddly all their determination to cure him is aroused, thus giving them further reason to continue to associate as a family.

The schizophrenic must also act quickly if the parents threaten to come closer together and be more affectionate, thereby provoking a change in the family (as well as panic in the parents). Should father almost reach out a hand to mother, the schizophrenic must promptly wet his pants, or he must say, "Oh, I want to visit Granny," thereby bringing father's mother into the scene, which always provokes an argument between the parents.

When the schizophrenic is old enough to perceive that his family is culturally defiant, he begins to function as the symbol of the family's differentness. The peculiar way he chooses to express himself on this matter will drive the parents closer together and at the same time attract community attention to provide some help for the family. His technique is to use parody. Schizophrenics have long been known as the most skilled people at parody in the world, and it has been said that they parody all the worst aspects of our society. This gives them too much credit; they are merely parodying their families. For example, if the parents insist that they are devoutly religious while behaving in a most unreligious manner, the schizophrenic son will begin to grow a beard and burn holes in the palms of his hands with cigarettes. Should this not attract sufficient attention—some of these parents will consider this only playful behavior—then the schizophrenic will take to strolling about the neighborhood carrying a large cross. The parents do not always take this as action in their best interests, particularly since they have a passion for secrecy about many matters, but in such a case they can hardly accuse the child of misbehavior when he merely is being more religious than they are. In a similar way, if the parents have unsavory minds while insisting that they are terribly puritan, the schizophrenic will loudly condemn dirty words, naming them and even writing them on the front sidewalk.

The skill with which a schizophrenic calls attention to a family problem while simultaneously declining responsibility for doing this is best illustrated by his verbal comments. The ideal comment is one which is as ambiguous as mother could offer—it must reach the parents in their souls but keep them uncertain whether an outsider gets the point. For example, a schizophrenic daughter listened to her parents describe how happy this family was except for this wretched daughter, and she said, "Yes, but wouldn't you and Daddy be happier if you didn't drink so much?" Granting that this calls attention to the parents' need for help, it was also a rather unskillful and crude thrust which does not merit being called schizophrenic. This rude directness might be attributed to the daughter's faulty control of her anger. The more experienced schizophrenic can completely control the expression of his feelings and offer flattened affect even when the doctors are sticking pins into him at medical demonstrations. One can only applaud another daughter who panicked her mother by saying flatly, "I'm going to call the police and tell them the house is dirty;" a son who sent his mother a Mother's Day card which said, "You've always been like a mother to me," and yet another daughter who arrived with her mother and stepfather in a psychiatrist's office and said, with inappropriate affect, "Mother had to get married and now I'm here."

When the family threatens to dissolve, the schizophrenic must be willing to go to any extreme, even insane activity which brings in the neighbors and the police. It is the willingness on his part to fulfill the function of holding the family together which explains why the schizophrenic—despite his skill, wariness, and keen perception—lets himself be cast into a mental hospital. His psychotic behavior is a last resort when a family crisis has reached the point where an unresolvable breach is about to take place. This final extremity drives the parents together because of their common burden of a truly unfortunate child, forces the parents into a common front against the community which is protesting that something must be done, and lets the family make the schizophrenic the patsy for all past and present difficulties. The psychotic episode is merely a more extreme version of other behavior of the schizophrenic at times of family crisis, but this time it precipitates him into a situation which calls forth all his skill—the treatment situation. Before describing the talent necessary for the schizophrenic to survive in the hospital setting, let us summarize the training the schizophrenic has had when he arrives, his face unwashed and his hair uncombed, ready for entrance into the institution which will become his tomb.

In sum, the schizophrenic must have come from the right sort of family, with appropriate parents as models. He must have learned to manipulate and balance complicated, conflicting family triangles, and he must be perceptive enough to keep his feet in a morass of trickery and despair. He must also have learned to deal with intensive attention; other children are ignored at times by their parents, but with the schizophrenic every move and word is taken personally. As a consequence he must become skilled in concealing his emotions, he must learn to indicate that whatever he did just happened and he is not responsible for it, he must perceive the threats in every situation, and he must achieve skill in stabilizing whatever system he is in by being a willing scapegoat to support the inadequacies of those around him. It should be immediately evident that few people can meet the complicated requirements of the world of the average schizophrenic. There is one final requirement which eliminates most contenders. Only certain of the great political and religious leaders of the past have had the character structure, the determination of the schizophrenic. He has the will to devote his life to an absolute and stubborn crusade. His crusade is this: never to let his family off the hook. The hundred million affronts he has suffered are never to be forgiven to the end of

his days. Even if the law should force him to separate from his parents, he must continually remind them, by bizarre letters if necessary, that they have driven him mad and he plans to continue in that state. His one risk is cure because if cured this means he has forgiven his family, and the true schizophrenic, his will power forged in the fire of a billion conflicts, will not offer that forgiveness even in the face of the most pitiable pleas. Just as the Crusader tenaciously pursued the Holy Grail over the bodies of the infidels, the true schizophrenic will remain attached to his family at all costs and by any methods so that on their deathbeds his parents still have on their conscience this parental disaster.

The Right Sort of Hospital

Only in the mental hospital can schizophrenia achieve its full flowering. Just as a plant reaches its greatest growth in well manured ground, so does the schizophrenic achieve his full range on the closed wards of mental institutions. Yet oddly enough the first reaction of the schizophrenic to hospitalization is a stout objection. Only when he has been incarcerated for a period of time does he recognize the merit of the establishment. Then he is almost impossible to remove. Nowhere in the world can he find an environment so similar to life at home and yet with opponents so much less skilled than the members of his family.

The average mental hospital has been extensively described in the professional literature. One can summarize these scientific reports by saying that the outstanding feature of a mental institution is a kind of formless, bizarre despair overlaid with a veneer of glossy hope and good intentions concealing a power struggle to the death between patients and staff, coated with a quality of continual confusion. The basic art of schizophrenia lies in a genius for dealing with power struggles, and of course in a mental hospital the problem of power is central. It should not be thought that the struggle between patient and staff is unequal. True, the staff has drugs, tubs, cold packs, shock treatments (both insulin and electric), brain operations, isolation cells, control of food and all privileges, and the ability to form in gangs composed of aides, nurses, social workers, psychologists and psychiatrists. The schizophrenic lacks all these appurtenances of power, including the use of gang tactics since he is essentially a loner, but he has his manner and his words and a stout and determined heart. He also has had extensive training in a family made up of the most difficult people in the world. A normal person might disintegrate or capitulate on any issue in the face of the organized assault by the staff of a mental hospital, but the schizophrenic at one glance can size up the situation and seize upon his opportunities. Even though disconcerted by being betrayed into the hospital, as he usually is, the schizophrenic can have family and staff embroiled in an argument before he has been stripped of his civilian clothes and had his money and driver's license confiscated.

The first lesson the schizophrenic learns in the hospital is that he must do what the aides tell him to do. His initial reaction is to decline, since he has never in his life done what he was told, it is against family tradition. However, the aides cannot permit recalcitrance since it is their duty to keep the hospital functioning. Therefore when the schizophrenic refuses to obey an order, the aide hits him as hard as he can in the gut. This astonishes the patient, and he muses over how to turn it to his advantage. He soon learns that he cannot, because being hit in the gut receives no publicity. Should the patient complain, the aide denies that it happens and the doctor pretends to believe him. That night the aide hits the schizophrenic as hard as he can in the gut twice more and calls him a squealer. From that time on the schizophrenic obeys the aide, although his courage is apparent even in these circumstances because he does what he is told in a desultory manner as if he has not heard a command and is only happening to follow it. In more modern and progressive mental hospitals the aides are not allowed to beat up on the patients. It is necessary for the aide to

report that the patient cannot control his hostility so that the doctor can bang the patient in the head with a shock machine. This procedure maintains the proprieties for medical investigating boards who know medical treatment when they see it. Recently institutions have attempted to incapacitate the schizophrenic by pouring drugs into him until his eyeballs float and he is uncertain what is up and what down. Drowned in sufficient powerful drugs, the schizophrenic's keen perception becomes impaired and he is less skillful in the hospital power struggle. However, over time immunity to the drugs begins to set in, and recently there has been a trend in hospitals to return to the shock machine.

After his first encounter with the brute force of the hospital structure, the wise schizophrenic casts his dull and calculating eye upon the basic game he must play to survive and keep his self respect. He soon learns that little is new; all is like life at home.

The first weakness the schizophrenic discovers in the hospital structure is the same one he found in his family; the hospital can be hoisted on its own pretense of benevolence. Just as mother defined all she did as done for his sake, so does the hospital define all it does to be for the benefit of the schizophrenic. Arrangements which suited mother's convenience were said to be for her child's best interests, and all hospital activity which is for the efficient operation or convenience of the staff, whether forcing patients to rise at six in the morning or cutting out random portions of the brain, must be said to be for the sake of the schizophrenic. It is when he is offered such benevolence that the schizophrenic manifests his most skillful appearance of confusion, disorientation, and delusion. If he is told he must be in bed at nine in the evening because of his need for rest (and not the convenience of the ward staff) the schizophrenic will experience night terrors which keep the ward in turmoil until his more reasonable bed time. Having forced the hard fist of the aide or the heavy hand of the psychiatrist on the shock machine to quiet him, the schizophrenic has won the acknowledgement that nine o'clock bedtime is a hospital convenience. Hanging a psychiatrist on his benevolence is best illustrated by the patient who was faced with a doctor who could not tolerate his patients milling about the ward indicting him for his inability to cure them. He therefore announced that for their sakes the patients must be out of the ward all day getting fresh air. This particular schizophrenic declined to leave the ward. When he was forced out the front door, he walked straight ahead until he bumped into a tree, remaining there outside the doctor's window with his forehead against the tree until the exasperated physician retrieved him later in the day.

The hospital also provides the schizophrenic with the comfortable feeling he is still at home with his family by the similarity in power structure. Just as mother maintained the pretense that father was in charge, while ignoring him, so does the nurse pretend the ward psychiatrist is in charge while running things herself. The schizophrenic soon finds that the ward psychiatrist is as unavailable as his father ever was, since of course the psychiatrist never has the time or inclination to talk to the patients. The schizophrenic finds too that his long training in stirring conflict between his parents is unusually valuable in the hospital where nurse and psychiatrist can be played off against each other with minimum maneuvers. The confusion between doctor and nurse over their official and actual power position can be touched off in quite simple ways. For example, when the doctor requires some activity of the patient, the schizophrenic can indicate that the nurse said he was not to do that. The doctor may reply that by God *he* is the one who makes such decisions, but he becomes uncertain in his dealings with the nurse, who feels in turn that she must have antagonized him in some inexplicable way. If necessary to go to extremes because of a dull witted staff, the patient can begin to scream whenever a particular staff member comes near him, thus making the entire staff look upon that person with suspicion.

The schizophrenic's training in manipulating coalitions across generations comes in appropriately in the hospital. He can join psychiatrist against nurse, nurse against aide, social worker against ward doctor, ward doctor against hospital administrator, staff against family, and so on. More skillful schizophrenics will escape occasionally and join community and police against the hospital. On the rare occasions when the schizophrenic is provided with a psychotherapist, he has the entire confusion in the staff power structure to play upon. The therapist, like mother, can be persuaded to request that the schizophrenic be given special treatment or at least be more fully understood, and the ward psychiatrist, like father, will bluster ineffectually that the patient must do what is expected of him, while the nurse protests that despite what the patient implied she wasn't out of her office for two hours leaving the ward unattended, and the aide will say that it's clearly a paranoid delusion when the patient says he was hit in the gut during the night. These periods of excitement alternate with long days of boredom for the schizophrenic, just as at home.

Whenever he is sufficiently bored, the schizophrenic can provoke action to enliven life on the ward. In fact, many schizophrenics have found they can provide some excitement by *not* doing anything. For example, they can stop eating. Just as mother went into a panic at home if her food was ignored and her poor child was wasting away to her shame, so does the hospital staff develop waves of anxiety if the patient ignores their food. They must have staff conferences, changes of drugs, physical examinations, the ever handy shock machine, extensive efforts to baby him into eating, and finally intravenous feeding. Before reaching the point of no return, the schizophrenic will usually begin to eat again. Some clever schizophrenics will time their resumption of food to coincide with a new drug the doctor has given them. Since the staff is always hoping for a pill which will cure all the staff problems, they rejoice with each success of a new drug—only to discover later that other patients do not respond to it and the responsive schizophrenics have duped them again.

The position and function of the schizophrenic in the hospital is identical with his position and function at home. The staff of a mental institution feel themselves to be outcasts in the profession, insignificant wretches incapable of human accomplishment. Therefore it is essential for their survival that they surround themselves with people who are more incompetent than they are. Living among the experts in failure, the schizophrenics, the staff can stand a little higher in the world. From the top administrator of the hospital who kicks his assistant when irritated, down through the hierarchy to the aide who kicks the patient when irritated, the structure requires that final someone that all else can feel superior to—and there we behold the schizophrenic. As at home, the bad feelings and difficulties of the staff members with each other can be excused as a product of dealing with such a difficult person as the schizophrenic, so that his valuable function as a scapegoat binds the entire structure together like an adhesive.

It should not be thought that just anyone, including people with other psychiatric problems, could fulfill the schizophrenic's function. Training, persistence, and ingenuity are required. There is also a need for courage because of the risks. The schizophrenic not only faces the daily possibility of the aide's fist and the psychiatrist's shock machine, but he also lives under the threat of total isolation in solitary confinement as well as the threat that the doctors will plunge a scalpel into his brain as a last resort. These dangers add spice to the schizophrenic's life, and they require a particular style of behavior from him. This style is known medically as symptomatic of the hospitalized person. Since clear rebellion or justifiable outrage against the institution provokes savage punishment for his own good, the schizophrenic must behave like a difficult person while indicating that it's not he who's doing it and besides he cannot help himself—this is the definition of mental illness. The staff is reluctant to give him the business since he cannot help himself and so they must

flounder in dealing with him—this is called treatment of the mentally ill. The most basic way to behave in a difficult manner and deny that it is your fault is to say that you are someone else and so aliases are common among schizophrenics. However, the mere alias is not enough, it should be one which is clearly an alias, such as a male patient calling himself Jacqueline Khrushchev. Alternatively, one can say that the behavior originated elsewhere, and therefore one should not be punished. A nice device to achieve this is to say that a "voice" told one to do it, therefore responsibility lies elsewhere. One can make any criticism of the staff, even accuse a puritanical nurse of unsavory thoughts, if one says that it is really the Lord speaking and one is merely an instrument for that voice. The nurse becomes uncertain about putting the Lord on the shock roster. Another procedure is to act clearly insane so that one is obviously not responsible for needling the staff. A way to do this is to appear to be disoriented in space and time, which is particularly effective if it carries within it an indictment of the staff. To say that the place is really a prison and it is the seventeenth century is to make it clear that one is too insane to be blamed for an act. Yet at the same time the resemblance to a seventeenth century prison is close enough to most hospitals to arouse the guilt feelings of the staff. One thereby can indict while disarming and escaping blame, all neatly in one maneuver. Sometimes the guilt can be aroused by more ironical disorientation; one can say, for example, that the hospital is a palace and the doctor a king, thereby dismaying the doctor with the comparison. A third procedure is to make caustic comments while giving a silly and delapidated laugh—who can punish such an idiot, and yet the comments simultaneously reach home. One can also indict by actions without ever waying a word. When a schizophrenic stands against the wall with his head hanging down and his arms outstretched, the staff suspects that they are being told they are crucifying the patient, yet they are told in a way that they cannot accept or deny the accusation, or blame the schizophrenic—here lies the true art of schizophrenia.

These few simple procedures may seem limited, but a skillful schizophrenic can provide tremendous variety in his use of them. Whenever he has finally driven the staff to bring brute force to bear, it could be expected that the staff does so with the guilty feeling that they are taking advantage of a poor, helpless victim who cannot control himself. However, to assume that the staff feels guilty is to underestimate their education. After all, psychiatrists have received a liberal college education, thorough medical training, and a full residency in the science of psychiatry. They are usually good-hearted men attempting to do their best, and they follow civilized rules in dealing with the human being. Because of their education and knowledge of the history of men, they are able to use a device which has always been used by civilized men caught in a death struggle for power with other men—they define the other men as not human beings, and therefore anything goes. The good-hearted Southerner can give the Negro his lumps and the good-hearted concentration camp guard in Germany can fling people into gas chambers as long as he can define those people as sub-human. Knowledge of this tradition has helped the psychiatrist, particularly those with a European orientation, to define the schizophrenic as not a person but a thing, an organic hulk who is out of contact with reality. Therefore civilized rules do not apply. By adopting this point of view and building it into a theory of psycosis, the staff can agree that the patient is not responsible for the trouble he is causing because he is not really a person and therefore regular bangs in the head with shock or an isolation room is obviously necessary to point the beast in a more amiable direction. Only by arguing that civilized rules do not apply to the schizophrenic can the staff meet the patient on at least equal terms, because the schizophrenic too is unwilling to follow civilized rules. Driven by his terrifying despair, he will go to any extremity of self abasement and therefore has a great advantage in such a struggle. The staff is faced with a person of extraordinary determination and skill in innovations. Even stripped nude and flung into a cell without furniture and soundproofed so that he cannot be heard, the schizophrenic is still not incapacitated. Ordinary people who must rely on friends, furniture to fling, or at least insults when they are in a power struggle would collapse in futile hopelessness in such a situation. Yet locked up alone and unheard, the schizophrenic still finds ways to express his opinion of the staff and arouse them further. He is willing to use the products of his own body and he will pee upon the door and crap upon the floor, cheerfully drawing pictures of the staff upon the wall in what he considers appropriate material.

Since there is some variety in the hospital environment, from reasonably pleasant wards for showing visiting dignitaries to the miserable back wards ruled by sadistic nurses and aides, it is important that the patient learn how to deal with the staff so that he forces them to behave badly to him but only if *he* has arranged it. He does not mind misery which he has provoked, but he does not like people to treat him badly on their own initiative. Therefore the schizophrenic must do a diagnosis of the staff to find the areas which are most suitable for provocations. The staff too must have an estimate of the range of skill of the schizophrenic so they can know what maneuvers to expect of any individual patient in this struggle. The need for a quick estimate of the schizophrenic has produced psychologists who are willing to do psychological testing so that the staff can diagnose the patient's weak points and thereby gain an advantage in dealing with him. Schizophrenics, however, are not put off as normal people would be by the aroma of pseudo-science exuding from the pores of the psychologist. The patients see immediately that this fellow who sits down pleasantly with them and asks them to look at blots of ink and talk about them is indeed a man who does not have their best interests at heart. In fact the schizophrenic knows what he says about the ink blot will be held against him and affect his career in the hospital in ways he cannot predict. Therefore the wise schizophrenic is guarded in his comments about the ink blots. Faced with the same kind of ambiguous situation he was raised in at home, with equally disastrous effects if he should say the wrong thing, the schizophrenic will avoid describing any coherent picture, because he knows this staff member may make ulterior use of the coherence. Instead he will point out little pieces of the ink blot here and there and make no connections between them. He will also avoid mentioning any of the human shapes he sees, even if they look like the psychologist, because he cannot be sure whether the human beings in power over him will take his comments personally. The more self-confident schizophrenic will toy with the test, reaching for bizarre points to see if he can shake the deadpan expression from the psychologist's face, playing with the idea of a bat since he is supposed to be bats, and occasionally making oblique references to violence to indicate that he knows that this threat lies behind the testing. Only indirectly will he indicate that looking at blots of ink seems rather silly and so he knows there must be some reason for it which is being kept from him. The psychologist is pleased with the schizophrenic's protocol because he can discover that the responses are not common, ignoring the fact that the situation of the schizophrenic is also rather uncommon. It is like the white man in the South who concludes that a Negro is ignorant because the fellow shuffles and scratches his head and says, "Yassah, Boss," ignoring the context which makes it wise for the Negro to behave in that way. Since psychologists have a trained incapacity to examine contexts, they write down in their report that the patient is confused and loose in his associations, has distorted perception, deeply repressed hostility, and a sprained ego. This scientific description of test results is given to the staff which uses it, as the schizophrenic knew they would, to determine where to place him and how to deal with him.

It would seem evident that schizophrenia can be a dangerous game, but it has its lighter side too. Occasionally, for example, the patient is given a chance to have psychotherapy. Although the ward psychiatrists are so flooded with patients they do not have time to talk with them, and would hardly know what to talk with them about if they did take the time, most hospitals report in their publicity brochures that they are not merely prisons because they have a therapy program. This consists of group therapy meetings led by social workers. It is the function of these meetings to (a) turn the schizophrenics upon each other so they will be less occupied with entrapping the staff (this is called the Keseyan function); and (b) provide the social workers with a feeling of being useful while also letting them vent upon the patients the feelings they have developed from attempting to deal with the patient's families. The schizophrenic usually uses these group meetings to sharpen and broaden his techniques of verbal comment. Often he uses them to practice subtle variations in his repetitious behavior; the schizophrenic is, of course, the master at repeating the same behavior until the staff is driven to distraction. A possible record is held by the schizophrenic who, in a period of only two years, said, "I think my thinking is not good," a total of two hundred million, seventy three times.

Occasionally a hospital will have a psychiatrist training program, and here the schizophrenic might have an opportunity for individual psychotherapy with a resident. The profession considers it wise to start these young fellows out on schizophrenics so that anything they meet later when making their fortunes in private practice will be anticlimactic. Psychiatric residents are a peculiar lot. Either they chose psychiatry because they thought they were going mad and it might help, or they could not develop a passion for some other medical speciality, like proctology, and so they fell into psychiatry by default. Once in training they discover that little of what their teachers say is of any use to them in dealing with a schizophrenic. Their instructors teach only part time and make their living in private practice where they entirely avoid schizophrenics (having had enough of them when *they* were residents). The basic problem of the resident is one of translation. His instructors talk in one bizarre language and the patients in another. While the instructors talk about dark Ids flooded with anxiety and the daffodil structure of ego syntonics, the schizophrenics talk about the influence of atomic energy upon the burontonic systems and the difference between hecocks and she-cocks. It is forbidden for instructors or residents to talk directly about the central theme of hospital life, the power struggle among staff and patients.

A typical beginning interchange between patient and psychotherapist can be presented to illustrate the kind of skill required of the true schizophrenic. The patient is brought to a room by an aide who mumbles something about seeing a doctor and then shuffles away. The schizophrenic waits, uncertain what new tactic the staff is offering and attempts to estimate its degree of savagery. At this point the door opens and a vacant-faced young man enters. He wears a suit and tie to distinguish him from the patients. "Hello," he says with false heartiness, "I'm Dr. Offgamay." The schizophrenic stares at the wall as if he has not noticed the intrusion. "Well," says the doctor, attempting to ignore being ignored, "I thought we might talk about things." This typical therapeutic gambit, the vague, ambiguous, open-ended statement interests the patient. It may even arouse his admiration since it is a degree of ambiguity he thought only his parents could achieve. He begins to test whether this man is really what he appears to be or is more dangerous by saying something like, "My tail light is on," or perhaps, "My head was bashed in last night."

"Well now," says the young man, uncertain what to do with that sort of statement, "I'd like to know a little about you, won't you tell me about yourself."

The schizophrenic, who knows perfectly well his record has been carefully examined for his history, has already understood the situation and he decides on a further test for confirmation. He says, "I want to do what you

do."

The doctor freezes—his status position shaken by this mild remark as if by an earthquake. "Oh," he says, his voice rather cool, "how long have you been a *patient* here?"

The schizophrenic has finished his testing, and he replies, "I was born here." He makes this statement with absolute sincerity, as if he fully believes it.

"Born here?" says the doctor, so confused by the sincerity that he can only inquire, "How old are you?"

"A hundred and eighty-seven," says the schizophrenic. The doctor suddenly has that lost feeling of one who suspects he is being put on and has been provoked into making a fool of himself and yet cannot be sure. The result is continuing suppressed fury and desperation as the game goes on and the doctor finds himself constantly provoked into saying what he would rather not say. He can only grab onto his shaky status position as a passenger holds the door handle on a wild ride down a mountain road.

This illustration of a typical interchange demonstrates the quick perception and interpersonal skill of the schizophrenic. If they had competitions, schizophrenics would vie among themselves to see who could discover most quickly whether he was dealing with a worthy opponent.

Once the therapy is off to this fine start, the only skill required of the schizophrenic is to keep it going. After all, the therapist is usually the only one in the hospital who will speak to him, except for the aides who have more muscle than wit. The schizophrenic must keep the therapy ongoing by not creating too much fear and despair in the therapist while at the same time not allowing anything which might approach success. Since residents change every few months, it is also good to give an impression of almost being cured so that this resident can encourage one of the next crop of residents to continue the treatment. Some schizophrenics can achieve strings of eight to ten psychotherapists over time, each one feeling that he is almost able to "reach" this poor wretch and a few more interviews will bring about a breakthrough.

The skill of the schizophrenic comes into play in several ways in psychotherapy. He must provide stimulation for the therapist and keep him coming, but he must also provide sufficient exasperating difficulties to help the therapist feel that he faces a worthy challenge of his abilities. Keeping the therapist on the hook requires an avoidance of any direct confrontation of the therapist with his miserable incompetence as part of a courtesy procedure. For example, if the therapist is late to an appointment and does not bother to apologize, it is not correct to directly confront him with his rudeness or he is likely to flee, as mother did when directly confronted with her misbehavior. Rather, the schizophrenic must tell a story which allows the therapist to correct himself if he chooses. For example, the patient can say, "I was out on my submarine this morning, and we were to meet the refueling ship off Madagascar, but unfortunately the ship had been struck by an atomic bomb and barely limped in late with its Chinese flagons at half mast." This rather complex statement, which any schizophrenic can quickly devise, allows the therapist an out. He can say, "I'm sorry I was late today," or he can argue, "Now Sam, you know you weren't out on a submarine this morning, you were right here in the hospital." The therapist's recognition that there might be more here than meets the vacant eye is usually represented by his following such an argument with, "Now let's try to get an understanding of why you'd think you were on a submarine. What does a submarine mean to you?"

A further requirement of the schizophrenic is an ability to find out quickly what the current psychiatric ideology is so that he can provide the young therapist with support for the theories he is learning. If it is a period when genital symbolism is the order of the day, the patient must discuss kings being overthrown and virgin queens married and vaguely rub his crotch whenever he mentions his mother. If genital symbolism is passe and

oral symbolism is being emphasized in training, the patient must quickly adapt to oral metaphors. He will discuss the cement in his stomach and the whiteness of milk, he can offer drawings which vaguely resemble breasts to the keen psychiatric eye, and he may make occasional sucking motions with his lips to stimulate the therapist. The skillful schizophrenic can read the interests of therapists from minimal cues, such as lighting up of the eyes when some obvious symbol that makes sense in theory is mentioned. The more Sullivanian fads require more skill from the patient. As the therapist struggles to handle his interpersonal defenses and to help the patient discover how he deals with people, the patient must offer interpersonal behavior which is easily enough interpreted by even a novice therapist. For example, he must fold his arms and cross his legs and turn his head away so the therapist can point out that he is building a wall between them and interfering with their interpersonal relationship. However, the patient must not merely help the therapist, he also must occasionally show the novice that he still has a great deal to learn. When the young fellow is feeling rather confident in his therapeutic acumen, the schizophrenic can stare thoughtfully at him and then look away and say, "There are some people in the world who have a homosexual fix." Such a comment will shatter any sensitive resident and leave him dragging through the day wondering about his unconscious desires.

The odds against a schizophrenic in a hospital meeting a skillful therapist of schizophrenics are so great that in the memory of those who keep track of these matters the last time it occurred was in Buffalo in 1947. Should this happen, the rull range of schizophrenic genius is necessary. He must play therapist against staff, make a thrust at every weak point in the man, pretend improvement when there is none, and generally fight for his life. After all, if he is inadvertently cured he must go out of the hospital to the family waiting for him at the gate. That family has discovered their child can be the burden which holds the family together while still being in the hospital with a hired staff to deal with the inconvenience, and so they protest how welcome he is without wishing him back. The occasional families who actually wish the patient to return home have marshalled their forces in his absence and plan to make up for lost time in giving him the business. Should the patient go mad and become normal, he also faces a society which will blacklist him for having accepted hospital treatment.

Psychiatry today is going through revolutionary changes, and we owe to the schizophrenic many of the advances being made. It is evident that the schizophrenic is responsible for the recent movement to close down all mental hospitals. The leaders of this movement, the more prominent psychiatrists in the field, are suggesting that rest homes should be created for the aged and emergency wards be set up in general hospitals for people to stay in for a few days during family crisis. Mental hospitals would be discarded with a state law that psychotic patients could not be kept in custody more than a few days unless they had committed a crime. The proponents of this scheme argue that schizophrenics should be returned to the families who deserve them and psychiatrists should be forced to deal with the insane and not avoid them.

Enthusiasts for the mental hospital, a group composed of families of patients, psychiatrists in peaceful practice, and those people employed in such institutions, argue that

such a radical change is fantastic. These patients are diseased and need medical care, they say, and besides they don't make sufficient income to pay psychiatrists for treatment. The moral wing of this faction also point out that it would be unfair to loose psychotics upon the the profession of psychiatry. Just as one would not put a man who runs the mile in four hours in the same race with a man who runs it in four minutes, so it is unfair to face the average psychiatrist with a schizophrenic or his family.

However, enthusiasts for closing down the hospitals argue in turn that such an act is necessary because of the skills of the true schizophrenic. As one proponent put it, "When patients were confined at home, it was thought they would improve with hospital treatment. Now let us admit defeat. Despite all attempts at reform and promising new methods of approach, the schizophrenic has beaten us. We should concede that fact and find other ways to deal with him." More active advocates of closing down mental institutions have created a slogan which can be seen on the signs they carry as they picket mental hospitals, "Let's get the patients off the back wards and back home into the back rooms!"

Reference

Laing, R. D., *Is Schizophrenia A Disease?* International Journal of Social Psychiatry. V. 10, 1974.

SELF TEST: MEASURING COMPREHENSION
"The Art Of Being Schizophrenic", By Jay Haley

1. What are the characteristics of the parents and siblings of the potential schizophrenic?

2. What role does the potential schizophrenic play within the family structure?

3. How is the situation encountered by the schizophrenic in the mental hospital similar to that of his home situation?

4. What criticisms does Haley make of the mental hospital and its staff?

5. In the final analysis, is the schizophrenic manipulated by those around him, or does he do the manipulating? Why do you feel this way?

THE PRINCIPLE OF NORMALIZATION & ITS IMPLICATIONS TO PSYCHIATRIC SERVICES

from *The American Journal of Psychiatry*

Wolf Wolfensberger, Ph.D.

In the concluding paragraphs of the preceding article, Jay Haley refers to a national movement to close down large mental hospitals. Deinstitutionalization refers to a movement to 1) provide appropriate mental health services in community-based systems, 2) assure accurate matching of client needs to available services, and 3) assure that potential benefits of deinstitutionalization justify the expenditure of community resources. This movement is progressing in America today. In 1955 there were 559,000 residential patients in state mental hospitals. In 1975 this number had been reduced to 193,000 patients.

Just as we have learned that putting a person in prison does not guarantee that the individual will be better able to function in society after his release (indeed, prisons often serve as finishing schools for criminality), we are realizing that mental hospitals provide incoming patients with large numbers of individuals who have assumed the role of being mentally ill, and "aid" the newcomer in assuming the same identity. Thus, the deinstitutionalization movement is a recognition of the failure of large mental hospitals to help patients, and a provision for new directions in mental health care.

The issue of deinstitutionalization is an extremely controversial one. Proponents of the movement argue that by allowing former patients to enter normal community settings, the processes of social adaptation and normalization will be enhanced. On the other hand, critics of deinstitutionalization refer to it as the "dumping" of sick, deviant individuals into communities where they are unable to function, are poorly cared for, are taken advantage of, and are unwelcome.

To emotionally advocate the closing of large mental hospitals is merely hollow rhetoric, unless realistic, comprehensive, normalization programs are developed as alternatives to institutionalization. In the following article, Syracuse University Professor Wolf Wolfensberger offers some concrete suggestions as to how the normalization of formerly institutionalized patients can be accomplished. He also discusses normalization regarding those patients who are sufficiently deviant to warrant continued hospitalization. The article is extremely relevant to the reader living in a community where deinstitutionalization programs are being carried out.

The "normalization principle" formulated by Scandinavian workers in mental retardation aims at eliciting and maintaining culturally normative behavior and using culturally normative means to this end. The principle is simultaneously simple and comprehensive, and it can constitute a unifying ideology for all human management areas. It provides guidance for decisions from the lowest clinical to the highest systems levels. Some specific implications for psychiatry are discussed.

The President's Committee on Mental Retardation recently sponsored a searching reappraisal of residential services for the mentally retarded.[1] In this report the history and evolution of residential models in retardation were traced; present practices were documented, assessed, and largely rejected; and a number of sweeping proposals were offered for the future. It is noteworthy that in the concluding and synthesizing chapter, Dybwad[2] identified the "normalization principle" as the keystone of a new approach not only to residential services specifically, but also to all services for the retarded. I submit that the field loosely referred to as "mental health" can profit as much from utilization of the normalization principle as the field of mental retardation.

The Normalization Principle

The normalization principle was first fully formulated in Scandinavia, and it has received little discussion thus far in the American literature. Yet the principle is consistent with and subsumes a number of concepts and principles that have gained ascendancy in sociological theory and human management practices and are widely known in the United States.

As a theoretical construct, the normalization principle is remarkably elegant and parsimonious and has profound implications for the management of persons who are likely to be viewed as "deviants" in a culture. In Scandinavia, especially in Denmark and Sweden, the normalization principle has not only

become a dominant theme in clinical practices but is also expressed and accepted increasingly by the citizenry. The principle has been incorporated most extensively in the area of mental retardation and has found its most recent legal expression in a new, comprehensive Swedish law (effective since July 1, 1968) about provisions and services for the mentally retarded (3).[2] Its expression in concrete service structures and delivery systems has recently been documented by Bank-Mikkelsen(5) for Denmark and Grunewald(6) for Sweden.

The principle of normalization is deceptively simple. Reduced to its essentials, it states that human management practices should enable a deviant person to function in ways considered to be within the acceptable norms of his society; by the same token, human management practices should enable a person who is not a deviant to continue being able to function within the acceptable norms of his society. As much as possible, the means employed should be culturally normative ones.

In terms of human management practices the principle has innumerable specific implications, some of which will be discussed later in this paper. However, the specifics can be classed into three broad categories:

1. Deviant persons should be helped to be able to become less deviant and nondeviant people to remain nondeviant; however, it should be noted that the goal is not to impose social conformity but to prevent or reverse involuntary or unconscious deviancy.

2. Deviant persons should be presented and interpreted to society in such a way as to emphasize their similarities to rather than differences from other people, and their positive aspects rather than negative ones. The use of culturally normative rather than esoteric means is intended to minimize the appearance of separateness of deviant individuals.

3. The attitudes and values of society should be shaped to be more accepting and tolerant of harmless types of differentness, such as differentness in appearance, demeanor, intelligence, speech and language, nation-

ality, education, race, skin color, ethnic background, and dress.

My first response to exposure to the normalization principle was "So what is new?" and I have found that most people respond as I first did, wholeheartedly endorsing the principle. However, I have also found that neither I nor most other professionals in the human management field could immediately grasp the sweeping implications of the principle, much less change daily human management practices so as to bring them into conformity with it. It is for this reason that I will spell out some specific management implications of the normalization principle.

Specific Human Management Implications

Normalization means that deviant persons should be exposed to experiences that are likely to elicit or maintain normative (accepted) behavior. These experiences can be derived from one's physical activities and from one's interaction with the physical environment (such as one's residence and its furnishings) and one's physical neighborhood. They can also be derived from one's interaction with the social environment, such as one's family, neighbors, fellow citizens, group members, and human managers. Social interaction with typical citizens under typical life conditions brings with it innumerable occasions and role expectancies that are likely to elicit normative behavior and normative role performance. Thus both physical and social environments must be structured in such a manner as to weigh their normalizing and de-normalizing elements, as well as those elements that are irrelevant to normalization.

Normalization has many subtle implications that require appreciation of other sociobehavioral processes. For instance, a common phenomenon in human management is for deviant persons to drift into employment where they work with clients who are deviant themselves. Thus the teacher who cannot cope with regular pupils is put in charge of a special education class; the physician who

does not have a license to practice in the community (usually because of inadequate training or skill, language problems, alcoholism, drug addiction, or physical or mental problems) is permitted to practice in institutions for the retarded or disordered; prisoners may be placed into training or work with the mentally retarded; retarded workers may be placed as orderlies in homes for the aged; and so forth.

Usually human managers defend these practices on narrow clinical grounds: The deviant worker can make a contribution by such an arrangement; he can be habilitated by it; and so forth. However, attention rarely is given to certain important and broad sociological considerations that lead back to the normalization principle. Three such considerations come to mind in this context.

1. When a deviant "reject" from society is employed to administer services to other deviants, it is inevitable that members of the larger society conclude consciously or unconsciously that the deviants who are served are of low value. For instance, a person not good enough to teach my normal child may be good enough to teach someone else's retarded child. Thus a juxtaposition of deviant workers with deviant clients devalues both of them even more, but particularly so the client. Inevitably, this devaluing perception will lead fellow citizens to behave toward the deviant client group in a way that is more likely to be "dehabilitating"(7) than normalizing.

2. When deviants work for and with deviants, almost inevitably a subculture of deviancy is created that exacerbates rather than reverses the deviancy of those within the subculture.

3. At a given time, a person generally has the potential of forming a limited number of social ties and meaningful relationships. Usually he will fill his "relationship vacancies" with the people he encounters in his social system(s). The likelihood of filling one's relationship needs with deviant persons probably stands in direct proportion to the percentage of deviants in one's social

system(s). Thus, by surrounding a deviant client with deviant workers, or vice versa, the chances of each group to socialize with nondeviant persons is lowered. Both the real and perceived deviancies of both groups are likely to be increased; and the chances of habilitation for either group, especially the much larger client group, are likely to be reduced.

It follows that instead of there being mutual benefits, both groups may actually lose—if not in each concrete instance, then at least in the long run of societal processes. Normalization principles would thus not only prohibit the juxtaposition of deviant workers with deviant clients but would dictate that as much as possible, deviant individuals be surrounded by nondeviant ones.

Let us return to the clinical considerations for a moment. Actually, juxtaposing deviant workers with deviant clients has been primarily a matter of convenience. If normalization principles were clearly understood and accepted and if a commitment were made to the discovery or creation of alternatives, such alternatives capable of optimizing normalization of all involved could be found, developed, and/or utilized.

Exposure to Normative Experiences

Since exposure to normative experiences is a crucial aspect of normalization, every effort should be made to avoid conditions that are apt to inhibit or even prohibit normalizing behavior. Thus psychiatric services should be structured so as to bring about the most feasible maximum integration of the deviant into society.

It follows that in a psychiatric service that purports to be habilitational, deviant persons should never be congregated in numbers larger than the surrounding community (usually even neighborhood) social system can readily absorb and integrate. How large such a number might be is ultimately an empirical question and depends much on local community factors. There is probably no neighborhood that can integrate 2,000 deviants,

although there are some that might be able to integrate 100 to 200. Generally, a psychiatric residential service or similar facility should probably not congregate more than 25 to 50 deviant persons. This implies a major rethinking and reorganization in regard to our residential psychiatric services, especially those that are defined as habilitation-oriented.

Generally, people in our society engage in age-specific associations and activities, and many activities and services are specifically identified in the minds of the public as appropriate for one age group and less appropriate or even inappropriate for another. Thus it is abnormalizing if we place persons into a context of activities or services perceived as age-atypical by a significant portion of the public.

This means that adults should not be housed closely adjacent to children and should ordinarily not be engaged in activities that are not considered appropriate for a typical adult. Thus while American society approves of recreation *after* work, it does not approve of recreation *instead* of work; the latter is viewed as childlike play activity.

A prime implication is that endless "recreational therapy" as well as the often euphemistically labeled "occupational therapy" of our psychiatric facilities are not culturally normative means and may have an effect opposite to their stated and intended one: They may dehabilitate and denormalize. Even if one were not willing to agree with this interpretation, one might consider whether meaningful work in a typical work routine would not be more culturally normative and therefore more effective than the ambiguously structured, defined, perceived, and valued recreational and occupational "therapies."

The conclusions that have been reached here can also be derived by considering other points that will be discussed shortly, such as the meaning of work in our culture and the nature of a normal rhythm of daily, weekly, and monthly activities of adults.

Normalization means that a person should live in a normal routine of life. In our culture most people live in one place, work or attend school in another, receive their medical treatments somewhere other than their residence (unless they are bed-bound), and partake of a variety of recreational activities outside their homes and places of work. Thus when we offer residence, treatment, work, religious nurture, and recreation all under one roof (as we usually do in residential treatment and service centers), we often denormalize.

To offer all services under one roof is convenient—although not always as economical as claimed. However, this convenience should be sacrificed if a useful principle is at stake. We should ask ourselves at all times whether any service provided in conjunction with a residential service could not be provided in a more normalizing fashion by drawing on extraresidential and community resources, thereby increasing the resident's integration and habilitation. Obviously, a community mental health center attempting to offer "comprehensive" services under one roof is likely to violate the normalization principle.

Most adults work eight or more hours a day, usually between 8 a.m. and 5 p.m., and usually outside their place of residence. Thus we should strive to provide a similar rhythm and arrangement and to involve adults in meaningful work, in as near a meaningful workday as possible. The idleness forced upon many of the consumers of our psychiatric services, especially residential ones, is clearly denormalizing; only slightly less denormalizing is "occupation" or work that is meaningless. This consideration argues strongly for the establishment of sheltered workshops that can be used by residents of psychiatric facilities—except that for most psychiatric residents these shops should not be on the grounds of the residential facility, as this would not be normalizing.

A normal rhythm of the day also means that most people under treatment should not have to rise significantly earlier than typical fellow citizens or have to go to bed at odd hours. It also means that they should be able to eat their meals at normal hours; few

citizens eat their supper at 4:30 or 5:00 p.m., as do residents in many of our treatment facilities.

Most people go on a vacation trip once a year, which breaks up the routine of life. Few things are as monotonous as long-term residence in a psychiatric facility. It is thus normalizing to provide annual trips for such residents to the usual tourist and vacation places. In Scandinavia even the severely retarded are taken on vacation trips—often abroad. Although cost may be a problem, at least some arrangements can be made, even if it is only a trip of two to three days' duration to a vacation home owned by the facility.

Normalization implies that generally, a person under psychiatric management lead an economic existence that is typical of the larger society. Once more, this implies that clients should have an opportunity to work and earn some income so as to exercise adult control over pocket money (not merely scrip or credit) and minor, everyday purchases. In Danish and Swedish human management services, clients who are impecunious or cannot earn money are provided generous allowances so as to increase dignity, assist in realistic social training, and foster independent choice behavior (6). "Poverty in a mental hospital is no less dehumanizing than in a slum"(8).

Although the normalizing nature of work has long been recognized in psychiatric practice, it has been greatly underutilized. One reason may be that in the acute stages of a client's dysfunctioning, the psychiatric manager may be impressed by the fact that the client's behavior has decreased or even eliminated his ability to carry out his *ordinary* work. The manager may then conclude that the same would be the case with all work, overlooking the possibility that the client may be capable of working, and being normalized by some other type of work activity. For instance, the certified public accountant, although momentarily too distraught to handle his ordinary job, may be effective in and normalized by the workshop assembly of relay switches.

Another reason may be that when work was assigned to psychiatric clients, it usually was work associated with the maintenance of the facility, e.g., in the laundry or library, on the farm or living unit. Such work has suffered from two aspects that have diminished its normalizing value. Such work was often exploitative, involving little or no pay and perhaps even leading to institutional peonage(9) rather than habilitation; conversely, work was often contrived or viewed with such an indulgent paternalistic ("therapeutic"?) attitude that it lost much of its work nature, thereby its sociocultural meaning, and consequently much of its normalizing effect.

Normalization also dictates that a person should be as independent, free to move about, and empowered to make meaningful choices as are typical citizens of comparable age in the community. As much as possible, his wishes and desires should carry the same weight as they would under ordinary circumstances outside of a human management context.

This means that unless it is essential, a person should not be submitted to a "mortification" process upon attaining "patienthood" (e.g., stripped of clothes and possessions, locked up) and that generally he should not be prevented by even nonphysical (e.g., social and psychological) means from exercising normal freedom of movement. Furthermore, a person generally should have reasonable control over his physical environment, including freedom to turn lights on and off, to open and close windows, to regulate the temperature in his room, and to decide whether he wants another person to enter or not. A nurse or other manager sweeping abruptly into a resident's room commits an act of denormalization. No person should be deprived of his physical freedom or his freedom of choice because he is housed in a facility with other people who appear incapable of exercising these freedoms.

A secondary implication is that residential facilities should achieve a greater degree of specialization of function. Instead of congregating the mildly disordered and the severely disordered together, as we commonly do at least during some (usually the initial) phases of a typical residential treatment course, we should group clients so that each group can be served with the minimum feasible number of restrictions and even personnel. Thus contrary to stereotype, a high staff ratio can imply an interpretation of the client as being more deviant than he is and can thus be denormalizing under certain circumstances.

Normalization means living in a bisexual world. In residential facilities this means that the building and the social structure should produce at least as much mingling of sexes as in a hotel, a mixed boarding house, or a home in which there live adults other than a married couple. For models, one need only think back to the extended households of some decades ago when families sometimes shared their homes with aunts, uncles, grandparents, housekeepers, govenesses, etc. A bisexual environment also means that there should be both men and women working with the clients.

Finally, an important aspect of normalization is to apply health, safety, comfort, and similar standards to mental health facilities as they are applied to comparable facilities for other citizens. This has implications primarily to residential facilities such as institutions and even more specifically to state-operated services that, in many states, may and do operate below the standards prescribed by law for private facilities. However, it also has implications to clinics. For instance, reception and waiting areas should be as comfortable, attractive, and private as typical citizens might encounter in comparable community services. By this criterion, the reception areas of many of our (psychiatric) clinics are *not* normalizing.

There are, of course, innumerable other implications from the clinical level to the level of large social systems. The examples given here represent only a selected and arbitrary sampling. However, they underline that many major and minor practices that are currently accepted and not found objectionable by proponents of other human management systems are, in fact, quite inconsistent with the principle of normalization.

Normalization Versus Other Management Systems

The normalization principle has powerful theoretical force vis-a-vis other human management systems, and despite its late emergence, considerable empirical evidence—primarily from social psychology and related fields—can be marshalled in support of it(10). However, upon first superficial exposure to the principle, one may well ask how it differs from a number of other approaches, as, for example, the therapeutic community.

The difference lies in the simplicity, parsimony, and comprehensiveness of the principle. The principle requires no assumptions that the consumer of human management services is, or is not, "sick" or a "patient." The principle is applicable not only to psychiatric populations and practices, both residential and nonresidential, but to many aspects of societal functioning and human management services as well.[3] The principle subsumes many current human management theories and measures—but goes beyond them in stipulating other measures that have been neglected so far. And the principle is easily understood once one has opened one's mind to it.

Occasionally, psychiatric orientations have been classified as being somatotherapeutic, psychotherapeutic, and sociotherapeutic. Although the normalization principle transcends psychiatry, it can be viewed as being most consistent with a sociotherapeutic approach in that it uses concepts and constructs rooted primarily in sociology. The emergence of this principle appears particularly timely now, both because of the apparent confusion and disagreement in the field in regard to human management ideologies and because the field appears to be ready to orient itself increasingly toward sociotherapeutic concepts(11, 12). While some management concepts, such as the therapeutic community, constituted a big step from a medical to a social model, the very word "therapeutic" still symbolizes medical model thinking. Now we should advance in our thinking from a "therapeutic community" to a "normalizing community."

A noteworthy aspect of the normalization principle is that it suggests action on three levels: clinical, public interpretation, and societal change. In addition to suggesting specific practices on all three levels, the principle also has relevance to the balance between them. At present, most mental health professionals work on the first level; very few work on the third. The normalization principle presents a powerful rationale for a redistribution of psychiatric priorities so that the second and third levels will receive at least as much attention as the first. After all, fellow citizens are the ones who ultimately define a person's behavior as deviant, and thus much deviancy is of our own making. Furthermore, by his involvement in sociosystemic action, a professional can often be instrumental in bringing about more individual benefits in a short time than he could in a lifetime of traditional clinical service.

From the larger viewpoint of how to move society toward effective support of necessary social action measures, the normalization principle has many advantages. Our society apparently has an inadequate understanding of current management measures in mental health (much less so than in mental retardation, for example), and this is an area where societal understanding will probably have to precede effective societal support. On the other hand, the normalization principle makes sense; it can be explained in a matter of minutes to an average citizen and usually finds at least partial acceptance. Thus it would appear that to the degree that the mental health field explicitly embraces this principle and its concrete implications, it may not only become more effective in its management and practices, but will also be able to marshal the necessary societal support for the action that is so urgent.

Footnotes

[1]The Webster's dictionary definition of management is "judicious use of means to accomplish an end." For the purposes of this paper I will define a concept of "human management" and of "human management services" as entry of individuals and/or agencies, acting in societally sanctioned capacities, into the functioning spheres of individuals, families, or larger social systems in order to bring about changes intended to benefit such individuals, their families or larger social systems, or society in general.

[2]The law is dated December 15, 1967, and is printed in the Swedish Code of Statutes, 1967(4).

[3]The principle can even be incorporated into some existing management theories, purifying and yet preserving them. For instance, the medical model is highly appropriate for certain types of problems, but it could be considerably improved by being suffused with the normalization principle.

"The Principle of Normalization And Its Implications to Psychiatric Services"
By Wolf Wolfensberger

1. What does normalization mean?

2. Cite specific ways by which the normalization of the deinstitutionalized patient can be enhanced.

3. Based on what you know about deinstitutionalization, do you feel that existing deinstitutionalization programs abide by the suggestions of Dr. Wolfensberger? Why?

4. Cite specific ways by which the normalization of those requiring residential care can be enhanced.

Chapter 9
CLARIFICATION

We have now covered the five major perspectives that have emerged as the dominant perspectives regarding the conceptualization and treatment of behavioral abnormality. As we covered the various perspectives, I trust it became apparent to you that the theory and treatment practices of each perspective were unique, and often directly in opposition to the notions of other perspectives. This was to be expected. It is uncommon to find experts in any field totally agreeing with other experts within the same field. If you are still somewhat confused about which perspective offers the most valid conceptualization and treatment of abnormality - don't dismay. There is no easy answer to this issue. In fact, if at this point you are confused about the relative merits of the individual perspectives, I feel that a major objective of this book has been met. I don't ordinarily derive pleasure from helping to confuse people, but for a student of abnormal psychology to appreciate the confusing, controversial nature of this field is of extreme importance.

The situation is not hopeless. We can make some sense of all this controversy and disagreement. It is the goal of this chapter to allow you to develop an understanding of the strengths and limitations of each perspective, so that you can come to some personal conclusions regarding the relative merits of the different perspectives. The purpose of this chapter is "to put the perspectives into perspective".

Based upon discussions with both mental patients and their families, I have developed the impression that commonly these people are not very knowledgeable about the various kinds of psychiatric and psychological treatments that are available. I perceive that they believe that all psychiatric treatment is the same, regardless of the hospital, staff, or clinician assigned to the patient. Obviously, this is not the case.

As pointed out in the chapter on the social perspective, the medical profession has replaced the church as the major source of social authority in modern America. This has often led people to place blind faith in the medical and psychological professions, and to trust without question, the directives of doctors. Obviously, the doctor should be the source of medical authority, but not to the point that whatever he suggests or directs is automatically accepted as valid. As evidence of the trust people place in the medical profession, I have on occasion heard patients and members of their family implore doctors to "cure" the patient. Upon hearing such requests, I feel compelled to inform the people that doctors have no magic wand to wave over the patient that will automatically cure him. However, for a patient to plead with a doctor to cure him is indicative of the total trust and faith placed in the psychiatrist, and the medical profession in general.

When patients enter psychiatric hospitals following psychiatric emergencies, such as suicide attempts, both the patient and members of his family are in confused, anxious states. These people ask numerous questions of the hospital staff. The questions are of immediate concern to them and of importance, but are not the most crucial questions to be asked in the admission situation. For example, they may ask "Does my insurance cover psychiatric hospitalization?", "How long will I be here?", "Who will take care of the children?", or "What will my boss think when he learns that I am in a psychiatric hospital?" These are indeed important questions, but questions related to the type of treatment the patient will receive are of greater importance.

As I have indicated throughout the book, the type of treatment a patient receives is dependent upon the orientation of his doctor. Patients come under the care of certain doctors in a variety of ways. Some seek the care of a certain doctor because a member of the hospital staff told him that the doctor was a "good" one. Others may come under a certain doctor's care because he happened to be on duty at the time of the psychiatric emergency. Commonly, neither the patient nor members of his family know very much about the therapeutic orientation of a doctor. They don't know if the doctor is a psychoanalyst, behaviorist, humanist, or a proponent of the illness or social perspectives.

Unfortunately, clinicians often rely too heavily upon the theory and techniques of the perspective in which they were trained and have practiced since their training. The result is that they often develop "blinders" around their "theoretical eyes" which hinder their ability to perceive the applicability of alternative treatment methods, even when these alternative methods may be more beneficial to the patient. Just as a shortage of medical general practitioners exists, so does a shortage of mental health general practitioners. The clinician should be familiar with the theory and techniques of all of the perspectives in order to select and employ the treatment that is of most potential benefit for the particular patient. Unfortunately, this is too seldom the case. Thus, knowing the orientation of the clinician is of extreme importance, because the type of treatment the patient receives is dependent upon the orientation of the clinician.

The best questions that can be asked at the time of admission to a psychiatric hospital are those that relate to the specific type of treatment the patient will receive. Questions such as "What kind of treatment is best for my particular problem?", and "Who on your staff can best provide this treatment?", are extremely relevant. Recipients of psychiatric services seldom view themselves as consumers of a service - a very expensive one at that. People who would become enraged if they purchased a defective toaster in the department store often passively accept any doctor to whom they have been assigned. People may fail to ask these crucial questions at the time of admission for a variety of reasons. They may be simply too anxious and confused at the time to think of such questions, not well enough informed to know which questions to ask, or have an inherent trust that doctors will make the correct decisions. The fact remains that often the most critical questions at the time of admission remain unasked and unanswered.

Let us now investigate the issue of which perspectives are the most appropriate in application to specific types of mental health problems, and also indicate situations in which particular perspectives may not be particularly relevant. The following discussion could be of great personal relevance, should you or a loved one ever be in need of mental health services. I will cover each perspective individually, indicating those instances in which the perspective is particularly relevant, and also point out limitations of the perspective in dealing with certain problems.

THE ILLNESS PERSPECTIVE

The illness perspective views behavioral abnormality as the result of genetic, biochemical, or structural disorder. The most valid application of the illness perspective lies in the treatment of disorders that have been definitely shown to have organic etiologies. For example, it has been conclusively demonstrated that general paresis (syphilitic psychosis) is caused by irreversible brain damage resulting from untreated syphilitic infection. Penicillin effectively prevents general paresis if it is employed before brain damage results from syphilitic infection.

Brain tumors, or other structural disorders of the brain, can cause psychiatric disorders. George Gershwin, one of America's most beloved composers, became increasingly restless, nervous and despondent in the last year of his life. He began seeing a psychoanalyst, but his condition worsened. He began losing consciousness for brief periods. His analyst suggested that there might be something physically wrong with him, but Gershwin maintained that his problems were related to the stress of his work. Although medical examinations revealed no abnormalities, his condition continued to worsen. Eventually he lost consciousness and slipped into a coma. Emergency surgery revealed a cystic brain tumor. He died shortly thereafter at the age of 38 (Goldberg, 1958, pp. 346-350). Obviously, the illness perspective would have been the most appropriate in application to Gershwin's condition. There was a definite organic etiology, although this etiology went long undetected. No form of psychotherapy would have benefitted his condition. Thus, psychosurgery emerges as a viable treatment for organic brain disorders.

Huntington's chorea, a degenerative nerve disorder that leads to psychosis and ultimately death, is known to be genetically transmitted through a dominant gene. Although there is no known effective treatment for Huntington's chorea, it becomes apparent that a medical approach is appropriate in conceptualizing general paresis, psychosis resulting from tumors, and Huntington's chorea, as there are definite medical etiologies for these disorders.

It appears that a biochemical breakthrough has been made in the treatment of manic-depression. Ronald Fieve and William E. Bunney are two of America's strongest advocates of the use of lithium carbonate to control the crippling moodswings characteristic of the manic–depressive. Lithium carbonate is a naturally occurring salt, which interestingly is present in the mineral waters that wealthy people have drunk for centuries for medicinal purposes. According to Fieve, "Lithium is the first specific prophylactic (preventive) treatment ever to come about in the field of psychiatry. It prevents the recurrence of a major mental disease - manic-depression" (The Thin Edge-Depression, 1975).

Bunney and his associates (1968) found that substituting controlled manic-depressives' lithium pills with placebos led to a return of manic symptoms in their patients within a 24 hour period. Bunney also feels that heredity plays a role in determining depression and manic-depression. He has stated that if one member of an identical twin pair is severely depressed, there is a 60-80% likelihood that the other twin will also be severely depressed. However, in fraternal twins, which are no more genetically similar than siblings, the concordance rate drops to only about 15% (The Thin Edge-Depression, 1975).

Popular singer Tony Orlando has suffered severe manic-depression which necessitated his temporary retirement from show business. He has been undergoing lithium treatment for his disorder. In an interview on the Mike Douglas television show, Orlando stated "Manic-depressiveness (sic) is . . . now controllable with a pill . . . A pill that can stabilize your mood until your blood goes back to its normal state . . . Biochemical therapy . . . is really the most contemporary way of dealing with emotional problems."

Famous playwright, Josh Logan, whose credits include "South Pacific" and "Annie Get Your Gun", had been plagued with recurrent episodes of manic-depression since 1939. He had tried various kinds of treatments with limited success. In 1969 he sought the care of Dr. Fieve and has since had his manic-depression controlled through lithium therapy. Referring to the period of his life since he began lithium treatment, Logan stated ". . . I just can't believe life could have been so enjoyable for that length of time if I hadn't been tempered, so to speak, by lithium" (Schanche, 1974). Today, hope remains high that the lithium is the "magic bullet" that controls manic-depression.

Unfortunately, biochemical research in the treatment of schizophrenia has not yielded the convincing results that lithium has in the treatment of manic-depression. Anti-psychotic drugs do have beneficial effects in the treatment of certain psychotic symptoms. However, these drugs only control the symptoms of the disorder, and do not attack its cause, just as cold tablets work on cold symptoms, and not the cause of the cold. No one medical treatment exists that consistently improves the conditions of large numbers of schizophrenics. Schizophrenia remains a puzzle; not only to the illness perspective, but the entire mental health profession. The illness perspective emerges as most appropriate in the understanding and treating of such disorders as manic-depression and those linked to heredity, or infection and disease of the brain.

A major limitation of the illness perspective lies in its inability to discover organic etiologies in all cases of behavioral disorders. It is my impression that proponents of the illness perspective often seek to apply the medical model in cases where no identifiable etiology can be discovered. In some of these cases the causes are likely to be strictly psychological. Ronald Fieve states that lithium is effective in controlling emotional illness in 80-85% of the cases it is employed. He also admits that he relies only upon biochemical treatments of affective illness (The Thin Edge-Depression, 1975). It seems plausible that the causes of the affective illness of the 15-20% of Fieve's patients whose moods are not effectively controlled by lithium are the result of psychological factors. It appears shortsighted to assume that all cases of a particular disorder are directly attributable to metabolic disorders, and therefore neglect the possible beneficial effect of psychotherapy.

Although drug treatment for psychiatric disorders is often beneficial, it also has its shortcomings. A major problem, which deserves more attention than it is currently receiving, is that of "legal" drug abuse in which the patient becomes addicted to prescribed medicine that was "just what the doctor ordered". I have encountered cases in which the patient had been prescribed the same drug for a prolonged period, sometimes as long as ten years. Such patients had become literally addicted to the medication and would experience withdrawal symptoms if the drug was changed or discontinued. Although anti-psychotic drugs often control psychotic symptoms, they may make the patient so tranquil that he feels continually exhausted and his cognitive ability becomes impaired.

A graphic example of "legal" drug abuse is Elvis Presley. In January of 1980, Dr. George Nichopoulos, Presley's doctor, had his medical license suspended for three months by The Tennessee Board of Medical Examiners for prescribing too many drugs to Presley. He had prescribed 10,000 pills to Presley during the last 20 months of his life.

One of the most widely abused legal drugs is the tranquilizer Valium. In September of 1979 a Senate subcommittee investigated the abuse of legal medications. Dr. Joseph Pursch, a psychiatrist at the Navy's Long Beach Regional Medical Center in California where Billy Carter, Betty Ford, and Senator Herman Talmadge have been treated for addiction, testified that many doctors don't appreciate the addictive properties of Valium and Librium. According to Pursch, "None of these drugs solve our problems. They make people feel better because they make you feel dull and insensitive. But they don't solve anything." More than 44.6 million prescriptions for Valium were filled in 1978.

In summary, the illness perspective is most valid in its application to the treatment of disorders that can be linked to identifiable organic etiologies. Its limitation is its application to disorders that have no definite organic etiology. However, even in cases where organic etiologies have been identified, psychotherapy should not be precluded as an adjunct to the medical treatment to assist the patient in coping with the psychological aspects of the disorder. Users of prescribed drugs should be aware of their addictive properties.

THE PSYCHOANALYTIC PERSPECTIVE

Psychoanalysis is likely to benefit a certain type of person with certain types of problems. Since psychoanalysis relies so heavily upon the importance of unconscious motives of abnormality, the patient should himself feel that unconscious explanations for his problems are plausible. Psychoanalysis also relies heavily upon the importance of unresolved childhood conflicts of a sexual nature in the development of pathology. Freud viewed any developmental event that contributed to the continuance of the human species as being sexual in nature. Thus, the way an infant was nurtured during infancy, toilet trained, and the way a child discovered human sexuality, were important events in personality development. If a patient feels that his problems are somehow related to difficulties of a sexual nature encountered during childhood, psychoanalysis may be a viable therapeutic option.

Psychoanalysis emerged during the Victorian period of European history. Victorian Europe was characterized by an extremely conservative attitude to human sexuality. In fact, a threat was made to call the police when Freud first began to discuss sex publicly. A major contribution of psychoanalysis has been to allow us to recognize and confront the strong influence sexual conflicts can have in the development of personality disorders. My personal observations confirm that patients are commonly troubled by sexual issues. Psychoanalysis is a type of therapy that allows the patient to deal with these sexual conflicts.

The success of psychoanalysis is not only dependent upon the type of relationship the analyst can develop with the patient, but also upon the type of therapeutic atmosphere the analyst creates. Psychoanalysis often has the reputation of being a mysterious type of therapy. Suggestion effects contribute to the effectiveness of psychoanalysis.

Shamans, or medicine men, have had the responsibility for treating the American equivalent of psychiatric disorders in their respective cultures for centuries. The success of the Shaman depended upon his ability to create the proper therapeutic atmosphere. The Shaman's hut was decorated differently from that of any of the other villagers. The Shaman dressed differently from the rest of the villagers, and was the only one in the village allowed to wear certain masks. He was the only villager allowed to perform certain rituals. These factors were considered as important if the Shaman were to rid the disturbed individual of his "possession".

The therapeutic atmosphere created by the analyst is in many ways similar to the atmosphere created by the Shaman. While psychoanalysis is not practiced in a hut, it is practiced in an office that is different from other offices. The rug is thick and soft, and a soft chair or couch is standard office equipment. Soothing background music may be piped into the room. The academic degrees of the analyst hang on the wall, indicating his competence. The mask of the analyst may be composed of a pipe, beard, and glasses. He may speak with a European accent. All these factors contribute to an atmosphere that appears to be conducive to healing and personal revelation. I am not being facetious in my comparison of the analyst and the Shaman. The therapeutic atmosphere created is an important factor in the effectiveness of psychoanalysis, as well as other types of therapy.

I will now describe a specific instance in which psychoanalysis seemed to be an appropriate type of therapy. While employed in a mental health clinic, I conducted an initial psychiatric interview of a 32 year old woman, who entered the clinic in an extremely emotional state. She was openly sobbing, and visibly shaking. She described her husband as being loving and hard working - the ideal husband, and that she feared she would abuse her son. She complained of an unsatisfactory sex life and of being frigid. She told me how she had been caught stealing money from her son's Boy Scout treasury. She said she did not need the money. She indicated that she didn't care if she lived or died.

Because of her emotional condition at the time, I invited the head psychiatrist to join us in the interview. He was Freudian in his orientation, and was to eventually become her therapist.

As the interview progressed, I became very much impressed with the manner in which the psychiatrist developed psychoanalytic insights into her problems. She reported her childhood as not being pleasant, although she had had ideal parents. She reported that her siblings were perfect in the eyes of her parents. However, she was always full of mischief, and enjoyed doing things that would anger and disgrace her parents. When in her early teens, she ran away from home. Everyone in her small home town knew she was missing, and she felt good that she had embarrassed her family. She felt this would revenge the fact that her parents had viewed her siblings more favorably, and show them that they were not perfect.

The analyst pointed out the symbolism of her stealing the money from her son's Boy Scout treasury. Just as she had run away as a teen to avenge her ideal parents' preferential treatment of her siblings, in what better way could she revenge her husband for being so perfect, than to publically disgrace his family by stealing from the Boy Scout treasury?

In explanation of her frigidity, the analyst pointed out her feelings of resentment over her husband's perfection could have been possibly converted into the physical symptom of frigidity (conversion hysteria). What better way to punish this ideal husband than to deny him the opportunity of having sex with his wife? The woman did not deny the explanations of the psychiatrist.

The woman became more emotional as the analyst continued probing her past. She began weeping uncontrollably, and then became hostile. She told us that she "felt like punching both of you in the face!" After a few moments of weeping and rage, she became much more relaxed. She stopped shaking and crying. She was more composed. It appeared as though through catharsis, Freud's term for the emotional release of previously repressed, unconscious remembrances, she had drained much tension from her psychological system. She left the session feeling much better. Plans were made for her to enter psychoanalysis.

Psychoanalysis seemed an appropriate treatment for this woman. She was troubled by childhood conflicts that plagued her into adulthood. She had become frigid, and this seemed logically explained by psychological factors. She was troubled by issues of a sexual nature. Personally, I felt more convinced of the validity of psychoanalysis. I must also confess that I was impressed with the accent with which the psychiatrist spoke. The stereotype of the analyst is that he speak with a German accent——this one spoke with an Oklahoman twang.

Psychoanalysis emerges as a viable therapeutic option in cases of neurosis in which the individual is plagued by painful emotions, anxiety, and symptoms of conversion hysteria. This is particularly true when unresolved childhood conflicts and problems of a sexual nature seem to play an integral role in the development of the pathological condition.

The psychoanalytic perspective was the first of the psychologically oriented perspectives to emerge. It was the first to offer a complex theory of personality disorder and its treatment. Thus, later perspectives have been afforded the luxury of pointing out weaknesses in psychoanalysis, and indicating how these more recent perspectives correct the perceived deficiencies of psychoanalysis. It is not surprising to find the criticisms of psychoanalysis are numerous.

The process of psychoanalysis is likely to be a lengthy one. Patients generally meet with their analyst a couple of times per week, and may continue to do so for years. As you can imagine, psychoanalysis is also likely to be extremely expensive. If a patient were to pay $50 per psychoanalytic hour (which in reality is often as short as forty minutes), tens of thousands of dollars could be spent in a few years.

The success of psychoanalysis is to a great extent dependent upon the development of a close, intense relationship between the patient and the analyst. This rapport often takes a long time to develop. The goal of any type of psychotherapy is to allow the patient to reach a point where he can function normally without the need for therapy. Should psychoanalysis continue for an extended period, there is a likelihood that the patient will develop a strong dependency upon the analyst, thus making the psychological "weaning" of the patient from the analyst a difficult task.

Psychoanalysis has also been criticized for placing too heavy an emphasis upon sex in the origin of personality disorder. The point has been made that man is not merely an attachment to his genitals, and that factors other than sex contribute to pathology. Since psychoanalysis was developed during the period of Victorian Europe, a time of sexual repression, it may not be as relevant in contemporary American culture, as we are no longer in a period of such sexual repression.

Should a person decide that psychoanalysis is the best type of therapy for his particular condition, he may have a difficult time finding a qualified analyst. It is estimated that there are only about fifteen hundred fully qualified psychoanalysts in America today. To become fully qualified as a psychoanalyst, the therapist must undergo his own lengthy analysis. Thus, many therapists employ the analytic model in their therapy, but are not technically fully qualified psychoanalysts.

In the previous section I described the skillful analysis performed by one particular therapist. It has been my observation that not all analytically oriented therapists are as skillful. In one particular case a psychiatrist, who interestingly does not claim to be overly analytic in his orientation, explained to me that a certain patient we were discussing had developed an ulcer because he had not received enough gratification during the oral stage (the first stage in Freudian psychosexual personality theory). When I questioned his assumption, he explained that ulcer patients are given milk to drink for the treatment of the ulcer. He therefore reasoned that this particular patient had developed the ulcer so that he could receive the nurturance of the hospital staff, and in this nurturant atmosphere, drink milk, thereby making up for the lack of gratification he had received during the first year of his life. I personally find such reasoning implausible. As in any field, some practitioners of that field are better than others.

It is difficult to evaluate the effectiveness of psychoanalysis as a type of psychotherapy. Freud did little to experimentally document its effectiveness. Some studies report about a 50% cure rate in cases in which psychoanalysis is employed to treat neurotic disorders. While a cure rate of 50% does not seem all that convincing (indeed many patients' condition would spontaneously improve without therapy), it must be kept in mind that the major goal of psychoanalysis is to affect a global, general cure of the person's condition. This is indeed an ambitious task.

Psychoanalysis does not work well in the treatment of psychotic disorders. Regarding the psychoanalytic treatment of psychosis, Freud stated ". . . we discover that we must renounce the idea of trying our plan of cure upon psychotics – renounce it perhaps forever or perhaps only for the time being, till we have found some other plan better adapted for them" (Freud, 1949, p. 30). However, we must recognize that all other perspectives have only had limited success in "curing" the psychoses, particularly schizophrenia.

Psychoanalysis emerges as a viable therapeutic option in cases of neurosis that seem to have deep-seated roots in early childhood conflicts of a sexual nature. In defense of its relatively low cure rate, it must be mentioned that the major goal of psychoanalysis is to bring about a general cure of the patient's neurotic condition, and not just offer symptomatic relief. A decision to undergo psychoanalysis must be made with the understanding that it is likely to be a lengthy, expensive process.

THE LEARNING PERSPECTIVE

The therapy of the learning perspective involves the application of the behavioristic models of learning (classical and operant conditioning) to the treatment of behavioral disorder. The basic notion is that all behavior, normal and abnormal, is learned. Just as a person learned to behave abnormally, he can learn to behave normally through the systematic restructuring of the conditions of reinforcement to which he is subjected.

As mentioned previously, a major goal of behavioristic psychology has been to make psychology a legitimate branch of science. Thus, the learning perspective has developed a convincing literature substantiating its effectiveness as a therapeutic model. The learning perspective has demonstrated that its principles can be systematically employed to obtain specific behavioral objectives in the treatment of a diversity of behavioral disorders.

The specific types of treatments considered to be behavioristic in nature are numerous. Behavior modification is often employed in institutional settings, where it is relatively easier to gain control over the conditions of reinforcement than in out-patient situations. Techniques may include the use of operant conditioning to strengthen desirable aspects of behavior. For example, specific desirable behaviors demonstrated by institutionalized schizophrenics may be rewarded with tokens, such as poker chips. The earned tokens are exchanged at a specified time to obtain soap, cigarettes, candy, or extended privileges. Patients may be fined tokens for undesirable behavior. Atthowe and Krasner (1968) established a token economy in a hospital ward consisting of 86 chronic schizophrenics. The average length of hospitalization for these patients was almost 25 years. In a relatively short time instances of breaking hospital rules decreased sharply. Many patients demonstrated improved social behavior. One patient became able to leave the hospital for the first time in 40 years.

Shaping techniques are often employed in behavior modification programs. Shaping involves the reinforcement of successive approximations to desired target behaviors. For example, in developing language skills, reinforcement would follow any verbalization of the patient initially. Eventually the verbalization must be more precise to obtain reinforcement. In other cases, aversive stimulation or non-reinforcement may be used to weaken undesirable behaviors.

The effectiveness of such behavioristic techniques in accomplishing desirable behavioral objectives has been well documented. In a comprehensive survey of research done in behavior therapy, Aubrey Yates (1970) has demonstrated its effectiveness in treating a wide range of behavioral disorders. These disorders include stuttering, sexual dysfunction, nervous tics, and criminality. He also verified the success of behavioral techniques in the treatment of neurotic disorders such as phobias and hysteria, and in accomplishing specific objectives in the treatment of severely impaired psychotics. Desirable outcomes are consistently reported in 60-90% of the cases in which behavioral techniques are employed.

Recent research is indicating that biofeedback training can be an effective treatment for both psychological and medical problems. Biofeedback machines allow patients to receive feedback, or knowledge of what is happening, regarding body processes that we ordinarily do not receive feedback about. For example, our bodies do not normally provide us with feedback concerning our blood pressure. However, if a person is instructed to lower his blood pressure, eventually, just by chance, it will lower to some small extent. When blood pressure decreases, a light on the biofeedback machine turns on. Although the person may not know how he does it, he eventually becomes capable of controlling blood pressure.

Biofeedback is based upon operant theory. A response (reduction of blood pressure) is followed by reinforcement (seeing a light turn on) that strengthens behavior (the ability to reduce blood pressure in the future).

Research in biofeedback has had encouraging results. Success has been reported in the treatment of muscle tension headaches by using biofeedback to teach the person to relax muscles in the head and neck. Migraine headaches have been successfully treated by teaching the patient to decrease the flow of blood to the head. Indications are that biofeedback may be beneficial in treating insomnia and epilepsy by enabling the patient to control brain wave activity (Mikulas, 1974, pp. 146-149). A clinic in which I worked used biofeedback training for a variety of disorders. The clinicians found that biofeedback was particularly effective in enabling neurotics to develop some degree of control over their levels of anxiety. Behavioral techniques can benefit a wide range of disorders.

Another advantage of behavioral therapy is that improvement commonly results in fewer sessions and in less total time than with other types of therapy. Psychoanalysis is likely to be a lengthy process, and its effectiveness is to a large extent dependent upon the relationship that develops between the analyst and the patient. While behavioral therapists would view the development of a close rapport between them and their patients as helpful, they would not view this rapport as essential for the success of therapy. The important factor is that the therapist is able to gain control over the learning conditions of the patient. Gelder and Marks (1968) showed that systematic desensitization, a type of behavior therapy, resulted in more improvement in four months than did two years of group psychotherapy in the treatment of phobias. Behavior therapy is relatively economical.

In "Behavior Modification with Children", presented in the chapter on the learning perspective, D. G. Brown refers to the serious manpower shortage in the mental health profession. He notes that for every mental health professional in this country there are thousands in need of services. The principles of behavior therapy can be employed by the lay person with relatively little technical training.

Thus, parents, spouses, siblings, teachers, and members of the hospital staff are all potential behavior therapists. It is plausible that some patients may be able to spend shorter periods of time in institutions if members of their family are capable of providing "booster shots" of behavior therapy at home. Through public awareness and utilization of the principles of the learning perspective, great steps can be made to alleviate the manpower shortage in the mental health profession.

Although behavior therapy has been demonstrated as effective in the treatment of a wide range of behavioral disorders, it is not without its criticisms. Critics point out that although behavior therapy does result in specific behavioral improvement in most patients' condition, it does not result in a cure of the disorder. For example, chronic schizophrenics may learn to wash and feed themselves and learn to use language effectively for the first time in their lives through behavior therapy. Although these are improvements in the schizophrenic's condition, they do not constitute a cure of the disorder. In rebuttle of this criticism, proponents of the learning perspective point out that behavior modification has at least enabled us to bring about some improvement in the condition of even severely disturbed patients. Since no treatment has been shown to consistently cure schizophrenia, symptomatic improvement is the most that we can currently hope for. In essence, it is a realistic approach to the treatment of schizophrenia.

Critics of the learning perspective also point out that improvement that results from the application of behavioral principles will continue only as long as the conditions of reinforcement of the patient are controlled. Likening behavior modification to psychological bribery, critics reason that just as a starving captured soldier divulges secret information to the enemy in exchange for food, mental patients "jump through the hoop" of the behavioral psychologist to obtain cigarettes or television privileges. However, once washing oneself is no longer reinforced with cigarettes, washing behavior will extinguish. Even staunch behaviorists must admit that this is a possibility.

The hope of the behaviorist is that intrinsic (internal) reinforcers will eventually replace extrinsic (external) reinforcers in maintaining the behavioral improvements in the future. Hopefully, the schizophrenic will realize that feeding himself, as opposed to having to be tube or spoon fed, can be rewarding in itself and give him a sense of pride and accomplishment. Thus, once the desirable behavior is developed, it will be maintained without the need for extrinsic reinforcers, such as cigarettes.

Perhaps the strongest criticism of the learning perspective is an ethical one. Critics argue that behavioral techniques are mechanistic and dehumanizing. Techniques that rely on reward and punishment are viewed as manipulative and controlling. They deny the patient of his freedom of choice. Behaviorists argue that the benefits gained through behavior modification outweigh the loss of individual freedom endured by the patient during the treatment. It is their contention that a schizophrenic who becomes able to take care of himself to some degree, does not engage in self-destructive behavior (such as head banging), and develops some language skills, is more fulfilled as a human being than a patient who is totally dependent upon the institutional staff, bangs his head into the wall until unconscious, and is totally non-verbal. Behaviorists have been willing to assume the responsibility for making such a crucial ethical decision. Behaviorists also point out that, like it or not, behavioral control is a reality of life. We all have our conditions of reinforcement controlled to some extent. For example, if we work well at a job, we are reinforced with pay and promotions. However, if our work is unsatisfactory, we may be demoted or fired.

While many types of less severe disorders are treated on an out-patient basis by behavioral psychologists, the treatment of severe disorders is more effective if conducted in an institutional setting. Proponents of the social perspective are quick to point out that the effects of long term institutionalization are devastating. The environment of the mental hospital is not a normal one, and the longer a person is removed from a normal environment, the less is the likelihood that the person will behave normally. This point must be heeded.

In summary, the strengths of the learning perspective are numerous. Behavior therapy works. Much empirical research has demonstrated its effectiveness in bringing about specific behavioral improvement. Improvement results in a relatively short period of time, and the patient need not "like" the therapist for behavioral techniques to be effective. Behavioral principles can be employed by other than mental health professionals.

Behavioral psychologists can boast of a high cure rate in the treatment of phobias and sexual dysfunction. Neurotics can develop some degree of control over anxiety through systematic desensitization. Biofeedback techniques show promise in the treatment of both psychological and medical disorders. Behavior modification employed in institutional settings predictably results in specific behavioral improvements, even in severely disturbed patients.

However, the effects of behavior therapy may not be permanent. Should reinforcement of desirable behavior cease, so may the behavior. Should aversive stimulation of undersirable behavior be terminated, the behavior may recur. The more severe the disorder, the greater is the amount of control needed to achieve desirable results.

Ultimately, behavioral techniques must be recommended for the treatment of a multitude of relatively minor behavioral disorders. Decisions to treat severe disorders with behavioral techniques in institutional settings must be cautiously made.

THE HUMANISTIC PERSPECTIVE

The major goals of humanistic psychotherapy are to enable the client to discover the significance in his existence, allow him to discover what courses of action are most appropriate in his life, and to assist him in the development of his fullest human potential. Humanistic therapists stress the importance of the development of a close rapport in the therapeutic relationship. Carl Rogers, in the chapter on the humanistic perspective, indicated that therapists should be warm, genuine, trusting, and understanding in their client relationships. They should also be empathetic, rather than merely sympathetic. Involvement in a non-exploitive, non-judgemental, open relationship is often of great benefit to neurotic individuals. Shlien and associates (1962) found that neurotic individuals treated with client-centered therapy for two months reported great decreases in self-dissatisfaction with their conditions. A one-year follow-up indicated the benefits were maintained. Humanistic therapy can be of benefit for neurotic clients.

However, humanistic-existential therapies seem best applied to certain clients referred to as YAVIS-type. YAVIS is an acronym, the letters of which stand for young, attractive, verbal, intelligent, and successful. These clients may be like you or me. There are numerous positive aspects of their lives, but they are simply not content with their present existences.

American technology has enabled us to mass produce goods in a relatively cheap, efficient, manner. Labor saving devices can do much of our work for us. Computers can instantaneously do work that previously consumed hundreds of man hours. We have put men on the moon, and have the nuclear capability to destroy an enemy nation within hours.

However, in the eyes of many, a spiritual nothingness has developed in the midst of our technological paradise. Man, as an individual, has lost his significance. We are referred to by social security numbers, and not by names. Numbers compute -- names don't. We are bored by assembly line jobs. How can a person be fulfilled if he spends half of the time he is awake doing something he absolutely detests? Our children lack legitimate heroes to emulate. Millions justify not voting, reasoning "My vote doesn't matter. What can one person do? The politicians will do what they want anyway." Our country has fought a war without the public's sanction. We are powerless, lost, and without hope.

The following scenario has become all too common in contemporary America. The young executive drives his late model station wagon, complete with imitation wood side paneling, into the garage of his suburban split-level home. The home is distinguished from those adjacent to it only by a different name on the mail box. He feels exhausted, although he has done no physical work. He tells his wife of the problems he encountered at work. She nods, but hasn't really listened. She tells him that new carpeting would make the house complete. He nods, but hasn't really listened. Although he has just been entertained by an episode of "The Odd Couple", and in the process gulped three martinis, he is still tense and nervous. With the help of Betty Crocker, dinner is prepared in a manner of minutes. As the couple eat their colorful, but bland dinner, they express hope that their upcoming trip to Miami will be enjoyable. Last year's trip to Aspen was a disappointment. He goes to bed early. Alone, she watches television until midnight. The next day is the same. So is the next. Fulfillment of the "American dream" has brought a nightmare of boredom and emptiness.

This situation is descriptive of YAVIS-type people, who have much in the way of material comfort, but whose lives seem without significance. They are simply not happy. They feel that something is missing from their lives. Humanistic therapy, which stresses the unique quality of the individual, and endeavors to aid the individual in his search for personal significance, is an appropriate therapeutic option for such YAVIS-type people.

The annual number of divorces in the United States has surpassed the one million mark. Displaced homemakers, or women whose lifestyles have been drastically changed following divorces, are finding it difficult to cope with single life once again. Some become depressed.

Although divorced men also experience problems, the divorced woman is in a particularly difficult situation because she may be faced with the necessity of entering the job market with few marketable skills. Her self-concept may suffer. She may come to feel that although she was a good wife and mother, she lacks significance as a person. Humanistic therapy can be of great benefit to her. It can help her to discover a new sense of significance in her life, teach her that she is not helpless, and that she is a valuable, worthwhile human being.

Seligman's work with learned helplessness was presented in the chapter on the learning perspective. Seligman's main point is that when we come to believe that nothing we do works, we learn to do nothing. We become depressed. Effective treatment for depression lies in the patient's realization that what he or she does matters, and that he or she is in control of his or her life. The techniques advocated by Seligman to combat learned helplessness and depression can be employed in a humanistic therapeutic atmosphere to effectively help the displaced homemaker.

In November of 1978, our nation was shocked by the suicide-murder in Guyana of about 900 members of the Peoples Temple, a religious cult. We have questioned the state of mind of people who would commit murder or suicide upon the direction of a religious leader, in this case, Jim Jones. Although it is tempting to think that these people were neurotic, psychotic, or psychopathic in the first place, such was generally not the case. While watching television interviews of defectors from the Peoples Temple, it became apparent that these people were not insane. They were essentially YAVIS-type people. Many were young, intelligent, conscientious people. They were vulnerable, misguided, and gullible, but not crazy.

Dr. Hardat Sukhdeo, chief of psychiatry of the College of Medicine and Dentistry at New Jersey Medical School, has interviewed a number of survivors of the Jonestown camp. He characterized the survivors as "polite, law-abiding, responsible and intelligent . . . they all had some humanitarian ideals. They want to work for people, to help people, to work for a just cause.

Young people are commonly attracted to religious cults because they have perceived hypocrisy in American culture. They feel alienated and alone. They have a need to belong to some group. They want to develop meaningful interpersonal relationships, and discover a purpose in life. Although in this case the results were catastrophic, cult membership often satisfies some basic psychological needs for its members.

Although it is common to hear that interest in organized religion is on the decline, the spiritual, existential components of our personalities remain strong. Indeed, some patients with whom I have worked have indicated that they used to seek clergy members when intensely anxious, but since they have gotten away from organized religion, now turn to the mental health profession for help.

Some people who have lost interest in conventional religion become involved in the intense study of humanistic psychology. Humanism becomes a philosophy of life for these people. Humanism becomes a substitute for religion. Many such people feel self-actualized, content, and at peace with the world. I cannot help believing that the events in Guyana could have been avoided, had the eventual victims sought answers to their existential questions in humanistic psychology, rather than in Jim Jones.

For the person who has turned away from conventional religion, feels alienated and without direction, and believes that there should be more to life than there currently is, humanistic psychology is of relevance. The individual need not enter humanistic psychotherapy, although it may be beneficial. The study of humanism can be undertaken individually.

Sensitivity and encounter groups, which have become popular today, are outgrowths of humanistic theory. A basic notion of Gestalt psychology is that the whole is greater than the sum of its constituent parts. Thus, when people come together in a group, the group represents more than merely the sum of its individual members. There is strength in numbers.

Sensitivity and encounter groups meet for a variety of purposes. Some meet with psychotherapeutic purposes. Some are designed for people having marital problems. Some are for people who are trying to "find" themselves. Business and industry often employ encounter techniques for the improvement of management-employee relations.

Self-help groups, like Alcoholics Anonymous, are somewhat similar to encounter groups. Both stress open and honest expression, and share the belief that people can develop unfulfilled capacities in a group setting. Humanistic theory has been applied to situations other than the treatment of personality disorder.

Regarding criticisms of humanism, it is often condemned as being overly optimistic and naive. While it sounds emotionally appealing to treat the neurotic client with upmost regard and respect in the therapeutic situation, the client will not likely receive the same kind of treatment in his daily routine outside of the therapy setting. Thus, the benefits of humanistic therapy are viewed as being short lived when the client reenters the "cold cruel world of reality".

While visiting a sheltered workshop for mentally retarded adults, I perceived that the staff of the workshop was rather demanding, unsympathetic, and cold in their relations with the clients. Troubled by this, I asked the director if he felt the staff should be more humanistic in its client relationships. He indicated that the purpose of the workshop was to prepare the clients for legitimate employment in the community. He also indicated that retarded adults are commonly singled out for ridicule by fellow employees. Thus, while agreeing that it would be desirable to treat the clients in a more humanistic manner, it may not be in their best interest. This is a valid point.

Humanistic psychology has also been criticized for contributing to the development of a permissive American society in which respect for authority, discipline, and personal responsibility have declined. While humanistic psychology does stress individual free will, it also stresses the full acceptance of responsibility for our actions. It is true that Gestalt psychologist Fritz Perls is the originator of the "do your thing" philosophy that became prevalent a number of years ago. Perls did mean that we all have the right to "do our thing", whatever it may be. However, he also stressed that once you have "done your thing", you must be responsible for your actions. "Doing your thing" is not to be used as a justification for shirking responsibilities that are rightfully yours, or for "ripping off" others. Unfortunately, Perls' message was largely misinterpreted by the American public.

In some cases, group therapy or training, advertised as being humanistic in orientation, have been severely criticized on ethical grounds. Some such expensive training has turned out to be little more than drug, alcohol, and sex orgies with little therapeutic benefit for the participants. In other cases, people have experienced psychotic episodes which seem to have been triggered by traumatic events encountered during training.

The human growth potential movement has turned into a multi-million dollar industry in this country. Where there are large sums of money to be made with relatively little effort, fraud will be perpetrated. By using the vocabulary of humanistic psychology, unscrupulous, unqualified charlatans have exploited people by promising unrealistic outcomes in unreasonably short time. People who would perpetrate such fraud are not humanists. They are criminals.

Unfortunately, people seeking legitimate group therapy or training experience must be cautious. Any legitimate therapist or trainer should specify his qualifications, and not be offended when asked to verify his credentials. The cost of the program should be specified beforehand. The goals of the training and the techniques to be employed should be explained. The consumer should be skeptical if any of the previous conditions are not met.

Humanistic therapy has not been demonstrated as being particularly effective in the treatment of psychosis. Humanistic therapy is dependent upon a high level of client awareness. To be effective, the client should be alert, coherent, perceptive, and in touch with reality. Psychotic patients do not demonstrate these characteristics. If they did, they would not be psychotic.

In summary, the humanistic perspective is most valid in its application to the existential dilemmas of the YAVIS-type client. I recommend the study of humanistic psychology as an alternative to cult membership for confused young adults seeking direction in life. Group training experiences can be valuable in fostering personal awareness and personality growth, but the consumer should be cautious. Humanistic techniques do not work well in the treatment of psychosis.

THE SOCIAL PERSPECTIVE

Unlike the other perspectives, the social perspective advocates no specific type of medical or psychotherapeutic treatment for the behavioral disorders. Throughout this chapter, I have pointed out that all of the perspectives have demonstrated some degree of success in treating neurosis and other less severe behavioral disorders. I have also pointed out that none of the perspectives can boast of consistent success in the treatment of schizophrenia. While the illness perspective has demonstrated some success in controlling certain psychotic symptoms with drugs, and behavior modification techniques have led to some specific behavioral improvements in the psychotic's condition, psychoanalysis and humanistic therapy are of minimal value in the treatment of the psychoses. The social perspective has been strongly critical of the mental health profession's inability to accomplish consistent, significant improvement in the treatment of the most severe disorders. It therefore calls for a restructuring of the mental health system and the services it provides.

To a great extent, the other perspectives have viewed abnormality as a quality of the individual himself. They have perceived something different about, or wrong with, the abnormal person. The roots of abnormality were viewed as stemming from within the individual. The illness perspective proposed that a person became mentally ill because there was something medically wrong with him. According to the learning perspective, social factors may have contributed to the learning of abnormal behavior; from the psychoanalytic point of view, other people may have contributed to the development of unresolved, unconscious conflicts that plagued the neurotic into adulthood. But in all cases, it was still the patient who was neurotic. While the humanistic perspective does view society as the source of feelings of alienation and emptiness, it is still the client who is not fulfilled or self-actualized.

The social perspective identifies society as the major culprit for creating mental illness. It is society that develops subtle codes of acceptable conduct, or residual rules, the violation of which constitutes mental illness. As Jay Haley pointed out in "The Art of Being Schizophrenic", it is the family of the schizophrenic that forces him into such an untenable position that he has no other alternative than to become insane. It is society that sanctions the mental health profession to stigmatize (through diagnostic labeling), institutionalize, and treat the residual rule breaker, thus leading him into a life of chronic deviance. The social perspective views mental illness as the result of external, societal factors, rather than internal ones.

The social perspective is also extremely critical of the devastating, denormalizing, effect long term mental hospitalization can have upon the mental patient. Erving Goffman (1961) has described the mortification process the patient experiences once he enters the mental hospital. The person must surrender most of his personal belongings. He is given a hospital gown to wear. He can no longer function in the social roles of husband, father or employee, having been removed from his family and job. His only close relationships are with other patients. He must conform to the demands and schedule of the institution. Non-conformity is not be tolerated. His decision making capabilities are taken away. Once the patient has been stripped of so much of his individuality and personal identity, only a naked skeleton of personality remains. The mental health profession has labeled this naked skeleton of personality schizophrenia. Long term institutionalization makes the person schizophrenic.

Once the patient is in the hospital, just about anything that he does can be interpreted as a symptom of his mental illness. After all, he would not be in the hospital in the first place if he weren't crazy. Tony Orlando, referring to his own experience in a New York mental hospital, elaborated on this theme in an interview on the Mike Douglas Show. He stated,

> "I noticed that every time I complained, there would be somebody with a pad that would be writing down, "Orlando complaining and may be a form of depression." So now, no matter what I did, if I went out to the window and looked at the ocean, "Orlando thinking of jumping." There was nothing that you could do that was not based on psychology."

Should the patient physically resist the attendants' attempts to manipulate him, he is viewed as potentially dangerous. Should the patient become a loner in this unpleasant situation, his withdrawal is viewed as a symptom of schizophrenia. Should he abide by the hospital rules and not question the authority of the staff, his complacency is viewed as an admission that he is mentally ill.

Because of the perceived failure of the mental health profession to help disturbed people, and of the debilitating effects institutionalization can have, the social perspective advocates the deinstitutionalization of chronic patients into small community based settings, where normalization becomes possible. By living in normal communities, performing meaningful jobs, associating with non-deviant people, and fulfilling normal social responsibilities, the process of normalization will be enhanced.

In Wolf Wolfensberger's article in the chapter on the social perspective, he noted the success of normalization programs in Scandanavia. The social perspective is optimistic that the time is now right to implement the principle of normalization in America. The movement has begun. The principle of normalization is simple. It is easily understood by the layman. It is an emotionally appealing principle. As taxpayers threaten to refuse to pay taxes, state governments look to deinstitutionalization as a way to reduce their mental health expenditures. The public has recognized the failure of the traditional mental health system to cure severe psychiatric disorders.

However, there are terrific obstacles to be overcome in the implementation of successful normalization programs. Critics point out that simply relocating former patients into urban, slum, ex-patient ghettos would be no more beneficial than to keep the patients in the institution. The movement faces the monumental task of educating the public to be acceptant and tolerant of these formerly institutionalized people. Although general public opinion may be in favor of the movement, strong negative reaction can be expected when people in individual communities learn that it is *their* community in which the program is to be implemented.

Another problem is that deinstitutionalized patients are often placed in nursing homes where adequate follow-up care is not available, instead of the residential facilities advocated by Wolfensberger.

Charles J. Hynes, New York State special prosecutor, testified at a hearing of the Senate Mental Hygiene and Addiction Control Committee in February of 1979. He proposed that adult homes be barred from caring for deinstitutionalized patients because, "In many cases, inadequate supervision or failure to react to danger signals has resulted in suicides or senseless accidental deaths." The normalization movement is in a curious dilemma: its implementation can wait no longer, but it must not proceed so rapidly that the programs are not comprehensive, thus defeating the purpose of the movement.

Ultimately, justification for the existence of a perspective cannot be based upon its criticisms of other perspectives. It must show that it is an improvement over the existing ones. Whether normalization programs will work in America remains to be seen. It is now the time for the social perspective to justify its existence.

The purpose of this last chapter has been to enable you to make a personal evaluation of the relative merits of the perspectives. I have indicated strengths and limitations of the individual perspectives. Hopefully, despite the controversy that exists within abnormal psychology, you have clarified and extended your understanding of the subject.

Should you or a loved one need mental health services, your understanding of the field could be of practical relevance. Knowledgeable mental health consumers can make rational decisions regarding which type of treatment is most likely to benefit a specific kind of disorder. You should know what questions to ask. If you have attained this level of understanding, consider your effort worthwhile.

However, if even now, you are still somewhat confused about abnormal psychology; if, in your own mind, you still can't definitely say which perspective is overall most valid and valuable——don't dismay. You see, you just can't get the experts to agree.

References

Atthowe and Krasner, Preliminary report on the application of contingent reinforcement procedures (token economy) on a "chronic" psychiatric ward, *Journal of Abnormal Psychology,* 1968, 73, 37-43.

Bunney, Goodwin, Davis, and Fawcett, A Behavioral-Biochemical Study of Lithium Treatment, *American Journal of Psychiatry,* 125:4, October, 1968.

Sigmund Freud, An Outline of Psychoanalysis (New York: W.W. Norton & Company, Inc., 1949).

Gelder and Marks, Desensitization and phobias: A crossover study, *British Journal of Psychiatry,* 1968, 114, 323-328.

Irving Goffman, *Asylums* (Garden City, New York: Doubleday & Company, Inc., 1961).

Isaac Goldberg, George Gershwin, *A Study in American Music* (New York: Frederick Ungar Publishing Company, 1958).

William Mikulas, *Concepts in Learning* (Philadelphia: W.B. Saunders Company, 1974).

Don A. Schanche, If You're Way, Way, Down—Or Up Too High, *Today's Health,* May, 1974.

Schlien, Mosak, and Dreikurs, Effect of Time Limits: A Comparison of Two Psychotherapies, *Journal of Counseling Psychology,* 1962, 9, 31-34.

The Thin Edge, "Depression", Produced by WNET, New York State Education Department, 1975.

Aubrey J. Yates, *Behavior Therapy* (New York: John Wiley & Sons, Inc., 1970).

Chapter 9

We have completed our study of abnormal psychology. You should have a basic understanding of the perspectives approach to the study of abnormal psychology. Now is your chance to apply what you have learned in the analysis of case histories. Let's play psychologist!

As you read the following case histories, look for bits of information that proponents of the various perspectives would consider as being important in contributing to the development of the described disorder. Also, think of treatment recommendations proponents of each perspective might make.

CASE HISTORY I

Patient's Name: Nancy K. **Date of Admission:** July 20, 1977

Age: 46 **Religious Preference:** none

Family History:

Parents:	Father, John J., age 71, good physical and mental health.
	Mother, Mary J., recently died at age 69 from heart attack. At age 50 she was treated by a psychiatrist as an out-patient. Diagnosis was manic-depression.
Siblings:	Brother, Arthur J., age 49, good physical and mental health.
	Sister, Eva N., age 47, good physical and mental health.
Children:	Son, Arnold K. Jr., age 23, college graduate, works as a computer engineer in Chicago, good physical and mental health.
	Daughter, Elaine K., 21, college student in California, good physical and mental health.

Marital History:

Nancy has been married to Arnold K. Sr. for 24 years. It has been each spouse's only marriage. Until the last few years, the marriage had been satisfactory to each spouse. Arnold then had an extramarital affair, and the couple were separated for a three week period. He stated that the reason he left her was that he couldn't stand Nancy's "crazy" behavior any longer.

Personal History:

Nancy was the youngest of three children in her middle class Caucasian family. During the seventh month of her pregnancy with Nancy, her mother had rubella (German measles). This did not apparently impair Nancy's physical or mental development.

Nancy's mother was the dominant person in the family structure. Her father was relatively passive, and was often not at home.

Nancy's older brother and sister were viewed as ideal children by their parents. They got good marks in school, and were seldom discipline problems at home. Nancy has remarked that she felt her parents had always shown preference for her older siblings.

On the contrary, Nancy was viewed as a discipline problem by her parents. She seemed slower to develop than her older siblings. She was not toilet trained until almost four years of age. Nancy's older brother recalls their mother scolding Nancy for making mistakes in her toilet training. He recalls her saying she was "fed up with washing diapers for all these years", and that "if Nancy was born first, there would have been no other children."

Nancy did not do well in school. She was a tense and anxious child.

When 17 years old, Nancy ran away from home. She went to Los Angeles. She became sexually promiscuous. She then became pregnant and had an illegal abortion. She also contracted syphillis.

After a year she returned home to "put her life back together". She had her syphilitic condition treated with penicillin. Her parents continually reminded her how she had disgraced them by running away.

Education and Employment:

Upon her return home, she completed high school. She then completed a nurse's aide training program and began working as a nurse's aide. She really enjoyed her work. She reported that for the first time in her life she felt that she was doing something worthwhile, as she was helping other people. She met Arnold Sr. at the hospital, where he was also employed. She married him when she was 22 years old, and has not worked since her marriage.

History of Arrests:

December 4, 1976 - Nancy was arrested and charged with disorderly conduct and shoplifting. She was apprehended in a department store. The store manager called the police because Nancy was screaming, crying, and throwing merchandise on the floor. The police discovered that she had filled her purse and coat pockets with cosmetics and jewelry. Nancy later said she didn't know why she had stolen the merchandise. She said she didn't have any need for the things she stole, and that she had enough money to pay for them right in her purse. She said she just felt compelled to do it. Charges were dropped under the condition that she not return to the store. Arnold K. Sr. reported that she had probably done this sort of thing before and not been caught, because her bedroom closet was filled with similar merchandise.

Events Leading To Hospitalization:

Until a couple of years before her hospitalization, Nancy had been an ideal mother and wife. She was very meticulous in her house cleaning, and made sure that everything was in its proper place. She would have periodic bursts of energy in which she would thoroughly clean the house.

Shortly after her youngest child, Elaine, left for college, Nancy's behavior began to change. She entered menopause. She complained of being bored. She stated that while she was caring for her children she was active and interested in life. After they left, she seldom left the house and spent most of her day watching television, waiting for Arnold to come home at 5 o'clock. She eventually stopped preparing meals and cleaning the house. She had no desire to have sex. She began drinking. Although at first she just drank once in a while, she eventually drank daily. Arnold stated that he found partially empty wine bottles hidden throughout the house.

Arnold became concerned about Nancy's condition, and suggested that she find a hobby. She began writing poetry. Arnold noticed that her poetry did not make any sense. He tried to get her to once again take interest in her home. She would explain her lack of interest by stating, "What's the use? The kids are gone. Every day is the same. You go to work. You come home. I sit here every day. It doesn't matter what I do. Everything will still be the same."

Nancy's drinking got worse. It became common knowledge in the neighborhood that Nancy took daily walks to the liquor store to buy wine. The neighborhood children began to ridicule and taunt her as she staggered down the street, talking aloud to herself. Arnold criticized her drinking and told her that their reputation in the community had been ruined. She began to express feelings of self-pity and persecution. She started to blame Arnold for her condition, and said that if he really wanted to help her, he wouldn't be so critical of her.

Arnold, frustrated, angered, and dismayed over the deterioration of his marriage, began having an affair with a nurse who worked at the same hospital as he. Initially, he excused his coming home late by saying that he had to work overtime. Eventually, Nancy became suspicious, and accused Arnold of having an affair. Arnold told Nancy that she was imagining things, and that he thought she was crazy. Nancy became increasingly more anxious and began drinking more heavily.

Arnold stopped coming home at all evenings. He finally admitted to Nancy that he was having an affair, and that he was going to live with the woman. A tremendous argument followed. As Arnold walked out the door, Nancy slammed it shut behind him with her right hand. Her hand felt numb, and she couldn't move it.

Arnold did not return home for three weeks. His affair was not working out, and he felt guilty about having left Nancy. Not much is known about what happened to Nancy in the meantime, but when Arnold returned home, the house was a complete mess. Empty wine bottles were all over the house. Nancy was laying on her bed, staring at the ceiling, babbling incoherently. She did not notice that Arnold had returned. Arnold called an ambulance, and Nancy was brought to the hospital. She was admitted to the alcohol detoxification unit. While there, thorough medical examinations could reveal nothing wrong with her. Her condition did not appreciably improve, so she was transferred to the psychiatric unit of the hospital.

Condition Since Hospitalization

Nancy was admitted to the psychiatric unit on July 20, 1977. After a thorough evaluation, she was diagnosed as schizophrenic. Nancy periodically experiences hallucinations and had delusional thoughts. Her right hand remains partially paralyzed. She demonstrates poor judgment and logic.

Behavior modification techniques have been employed on her, and she has become able to attend to her personal care and hygiene to some extent. She is able to feed herself, take care of her room, and perform her ward duties. However, her social adaptation, as judged by her staff and patient relations, is poor. She has remarked how crazy the other patients are, and how well she fits in here.

Last month Nancy attempted suicide by slashing her wrists with her shaver. Following the attempt she stated that she wanted to die because she was so bored and her life was so worthless. She was critical of the hospital for not helping her. In a semi-conscious state she mumbled that mental hospitals only make people sicker. After recovering for a week, she recalled that the night prior to her suicide attempt she had had a terrible nightmare in which her mother was scolding her for not being as good as her brother and sister.

Her family visits her periodically, but she is generally not responsive to them. Her overall prognosis is poor.

Each of the perspectives would conceptualize Nancy's condition differently. Using the terminology of the perspective, explain how a proponent of each perspective might explain the causes of Nancy's condition. Consistent with the theory of each perspective, describe a plan of treatment for Nancy.

Illness Perspective

Psychoanalytic Perspective

Learning Perspective

Humanistic Perspective

\

Social Perspective

CASE HISTORY 2

Patient's Name: Kevin C.

Age: 22

Religious Preference: Baptist

Date of Admission: Admitted to hospital October 27, 1979. Admitted to psychiatric unit November 2, 1979.

Family History:

Parents:	Father, David C., age 53, good physical and mental health. David is a physician with a demanding practice in a large urban area.
	Mother, Delores C., age 51. Delores has been periodically treated for depression for the past 20 years. First episode followed the delivery of a stillborn child a couple of years after Kevin was born. Kevin feels that there is nothing wrong with his mother and that she sees a psychiatrist because it is "the fashionable thing to do".
Siblings:	None living
Children:	None

Marital History:

Kevin has never been married. He had been going steady with his high school sweetheart, Holly, from age 17 to 21. They planned to marry when Kevin completed his bachelor's degree.

Kevin became very close friends with his college roomate, Erik L.. Kevin was very homesick when a freshman in college, and Holly was happy that Kevin had found such a good companion in Erik. Because of the distance between Kevin's college and home town, he could only see Holly about once a month. However, Kevin and Erik came to realize that their attraction for each other was more than platonic. Erik had had previous homosexual experiences, and convinced Kevin to form a homosexual relationship with him. This relationship lasted for more than two years. Holly was unaware of Kevin's homosexual relationship with Erik, but became suspicious during spring recess of Kevin's junior year in college when he spent the vacation with Erik rather than coming home to be with her. Following spring recess, Holly unexpectedly visited Kevin. She knocked on his door, but nobody answered. The door was not locked. She thought Kevin must have been sleeping, and walked into the room. She found Kevin and Erik sleeping together, wrapped in each other's arms.

Later that day Holly told Kevin that she still loved him, but that she would never see him again unless he promised to move into another room and terminate the relationship with Erik. Kevin agreed.

Holly went home and Kevin began moving his belongings into another room. Erik was extremely disturbed that Kevin was terminating their relationship and told him that if he left, he would kill himself and it would be Kevin's fault. Kevin told Erik that he couldn't "psychologically blackmail" him, and that he didn't want to lose Holly. He left the room. Erik was found dead the next morning after a fall from the dormitory window. Although Erik's death was officially listed as accidental, Kevin knew what had really happened. Kevin felt terribly guilty. Thereafter, Kevin and Holly's relationship was never the same. Kevin has had no serious heterosexual or homosexual relationships since.

Personal History

Kevin was an only child. His parents were wealthy, and he had every material comfort as a child. His father, David, was a prominent member of the community. Because of his medical practice, David worked long hours and was seldom home to interact with Kevin. Kevin's mother, Delores, was frequently engaged in social activities and viewed caring for Kevin as demeaning and boring. Kevin was cared for mostly by domestic helpers during his childhood.

Delores reported that she felt Kevin had been sexually assaulted by one of his caretakers when he was three. She found unexplained bruises on his body. She recalled Kevin describing the assault, although he didn't understand what had happened to him. The domestic was fired, but no charges were filed in order to avoid undesirable publicity for the family.

Both David and Delores encouraged Kevin to do well in school. Both had wanted Kevin to be a doctor since he was born, and he was strongly influenced toward academic pursuits. Kevin reported that his birthday present for his fourth birthday was a set of encyclopedias, and his parents became angry with him if he did not "study", even though he could not yet read. He did exceptionally well in school. Although he was not really an introverted child, he had relatively few friends. He often complained that his classmates ridiculed him for being a "bookworm". Kevin did very well academically throughout high school.

It was during Kevin's junior year in high school that he started dating Holly. The two spent most of their free time together. They were frequently alone at Kevin's house, as David was working and Delores was busy with numerous social activities. Kevin and Holly became sexually intimate, and began experimenting with drugs that Kevin took from David's home office. Kevin reported that they used amphetamines because they felt the drugs enhanced their sexual experience. Kevin never drank alcohol. Delores was proud of this because it gave her an opportunity to boast at church functions that "our son doesn't touch a drop of alcohol".

Kevin graduated from high school as the valedictorian of his class. He was also voted "most likely to succeed" by his peers. David bought Kevin an expensive foreign car as a graduation present. Kevin remarked that the only time his father ever showed him any expression of affection was when he shook his hand and put his arm around him following graduation.

During the spring of Kevin's senior year, he was accepted for admission into a premedical program at a prestigious eastern college. The school was the alma mater of David, and the one he wanted Kevin to attend.

Kevin's freshman year in college was a successful and happy one. He did very well academically, and got along well with Holly when he saw her on weekends. Despite being homesick, he had found much desired companionship in his roomate, Erik. His parents, although not very affectionate toward him, were proud of his academic achievements. David would often say things like, "It looks like there's going to be another doctor in the C. family in a few years."

Some major problems began developing during the spring semester of Kevin's sophomore year. He began questioning if he really wanted to be a doctor. He began feeling that the only reason he was in college was to please his parents. He felt that he could not be himself because he had so much pressure on him to be what his parents wanted.

His homosexual relationship with Erik had begun, and as this relationship intensified, he felt increasingly more guilty about cheating on Holly. He feared that she would find out, and that his parents would eventually learn of his homosexual relationship. Although Kevin resented the fact that David was never very affectionate toward him, he felt that he would be totally rejected by him if his relationship with Erik was discovered. He experienced much anxiety over this dilemma.

As he doubted his motives for becoming a doctor, his grades started slipping. His usage of drugs, which until now had been moderate, increased. When home on weekends, Kevin would take as many drugs from his father's office as he thought he could, without causing David to be suspicious. Kevin and Erik took the same classes. As important exams approached, they would take amphetamines so that they could stay up all night to study. However, Kevin could not sleep nights following the exams because of the large amount of drugs he had been taking. He began taking barbiturates to enable him to sleep. This cycle of alternative use of amphetamines and barbiturates became common practice for Kevin. He developed a serious drug dependency problem.

His grades continued to worsen during his junior year. His parents became critical of him. Kevin came to believe that the only reason his parents had been proud of him was that he had been doing well in school, and now that he wasn't, they could not accept him. He came to resent his parents, his father in particular. He more firmly believed that he was never allowed to be what he wanted because of the pressures placed on him to be like his father.

David came to suspect that Kevin was using drugs. He noticed that the drug supplies in his office were disappearing without explanation. During Christmas vacation, David locked the door to his office so that Kevin could not get into it. Kevin experienced withdrawal symptoms. During the month vacation, David secretly treated Kevin for drug addiction.

Kevin returned to college in late January for the spring semester of his junior year. He had not taken drugs for a month, but began again, as Erik had returned to school with an ample supply. Kevin's homosexual relationship with Erik remained intense. His interest in school continued to diminish, and his grades were now failing. Following the previously described discovery of Holly of Kevin's homosexual relationship with Erik, and Erik's suicide, Kevin dropped out of school and returned home. He felt extremely guilty and viewed himself as a total failure.

Kevin's parents were now highly critical and ashamed of him. Holly began to make excuses for not seeing Kevin. They drifted apart and their relationship soon ended. Kevin felt abandoned by her. He resented more and more the competitive, materialistic lifestyle of his parents.

One summer's afternoon, as Kevin was walking downtown, he was approached by two young women who asked if he would like to talk to them. They were very friendly and told him that he was a beautiful human being, and that they cared for him very much. Kevin was very impressed by the girls, as he felt they were genuinely interested in him as a person. He began making trips downtown purposely to meet with the girls, who could be found any afternoon in the downtown area. He did not care that they frequently asked him for money to "help them get by".

The girls eventually asked Kevin to come "home" with them at the end of the summer. They described "home" as a place in the country where a hundred friends live together as one big family. Kevin contemplated leaving with them for a few weeks. He continued to visit them regularly. Toward the end of September, the girls told him that they were leaving. They invited him along, but told him that he had to come immediately, and tell no one that he was leaving town. Kevin was so dissatisfied with his lifestyle that he went with them.

After four days of hitchhiking, the three ended up in a desolate area of a Western state. "Home" was three dilapidated buildings five miles from the nearest road. Upon their arrival, they were greeted by a group of "friends" who welcomed Kevin. They told Kevin that they were glad to see him, and that they would help "educate" him. Kevin was unaware at the time that he had entered the training center for new members of a wealthy, urban-based religious cult.

After a week of instruction, during which he was told to do whatever the leader ordered, he was taught begging and panhandling techniques. Although Kevin was vulnerable, he realized the plans the group had for him. He escaped in the night and returned home to his parents.

Education and Employment:

Kevin completed two and a half years of college. He was dismissed for academic reasons following his leaving school during the spring semester of his junior year.

Kevin worked for two summers during college as a clerk in a pharmacy. He was fired when the owner suspected that Kevin had been stealing drugs. The owner did not press charges on the condition that Kevin never enter the store again. Kevin admitted that he had been stealing the drugs.

Events Leading to Hospitalization

Kevin returned home from the commune with his life in a shambles. His parents were thoroughly disgusted with him, and continually reminded him how they had been embarrassed by his running away. The police had been notified and the community was aware that he was missing. He tried to renew his relationship with Holly, but she was going with another man and planned to get engaged in the near future. Returning to college was out of the question, as he had been dismissed.

Kevin became increasingly more despondent. Since David kept his office locked, Kevin started purchasing drugs from a pusher. Late one night in late October, while on LSD, Kevin crashed his car. He had been driving at an unreasonable speed on a familiar, winding road. He was admitted to the emergency room of the hospital with a concussion, numerous contusions and a broken arm. When Kevin first regained consciousness he said to the attending doctor, "Why didn't you just let me die? I am no good to anyone. I'm a disgrace. Nobody cares about me. The crash was no accident!"

Condition Since Hospitalization

Kevin was transferred to the psychiatric unit of the hospital when his condition stabilized. He was diagnosed as depressed with suicidal tendencies.

Kevin's parents have visited him regularly since he entered the hospital. They seem to realize that they neglected him emotionally during childhood. They seem to understand that Kevin must find something in life that is meaningful to him, and that what Kevin chooses to do with his life may not be compatible with what they want. Holly has come to visit him, although she has no intentions of dating him again. Kevin was very pleased to see her.

Kevin demonstrates numerous depressive symptoms, but his outlook seems to be improving. He is thinking about his plans for when he leaves the hospital. He seems to be committed to conquer his drug problem. He has promised himself to join a group for recovering drug addicts that meets at his church. Although he does not feel it is realistic to plan on completing medical school, he thinks that he might like to take up nursing at a local community college. He realizes that his recovery process will be difficult.

Although his depression is still serious, there is reason for cautious optimism about his eventual recovery.

Discuss the etiology of Kevin's condition. You may choose to explain the condition from one particular perspective, or to integrate a number of different perspectives into your explanation. Develop a treatment program for Kevin.

Develop your explanation of Kevin's condition and recommendations for his treatment in the following space.

INDEX